Hometown Boy

Other books from *The Baltimore Sun*:

Dining in Baltimore

The Wild Side of Maryland: An Outdoor Guide, 2nd Edition

The Great Game of Maryland Politics

Raising Kids and Tomatoes

Gaining A Yard: The Building of Baltimore's Football Stadium

Motherhood is a Contact Sport

The 1996-1997 Maryland Business Almanac

Cal Touches Home

Other books by Rafael Alvarez:

The Fountain of Highlandtown, Woodholme, 1997

Orlo & Leini, Woodholme, 1999

This *Baltimore Sun* book was published by SunSource, the information service of the *Sun*. To order any of the above titles, or for information on research, reprints and information from the paper's archives, please call 410.332.6800.

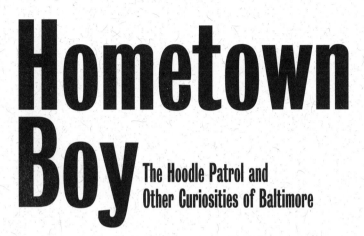

Hometown Boy

The Hoodle Patrol and
Other Curiosities of Baltimore

Rafael Alvarez

THE BALTIMORE SUN

Copyright ©1999 The Baltimore Sun

Published by
The Baltimore Sun
A Times-Mirror company
501 N. Calvert Street
Baltimore, MD 21278

Edited by Scott Shane
Layout and design by Jennifer Halbert
Photograph of Rafael Alvarez by Jim Burger
Cover photograph by Amy Davis

ISBN – 1-893116-01-8

Hometown Boy: the hoodle patrol and other curiosities of Baltimore: a publication of the Baltimore Sun Company - 1999 - Baltimore, MD: Baltimore Sun Co.: 1999

In memory of

James H. Jackson

1929 — 1992

Baltimore Sun sportswriter

"Atta way, baby!"

Contents:

Foreword

IN THE FALL OF 1978, AFTER A YEAR OF DISPATCHING TRUCKS IN THE *SUNPAPERS* circulation department and using the office's electric typewriter to write fiction once the bosses had gone home, I landed a job as a clerk in the sports department.

I was 20, with a year of writing for the *City Paper* behind me. A few weeks before, I'd scored my first byline in *The Sun* after squeezing in an interview with Studs Terkel between Rolling Stones concerts at Soldier Field.

They put me on the horse race desk.

My first week in the newsroom, thrilled to be compiling results from Pimlico and on fire for the day when they might pay me to write, I walked up to an immense, Gleason-esque barrel-of-a-man banging away at a keyboard with a cigar in his mouth. His name was Jimmy Jackson and, like Gleason, he was one of the Great Ones.

I didn't know Jimmy at the time, but it wasn't hard to know or love him and I found myself blabbering about how blessed we were to make our living with the English language. Jimmy sized me up, removed his cigar and roared.

"Kid," he said. "We're just a bunch of hacks and the sooner you realize that the better off you're gonna be."

I think Jimmy was typing in lacrosse box scores that afternoon and in the time it took him to chomp back down on his cigar, I went from Alvarez agog to Alvarez aghast.

How could anyone speak this way?

That was more than 21 years ago.

Jimmy has been gone for a good while now, and, with several hundred weather stories and twice as many obituaries in my file, I know exactly what he was trying to tell me.

This ain't religion.

Since then, I have covered the blues and public libraries; Elvis and the Jews; heroes and hoodles, all in my own backyard.

I've spent many a night grinding sausage and sewing silk purses on rewrite;

barged into the lives of innocent people who didn't deserve it; managed to avoid a regular beat for two decades; and still write fiction after everyone else has gone home.

It was never my dream to be a reporter. Not in high school, not in college. Not ever.

But it happened and I am glad of it. I learned to write on the City Desk, was given the freedom to wander the city on company time and had license to walk into strangers' homes to see what hung on their walls and stewed in their pots.

For this privilege, I thank Gilbert L. Watson, III, who was *The Sun's* metropolitan editor when I jumped from sports to city side in 1981, the year I was promoted to staff writer. Gibby took the chance of sending me to Ocean City for a long summer of reporting when I was 25 years old. It was my break and I'll never forget him for it.

Everything I have — from my rowhouse on Macon Street to the braces on my children's teeth — has been purchased with words. Some 95 percent of those words were published in my hometown paper. It's a good feeling.

There is a quote attributed to Hemingway that says newspapers are the place for an aspiring writer to learn to write a clean sentence before taking that trick out into the larger world.

I don't understand why I am still on Calvert Street any more than I know how I got here.

Except that this is Baltimore and no one really leaves.

Shalom,

Rafael Alvarez
Baltimore
Feb. 25, 1999
George Harrison's 56th birthday

Introduction

IT'S A SAD REFLECTION ON AMERICAN JOURNALISM THAT THE APPEARANCE OF genuinely good and original writing on a modern newspaper page can only occur as an act of institutional subversion. For a writer to practice his craft unencumbered at most large dailies, rules need to be broken; standards ignored. By necessity, a contempt must be nurtured for the dutiful professionalism of any self-respecting news organization's stylings, which invariably amount to a fill-the-columns triumph of crippled, pyramid-structure news accounts, constant attribution, belabored anecdotal leads, and, of course, the feigned objectivity and nodding, analytical tone that screams Trained News Provider. For originality to survive such a construct, line editors will have to be ignored or placated; the copy desk will have to be thwarted. And, in the end, the best stuff still ends up on the composing room floor.

By this measure, Rafael Alvarez is more than a little subversive. On a good day, with a good story to tell, the man is a freaking Communist.

His work at *The Baltimore Sun* is one of the few things that still defines that newspaper as an organic product of its strange and improbable city. As a writer and reporter both, his best argument is that what is true and real in the world cannot be condensed to what-happened-yesterday and what-has-impact journalism. The small moments matter. The ordinary is anything but. And the broken quotes and rag-tag street talk are always more eloquent than a thousand well-crafted press statements.

If we can be sure of anything at the end of this failed century, it's this: The great doings of our day — the violence, the politics, the social upheaval, the trials and tribulations of the famous and notorious — leave only a long wake of action and emotion signifying less and less. Nations implode, governments fall, and human beings succumb to deaths, defeats and embarrassments that are, at best, random and interesting. But none of it gets close to anything that we know in our hearts to be truth.

Truth, if it can be found at all, comes in the quiet moments, the fragile moments. A woman on her knees at the shrine of St. Jude, calling on hope. A club of aging Highlandtown ladies, affirming qualities of a confederate's mandarin orange cake. A Mississippi bluesman on his front porch, contemplating the timeless honesty of his twelve-bar art. The journalism of Ralph Alvarez seems at first glance deceptively simple, a backwater, back-page respite from the high drama of that which passes for important news. Yet at its core, this collection makes the argument that on any given afternoon, more truth can be captured in a Morrell Park kitchen that in any great nerve-center of post-industrial society.

The writing in this book keeps to the simple clarity of a good newspaper-man, but still challenges the painful reductivism of modern newspaper structure. In today's journalistic climate, it's fair to say that the best work of Mencken, Swope, Twain or Runyon would find itself spiked, savagely rewritten or condemned to the op-ed page. Yet Alvarez somehow endures in *The Sun's* news sections. He is a master of the never-start-at-the-beginning, backwards-ass, I'll-tell-the-tale-as-I-damn-well-please manner of American narrative. Like Twain or Melville, he is not interested in getting to the point when, in fact, it is the unfolding of a fresh, new world and the intimacy of ordinary lives uncovered that is the point. The best of his stories stumble into the light as if they are being offered up over whiskey in a Fell's Point bar, or over homemade ravioli at a St. Leo's lunch.

Consider this very typical Alvarez beginning: "The Chitter Chatters save their retirement nickels for bus trips to Wildwood, N.J. but they don't get in the water. As 77-year-old Dolores Rogers puts it: 'Nobody's seeing my body but the undertaker.'"

Admit it. You don't have a clue where you're going.

To which Alvarez himself would likely reply: Keep reading, bunky.

The joy of it is all for you, the consumer of some very fine, very real stories about the unlikely harbor town of Baltimore, Maryland. The nightmare is for the trained newspaper editor, and after him, the trained copy editor, who have misspent their careers trying to compress the essences of a confused, corrupted and completely idiosyncratic city into bite-sized, easily digestible pieces of interchangeable newspaper copy. There is a cool, reductive logic to most journalism. The information can be catalogued, grouped and regrouped so that in the end, the story is no longer the point. Just the facts, ma'am.

An editor in service of such logic is always at a loss when it comes to the real. And take a moment now to pity all the poor bastards who picked up a piece of Alvarez copy on deadline to discover that the lead was not a lead and the quotes were filled with Bawlmerisms and, goddammit, yet another train had left *The Baltimore Sun's* main track. Once, when forced to write an anguished, hackneyed tome on a Washington's Birthday celebration, Alvarez turned in a piece of copy with the following phrase buried many paragraphs down:

"Washington, who would have been 282 yesterday, had he lived..."

Sheer genius. Which is to say, the weekend editor cut it right out of the story.

Nonetheless, there is no way to keep a good man down and Alvarez is still on the pages of *The Sun*, peddling something far more precious than the facts, far more elusive than something that can be hammered into a seven-part series of high-impact information that *The Sun* Has Learned and hopes to submit for a major journalistic prize. To his great credit, Alvarez is bringing you life, as it is lived, as it is felt in the streets and homes and storefronts of his city.

So enjoy. But keep in mind that this is a collection that demands to be perused by real people in real places. Free yourself of your dens and libraries and drive downtown to those aged and battered places where all the houses share their walls and all the steps are white marble (even if they don't polish them the way they used to). These are stories that should be read on the waterfront benches at Fort McHenry, or by the pagoda in Patterson Park, or beneath the drab gray cranes and masts of the S.S. John Brown on South Clinton Street.

In such places, you can throw down a coddie, a beer and a chocolate-top cookie for dessert and discover that there are moments when some of the verbiage in the hometown rag actually sits upright and behaves like literature. A beer or two more and you'll forget that anything you're reading ever existed as newspaper copy. You'll be lost in the stories themselves, which, for Ralphie, was always the point.

David Simon
Baltimore
March 3, 1999

David Simon is the author of Homicide: A Year on the Killing Streets *and* The Corner: A Year in the Life of an Inner-City Neighborhood.

Chapter 1

Family

Remembering Christmas with Grandmom on Eastern Ave

THE YEAR AFTER MY GRANDMOTHER DIED I WENT LOOKING FOR THE SPIRIT OF Christmas on Eastern Avenue.

Frances Prato Alvarez, my father's mother, was a soft, round little Italian lady whose love for her family and skill with food have come to define Christmas more for me than the round man in the red suit.

Perhaps our relationship was special because I spent more time at her Highlandtown rowhouse on South Macon Street than any of the other grandchildren. Perhaps it was because I, the first male grandchild and the first born of her first son, was named for her husband. Perhaps I don't really know why, except that I have been told I was her favorite.

After she was gone, instead of visiting the cemetery or staring at old photos, I believed I could give life to the things that made her special by walking the Avenue (as we called Eastern Avenue) I had walked so often with her as a little boy. Especially around Christmas.

It is 1976, just before her 70th birthday, the year I graduated from high school. In June, I was sailing through the Gulf of Mexico with the Merchant Marine as "Grandmom" lay dying in the old City Hospitals.

Trapped on board the rusting hulk of a Puerto Rican container ship, I floated between the Gulf and Baltimore as the rest of the family realized the end was near for her. Everyday she would ask my Mom when I was coming home, and everyday Mom would say soon, real soon.

I made it to her bedside. What we said I don't remember. In a day, I'd have to report back to the ship. In a day, she'd be gone.

My father, a former seaman and tugboat man, gave me the choice of returning to sea, where I was making money for college tuition, or staying for Grandmom's funeral.

Because I decided to sail, my last memory of Grandmom is a living one.

Not that it helped when I went searching for the soul of a youngster's Christmas by walking the Avenue, past Dietz's, where she bought many of my childhood clothes, by Kramer's Popcorn, where we'd stop for caramel corn, and in one of the five-and-dimes where I'd pester her to buy me Beatles records.

2

I pressed my nose to the windows, but nothing was happening. The Avenue was gray, and the cold weather wasn't brisk and invigorating, it was just cold. The decorations strung across the lightpoles in the shopping district looked cheap and dingy, and the people walking by seemed luckless.

As I walked, I thought about the magic of our traditions, which my dad has always said is nothing more than hard work and preparation, and I thought back to the Christmas Eves of my childhood.

It meant running to the store for the adults as they cleaned fish, deep-fried anchovies wrapped in dough ("alisce cakes") and prepared empanada, a Spanish fish pot pie. It meant running up and down the steps at Grandmom's home to fetch pots and utensils, and it meant watching the slowest clock in the world, for it would be midnight before any gifts would be opened.

At about 3 p.m. everyone would go home to get ready for the dinner, leaving me alone with my grandparents. They'd coax me in for a nap, and after snooping through some closets to see if Santa had anything on lay-away, I'd rest until about 5 p.m., get dressed and help Grandmom set the long table in the basement (actually three tables shoved together), setting out the plates, the silverware, lupino beans, and little dishes of celery swimming in oil, vinegar, and black pepper.

Then I'd wait in the front room upstairs, and stare out the plate glass at the twinkling lights in the clear darkness. The rest of the family and our guests would arrive, old Spanish men with big cigars, women with shopping bags full of presents, my parents, my brother, and my cousin. We'd eat, watch the clock, and wait while the adults celebrated. It was wonderful.

None of this was on the Avenue in 1976. If I'd have been thinking, I would have given up the idea, walked east past the Highlandtown underpass, up the hill to Macon Street to sit with my grandfather to drink a few glasses of wine and chat.

Instead I stumbled into Stella Foods at Eastern Avenue and Eaton Street.

You walk into "Stella's" and all the Mediterranean kitchens of Europe let loose their aromas at once. Cheese and sausages hang from the ceiling, fresh bread bakes in the back, the shelves are stuffed with cookies, wines, pastries, liqueurs, and torrone, the Italian nougat my grandmother loved. She was close by. I was beginning to feel it. Behind the counter was a cute Greek girl, maybe my age, waiting on customers with her parents. I began explaining how I always came here with my grandmother when I was a boy. Did they remember?

"Sure we remember her," they smiled. Maybe they did, maybe not. I wanted them to, so I believed. I slowly walked around the store and looked at everything. I picked up loaves of bread and just held them, and stared at cans of garbanzo beans like a fool. I bought a gallon of "good" olive oil for my grandfather, a few things for the table, and hopped back in the car to drive home to Linthicum where I lived with my folks.

Linthicum is where Christmas was held that year, the first time the feast would be held away from Macon Street in 40 years. For me, it was an awkward transition.

As the adults sat downstairs and chatted, upstairs I filled the void with a gaggle of friends who were never associated with our tradition, a case of beer, and the stereo blasting. Fine for New Year's Eve, but a bit out of place on Christmas Eve.

But out of this confusion, somehow, has come new order and a fulfillment of what we lost in 1976. One of the new friends invited to dinner that year was a girl I had met a few months earlier in college.

Today she sits at our Christmas Eve table amid highchairs and bibbed children, making sure they eat their food and behave because Santa only comes for good little boys and girls. She quiets them when they cry to open their presents, comforts them, loves them.

My children know nothing of my Grandmom, but they know and love all of their grandparents; they know nothing of a glowing Christmas Eve basement on Macon Street, but they know Linthicum is the only place to be on that special night.

And when they're in the car with me, when we're driving down Eastern Avenue to visit my grandfather during the holidays, the dingy decorations strung across the Avenue don't look so bad after all.

I love you, Grandmom. You are with us tonight.

December 24, 1985

Cannery Rows

MY GRANDMOTHER WAS A BEAN SNIPPER.

The New World daughter of Old World Poles, Anna Potter Jones started making her own way in life as a child. At 9, she lost her mother to cancer and her father promised never to marry again. With her 11-year-old sister, Anna helped raise three younger siblings and began a lifetime of work.

I knew that my grandmother had been a flapper during the Roaring '20s, had sewn sandbags for the Allies during World War II, and that she had once taken my mother to see Lou Costello in person at the old Hippodrome Theater.

But I never knew she was a bean snipper in a packinghouse.

Stories float through my family like prayers drifting through the cosmos, and the ones told in the neighborhoods of Baltimore's immigrant holy land — Highlandtown, Broadway and Canton — were magnificent.

Growing up I heard tales of bicycles carved from wood, of distant teen-age relatives who died fighting Franco, of sea dogs who built cabin cruisers in their living rooms, and about soup made with prunes and the fresh blood of ducks.

Through the weave of such yarns there would be talk about "the packin' house," the place where Anna Jones worked for nickels during the Depression.

When I later found out that almost every Polish woman of her generation labored in Baltimore's canning industry — that the story of my grandmother was stenciled across the harbor landscape a thousand times over — I set out to preserve it in the words of the survivors.

To find these women, I walked along the streets and alleys of the old Polish neighborhoods and started knocking on doors, just the way a man known as Mr. Roberts did in the 1930s. I began at my grandmother's little brick rowhouse on Dillon Street.

In 1937, as the Great Depression rolled through its eighth year, Mr. Roberts came begging women to work for him.

My grandmother listened to his pitch while a little girl hid behind her skirt. "He needed help bad," she said. "But my Gloria was only 3 years old and I told him: 'I got a young baby at home, I can't work.' And he said I could bring Gloria with me, so I did. She sat next to me while I worked in the packinghouse."

My grandmother, one of thousands of Poles living along the Southeast Baltimore waterfront before World War II, married as a teen-ager and had three kids before she was 23. An offer to make a few bucks without having to hire a baby sitter was perfect and, taking him up on the offer, Anna Jones embarked on a working-class career that lasted 35 years at East Baltimore factories making everything from canned goods to slipcovers. The money helped add to the few dollars my grandfather made as a journeyman laborer.

The little girl at her skirt was my mother and the Roberts packinghouse was her first playground.

The Roberts family owned the fruit and vegetable cannery around the corner on Binney Street, a block-long, unheated wooden building in the looming shadow of the American Can Co. It was one of many similar buildings in the long-vanished Baltimore that was once the nation's great canning center for everything from oysters to pineapples.

At the packinghouse, my grandmother stood over a table cutting the ends off of string beans the snipping machine had missed. Next to her sat my mother on an upside-down bushel basket.

"Some of the baskets would be stacked 20 high and we'd move them around to build houses with doorways and play out on the sidewalk," my mother recalled. "And to keep us out of his hair in the summertime the foreman would let us cap strawberries for pennies."

The packinghouse was open to the street and the older children who spent the day praying the rosary in Polish and learning to read at St. Casimirs School around the corner often came over during lunch.

"I remember going over there lots of times just to talk with her," my mother said. "We could always just run in and out. You walked in and you knew that your mom was sitting over at the bean belt."

"It was a good job if you had kids because you could run home at lunch when they came home from school and eat with them," my grandmother said. "And when they went back to school, you went back to work."

The job paid on "piece work" and the women made so much per bucket of tomatoes, or pound of spinach, or basket of strawberries, receiving tokens that were redeemed for cash at the end of the day. "We made a quarter an hour," she said.

On Saturday the women worked until all of the produce had been processed so the plant could be hosed down before Sunday, the only day off at the packinghouse. "I remember standing up around the snipper all week, and my feet would swell up," she said. "And on Sunday the kids would want you to take them out somewhere, but my feet hurt so bad you'd almost have to do nothing on Sunday just to be ready for Monday."

My grandmother remembers trucks loaded with fruit and vegetables coming in "from little farms around town"; farms that were out "in the country" — the term city folk used in the first decades of this century when talking about any place north of Towson, south of Curtis Bay, east of Highlandtown or west of Catonsville.

"The trucks would be lined up outside the packinghouse in the morning and we used to count [them] to see how long it would take us to finish," my grandmother recalled. "You had your season for tomatoes, for spinach, for string beans and a season for strawberries. Every thing came around in season."

In 1873 Mark Owings Shriver invented the pressure cooker in Baltimore and the new way of steaming allowed food to be cooked four times faster than previous methods. It so changed the canning industry that a few years later there were more than 100 canneries ringing the harbor from Locust Point to Canton.

Although black women also labored there along with a few men who shucked oysters, the work in the canneries was mostly done by Polish women who lived along the narrow waterfront streets a block or two from the packinghouses. The job of skinning tomatoes, snipping beans and cleaning spinach was considered unmanly.

The women of the packinghouse brought out-of-season nutrition to soldiers, westward pioneers and ordinary people used to enduring endless meals of cabbage, potatoes and salted meats, foods that would keep over a long winter in the basement. Before man figured out a way to preserve fruit and vegetables in tin, scurvy was a menace. But a couple of cans of Eastern Shore tomatoes had enough vitamin C to keep illness at bay.

And whether they live on Dillon Street, a mile west on Bond Street, or up on the hill that gives Highlandtown its name, the refrain of the surviving packinghouse veterans is the same: The work was hard. Honest labor brought independence a few dollars at a time. Those days are gone, and no one wants to live through them again.

"They're the good old days for the ones who never lived it," says Florence Plociennik, 71, who lives on South Kenwood Avenue. "I was making 25 cents an hour, but you had nothing because you came home and gave your mother everything you made."

Montford Avenue's Mary Ljek Eber, 76, can rattle off the factory names without blinking.

"There were packinghouses from Aliceanna Street clear over to Kenwood Avenue: McGraff's, Boyer's, Roberts', Webster's, Gibbs', Langrell's, Foote's, Lord Mott's... I worked in almost all of them," she said, looking out of her front window at a stretch of luxury homes along a marina that took the place of Boston Street's canneries.

During the Depression, Mrs. Eber would put in a few hours at a packinghouse and then go up to the Varsity underwear factory at Eastern Avenue and Port Street to help her parents support a family of 10 children. She started out working the strawberry line in her early teens before the floor walkers discovered her talent for separating a tomato from its skin. "I was a hog-eye on tomatoes, I could skin 'em fast, I could do the work of two women," she said.

"I wouldn't say it was a rich life, but it was a good life," Mrs. Eber said. "We never went hungry and my mother made sure we had something to eat all the time. At Langrell's the farmers would bring corn or half-green tomatoes and you'd buy 'em for almost nothing. We used have tomato trucks sitting around here, all along Boston Street. The farmers would pick the nice ones off the top and give 'em to you."

Not all of the tomatoes eaten on the eastside were given away or paid for.

Near the beginning of my life and the tail end of Baltimore's canning era, I remember swiping one and biting into it on the sidewalk, a big kick for a kid raised in the suburbs where you bought tomatoes at the supermarket, and I remember the juice, warm and sweet, running down the corners of my mouth as I stood on Binney Street eating a stolen tomato.

For me it was an isolated thrill, but for generations of eastside "hoodles" — waterfront kids who played street football, swam naked from the end of the wharves, and broke soda bottles against sewer grates — stealing tomatoes off a truck was an everyday thing.

As a kid who hankered to play with the hoodles on weekends and get in their games, I didn't pay much mind to the sour-faced women who stared at us out their front windows when the ball bounced up against their storm doors.

Back then I didn't know them, I didn't know how hard and how long they had worked to say with pride that their house was their own: little rowhouses paid for in sweat by women who put spinach in cans.

Women like Sophie and Helen, the tomato-skinning daughters of an oyster shucker from Poland named Frances Wolaniec.

"I worked hard all my life, that's why now I got a nice pension and don't have to depend on anybody," said 82-year-old Sophie Jender, who lives in a little alley called McKay Court a few blocks north of my grandmother's house on Dillon Street.

Her pension comes from 38 years at the National Can Co., where she made beer cans on a "double seamer," but her vivid memories come from days picking fruit and vegetables "down the country" and putting the harvest into tin cans at the neighborhood packinghouse.

"I been working since I was 8," she said. "When I was about 14 I made out that I was 16 so I could get a job down the packin' house. I had to go because my daddy — he worked in the licorice factory — got a heavy cold and died, and my mother made me quit school. She needed me."

Her little sister, 80-year-old Helen Sadowski of Macon Street in Greektown, followed the family's footsteps to the edge of the water in 1932, skinning tomatoes and running back home on lunch hour to nurse a baby.

"I remember my mother shucked oysters for Langrell's. It was cold and they wore rags around their shoes to keep warm — all bundled up and all day shucking," she said. "That was hard work, babe, but it was easy to get work in them days."

Anna Potter Jones worked at the packinghouse around the corner from her Dillon Street home for about five years. She quit skinning tomatoes when the Depression lifted and took a job sewing sandbags for the Allies. By the 1950s she found steady work with regular raises, protected by the International Ladies Garment Workers Union.

She worked long enough to earn a pension and Social Security.

"It gets me mad now, how people praise these women who go out and work," she said. "How about us poor old women in the olden days, getting up at 4 in the morning? It was cold working that spinach and them string beans in the winter. Us women had to work," she said. "Just like now."

All but one of Baltimore's canneries are gone today, vanished as new plants were built closer to the crops on the Eastern Shore and Florida. The wooden packinghouse where my grandmother worked between 1937 and 1942 is now a cinderblock warehouse, a 26,000-square-foot building where vending machines are stored.

And when she steps out of her front door to look at it, she looks back on her days there as an entry into a life of hard work that made her independent.

Being independent meant paying your bills, owning your own home and having a couple of dollars extra on the weekends to take your grandchildren on a bus uptown to see a movie on Howard Street.

And whenever she opened her change purse, there were always dollars inside, endless dollars for hamburgers and popcorn and soda; dollars to be given away to a kid like me who never questioned or knew where they came from.

Now I know.

February 16, 1992

OK, Mom, right to the moon

THE WORLD BELIEVES THAT NEIL ARMSTRONG WAS THE FIRST HUMAN BEING to walk on the moon. But the world, as so often happens, is wrong.

It was my mother.

That's right. One small step for Mom.

And one giant leap for the way I would forever view life on Earth.

She didn't do it for the glory or the march of science.

Mom traveled 240,000 miles into space and back for the same reason she did everything else: to teach me a lesson.

"Do something," she said before blasting off. "Do something that matters."

Mom liked to preach. She preached, in fact, until she was blue in the face.

When the ecology movement was just a seedling, she said: "You want to clean up the environment? Start in the garage."

Now, many folks today fancy themselves children of the '60s, but I was a child in the '60s. And by the summer of 1969, I yearned to be cool more than anything in the world.

I wanted a poster of Frank Zappa sitting on a toilet with his pants around his ankles. "Not in my house," said Mom.

I wanted to hitchhike to Woodstock. Mom wouldn't let me ride the bus to the mall.

I wanted to drop acid and dance in the mud with bare-breasted young women. I was 11.

Do you know how hard it was to be groovy with a wiffle haircut?

"Forget those stinking hippies," said Mom. "And get your feet off the table."

You could say that my mother found the counter-culture a bit alien and her son's desire to embrace it more than a bit unsettling. Although we lived in the suburbs with central air-conditioning and a manicured lawn, Mom brought the Great Depression to our cul-de-sac.

This is a woman who grew up thinking that black bread spread with lard and sprinkled with sugar was a treat. Mom's favorite expression? "You've had enough fun for one day."

But because her working-class childhood of Hoover and Roosevelt was a place where idealism was not a hobby, she knew how to combine good deeds with hard work.

Long hair and dope and people tearing things down that other people had worked their whole lives to build held no charm for Mom. Her only opinion on the Vietnam War was to thank God I was too young to fight in it or protest it.

But for a woman who grew up thinking she was lucky to have a radio in the parlor of her Canton rowhouse, America's race for the stars was something to take pride in.

One day she was vacuuming behind the sofa.

The next day she was vacuuming the face of the moon.

On that long and humid Baltimore weekend in July 1969, I was playing Beatles' records backward and staring out my bedroom window, chanting: "Koo-koo-ka-choo......koo-koo-ka-choo..."

The world was changing every hour and if I couldn't become the youngest sibling in the Fabulous Furry Freak Brothers, I didn't want to do anything.

Mom hated idleness. It wasn't that devil's workshop foolishness, she just couldn't stand to see anyone sitting around when there was so much to do.

She said: "Why don't you go outside and get some fresh air. When I was your age we used to punch holes in the bottom of a coffee can and run the hose through it for a sprinkler."

Fresh air? It was 97 degrees. I rolled my eyes and turned the music up and Mom lost her temper.

Yanking the plug on my record player out of the wall, she snapped: "You want something to do? I'll give you something to do."

I was grounded for the rest of the weekend and told to clean the house. Mom left so fast (she said she was so mad that she couldn't see straight) that she didn't even tell me, like she always did, where I could find the bucket and scrub brush.

And then she was gone.

Dad came home around 4 o'clock, after working overtime down the waterfront. "Where's your mother?" he asked, getting a beer out of the fridge.

"I don't know."

"What'd you get punished for?"

"Being alive."

Dad smiled, pointed to a corner of the kitchen floor and said: "You missed a spot."

He told me to forget about cleaning and grab a bowl of ice cream.

"Let's watch a little TV," he said. "They're gonna be landin' on the moon any minute now."

We turned the TV on just in time to hear Walter Cronkite confirm it.

Someone in a bulky suit hopped backward off a little ladder, jumped up and down in the gray dust and waved from behind the curved windshield of a space helmet. The wave turned into a shaking finger, a scolding finger —

a finger pointing down from the heavens.

Through the electronic crackle of the transmission from Tranquility Base to Mission Control, a voice that could only come from one place in the entire universe — a small patch of terra firma nestled between Eastern Avenue and the Patapsco River — spoke to the people of Earth: "See what you can do when you get up off of your rear end?"

I was speechless. But Dad managed to get out a few words after draining his National Boh can.

"Let's get upstairs," he said. "We better get dinner on the table before your mother gets home."

May 19, 1995

Thirteen: A soundtrack in search of a movie

MY SON TURNED 13 THIS SUMMER. AN ADULT IN SOME CULTURES, STILL A BOY to his father. A good boy and, I think, a happy one.

I became a teen-ager 25 years ago in 1971, the summer that George Harrison, the quiet Beatle, invested his stardom in a concert to relieve the people of Bangladesh. The title song from the concert reached No. 23 on the American charts and it's always thrilled me the way George's Liverpool accent lyrically added another syllable to the beleaguered Pakistani region: "Boun-gah-la-desh . . . BOUN-GAH-LA-DESH!"

Ringo was there. So was Dylan, but Bob was just a name to me then and it would take another decade before the Dylan door opened for me. What mattered to my adolescent soul was that Beatles were appearing on stage.

And I couldn't wait to taste it.

I've known plenty of kids who couldn't wait to grow up, most of them first-born like myself; nearly all eager to take reckless chances, as I did, to get where they needed to go, where they had to go, even if they didn't know where that was. (Baby if you wanna be wild, you've got a lot to learn.)

By the summer of 1971, I could not wait any longer and so, at 13, I got bombed for the first time in my life.

What makes a kid about to enter the 8th grade go into the woods and drink until the world passes away? I think I know now, but back then it wasn't an action based on thought. I sensed that something important and exciting was going on without me, somewhere just beyond the radio waves. Does there exist a place with a pull more powerful than somewhere?

And since I couldn't hop a bus to New York to see George and Ringo sing their hearts out with freaked-out friends like Billy Preston and Leon Russell, I determined to ready myself for the day when nothing would hold me back.

My parents weren't prepared for their 13-year-old son showing up drunk for dinner. With the sun still shining in the backyard, they sent me to bed and decided to put some distance between me and my wayward friends. I was shipped into the city to stay awhile with my grandparents in Highlandtown.

Down on Macon Street, the air above the rowhouses was charged with the same current of discovery. Sounds and colors and sensations waited only for me to catch up to them. Even the magic of Grandmom's kitchen — where the sight of her frying eggplant in olive oil is a memory for which I'd trade all of rock and roll to relive for one day — could not compete with the soundtrack in search of a movie in my head.

Foster Avenue dead-ends into railroad tracks around the corner from my grandparents' house and back then, as now, kids played baseball there. I hung out with the older boys, hoping to learn something, and never had any trouble getting in a game.

One afternoon, instead of playing ball, the guys asked me to stand look-out in the street while they ducked into an alley. I wasn't exactly sure what they were up to, but I had a good idea and I remember, while stealing glances over my shoulder, wanting desperately to be in on it.

I was 13 years old and it was right around the corner.

It took me years after turning that corner to understand why a boy would willfully chase poisons. It wasn't knowledge deduced from reason, but more of an epiphany — a blessed moment of clarity that opened without notice one day after I'd walked into the same wall over and over and over again.

It was the beginning of learning my hard lessons and because of that moment, I don't do the things I used to do anymore.

This summer, my son and I went to a party where, aside from him, I was the youngest guest by half a generation. It was a small, elegant gathering of middle-aged artists, old friends who had survived the Sixties together and couldn't believe that a quarter-century had passed since the concert for Bangladesh. None of them even knew anyone who had shown up to help George save some lives at Madison Square Garden on August 1, 1971.

Beer and wine were plentiful, but no one seemed to get drunk, even as the evening moved toward midnight. My son and I shared a few cans of soda, taking turns pouring it for each other as the evening percolated gently around us.

Late in the party, I glimpsed a white-haired man hunker down with a match over a small wooden pipe and inhale a substance the Beatles experienced for the first time courtesy of Robert Zimmerman. There were others nearby (my son wasn't around), but no one joined the toker. Some averted their eyes, but I made a point of looking long and hard, to see clearly. I saw a man alone, coughing out gray smoke that read to me like death.

Walking home, my son and I chatted about what a nice time we'd had: the twinkling lights strung through the trees, the pungent pies of Arabian zahtar, and how much we admire folks who turn their homes into works of art. We had passed an evening with cool people: smart, passionate intellects who'd lived lives that made for good conversation.

As we approached the house where my son lives with his mother and sisters — he is the middle child, seemingly content with life as it is and not as he would have it be — I heard myself talking about drugs and alcohol. It wasn't the first time we'd discussed the subject, but with the enemy looming, my cautions were more urgent than before. I told him: It's all out there, waiting, and you will have to decide for yourself whether or not to cross over.

He was adamant: "Dad, I'll never do those things."

I'd believed the same thing when I was a haircut younger than he and the swiftness of his reply unsettled me. I don't doubt his conviction, only that he might underestimate the wiles of the monkey.

Yet he'd given his word — the word of a man in some cultures — and as we hugged I told him that I loved him, knowing too well that if the voices start calling his name, there isn't much I can do beyond persevere and pray.

July 26, 1996

Chapter 2

Trades

After paying dues 45 years, piano player gets a break

EVELYN IS SAYING HER GOODBYES.

Moving between tables with her arms open and a wide smile, she asks folks if they had a good time, tells them to drive carefully, and promises a certain few she'll remember them in her prayers.

It's closing in on 2 a.m. at Rickter's Cafe, a neighborhood tavern in Northeast Baltimore, a working-class, good-times saloon so typical of this town that it seems the Orioles are always on the TV, the crab cakes are always fat, and the beer — big, cheap pitchers of it — is always cold.

As the older crowd — here, people in their 40s are considered youngsters — files out the back onto Parkside Avenue, Evelyn continues to chat, giving a hug or a kiss to those who linger before calling it a night.

An Italian lady, speaking in slightly broken English, takes Evelyn's bright, broad face in her hands, moves it closer to her own, and speaks warmly.

"Evelyn," she says to her 61-year-old friend, "you look beautiful tonight. This week I light a [church] candle for you."

"Aww," says Evelyn, with a blush. "God love ya."

It's the end of another Friday night; the end of another small chapter in the 45-year career of Evelyn Butterhoff, barroom piano player.

Once again, as she has done nearly every weekend at Rickter's for 13 years, Evelyn has mined American pop music to fill the bar with good cheer and its customers with warm memories.

As usual, a few people get up to put one hand atop Evelyn's rickety upright and begin singing. On key or off, in time or out, Evelyn follows along, never allowing her own skills to overwhelm or embarrass the crooners.

She makes them feel like stars, and they love her for it.

But what many people don't know — not at Rickter's or the handful of other neighborhood bars where Evelyn has worked over the years — is that the woman who keeps them rollicking with happy sing-along tunes, the lady who takes them away from their troubles for a few hours, has had considerable heartache of her own.

You see, Evelyn the piano player is also Evelyn the scrubwoman, using fingers more suited to charming a keyboard to instead grip a brush or a mop to make ends meet.

For as much as she loves music, dedicating her life to it from the age of 7, the spirits of melody and rhythm have been somewhat fickle in return, rewarding Evelyn with many friends but few dollars.

"Let's just say I've learned a lot and leave it at that," Evelyn said.

But Agnes Beck, Evelyn's 83-year-old mother and the woman who ordered piano lessons for her first-born after listening to a radio ad in 1932, can't quiet her frustration.

"That girl can play, I don't care what anybody says," said Mrs. Beck, still living in the North Curley Street home where Evelyn was raised. "She plays for a few lousy dollars at that tavern, and it breaks my heart to see these other people with no talent who have two or three homes and cars.

"She says she don't want all that. She says, 'Ma, look how they end up.' But every day I think that girl should get a break," Mrs. Beck said. "She's been a good girl all her life and there isn't a thing she couldn't play.

"I don't want her to be a star, but I'd like to see something better for her," she continued. "She cleans houses for people and it's a darn shame 'cause she's all heart. I picture her standing on corners waiting for buses and cleaning up for people. It's a shame, but she says she's satisfied the way she is."

Evelyn lives alone in an apartment near the intersection of Harford Road and Cold Spring Lane. She has a piano there and sometimes stays up until 4 a.m. playing and writing.

She belongs to a Christian prayer group, takes buses everywhere or walks, is fond of strolling through the Inner Harbor, and tries to see her children as much as she can.

Evelyn has been separated from her husband for 17 years, and although she won't elaborate, it seems her husband couldn't accept a wife who made a living playing the piano in bars, or anywhere people wanted to hear good music.

"I don't want to say anybody held me back because I love them," said Evelyn. "But I was trying to mix it together, have a career and still stay at home."

The mix was too much, and Evelyn chose music. "I spent half my life playing music," she said. "I didn't see no good reason to stop."

Her music has taken her all over the state for dates as diverse as executive parties on Gibson Island and cheering-up jam sessions at the Fort Holabird Veterans Administration Hospital.

And just now, through coincidence or — as Evelyn prefers — the Lord's blessing, things are starting to happen for her. One recent night, a recording-studio owner sitting at a table at Rickter's was impressed enough that she hired Evelyn to help complete a recording. This, after a lifetime of long rehearsals and one-night stands in churches and nightclubs.

The road to her first record, cut with a local gospel group last month, began in East Baltimore when she began taking 50-cents-an hour piano lessons from an "old maid" in the neighborhood, according to Mrs. Beck.

At 12, Evelyn switched to lessons in the back of the Hammann Music Co., in the 200 block of North Liberty Street, from Jack Rohr — her biggest influence.

"Jack really socked it to me," Evelyn recalled. "I had to start all over because I couldn't play in time. Jack Rohr got $2 a lesson, paid a month in advance whether you showed up or not, but he taught me sonatas, Beethoven, how to change keys, improvise and fake it."

After five years with Mr. Rohr, Evelyn was ready to turn professional, taking her first job with a Polish band that played on WCBM radio.

Led by Frank Skolsky, the band played weekend gigs at the Polish Home Club on Broadway, where Evelyn, then 16, made $2 plus food and drinks.

In 1949, Evelyn joined a "dinner music" trio that included a woman who played the musical saw.

The next year she landed with the group that would take her to hotel ballrooms, car dealership grand openings, wedding parties, local Army camps, and retirement parties.

"I answered an ad in the paper, and that's how I got to playing with the 'Queens of Rhythm,'" an all-woman orchestra that specialized in the Big Band sound.

Evelyn stayed with the Queens for 15 years, playing piano as she raised her family, often collapsing into bed late at night, exhausted.

She began working in neighborhood bars in the 1960s, mostly in North and Northeast Baltimore, finally landing at Rickter's Café on Belair Road about 1972.

"Sometimes I'm tired as anything, but I'm swinging anyway," said Evelyn, who gives highly animated performances, sometimes in costume. "I guess the music just takes over. I'm playing a part and I give it all I've got. I kept on stomping through the floorboards, so they put a steel plate under me."

One night not long ago, Mary G. Mullaney happened into Rickter's for dinner and caught Evelyn's act.

"She was just playing her heart out," said Ms. Mullaney, owner of the Starship Record Co. "It was a homey atmosphere and she knew everybody, had them right in the palm of her hand."

At the time, Ms. Mullaney was looking for a pianist to add background tracks to a gospel album being recorded by the Welcome Travelers, a local group.

Within the week, Evelyn was in a recording studio for the first time.

"She showed us she can do it all," Ms. Mullaney said. "From ragtime, to blues, to country, or old standards, she's just a fantastic musician.

"Her ear is tuned into music like you wouldn't believe," she continued. "She's concerned about timing, phrasing, and a real fanatic about tone. I work with nothing but musicians, and I've never seen anyone like her."

With Ms. Mullaney's enthusiasm has come more work for Evelyn, both in the studio and live, with a June 1 gospel concert planned for Eastern High School.

Coming so suddenly after years of being paid in tips, free drinks and a few dollars, the good fortune has left Evelyn thankful but not too surprised.

"I'm sure I'm going someplace, I don't know where, but somewhere," she said. "I don't want to waste what God gave me on people who don't appreciate it, who'd rather drink beer and smoke cigarettes than listen.

"I want some fulfillment of my own."

And with a wink, Evelyn says that she won't ever stop going for it. "Hon," she said, confidentially, "I got a story that never ends."

May 12, 1986

Graves are a fine and private place
for caretaker couple

SOME COUPLES DRY OFF WITH HIS-AND-HERS BATH TOWELS MONOGRAMMED IN Gothic script. Other husband-and-wife teams cruise town in identical luxury cars, and many work side-by-side in businesses from law offices to pizza joints.

But out on a stretch of O'Donnell Street in East Baltimore, where Highlandtown slopes down from its hill toward Dundalk, there lives perhaps the only couple in America to preside over his-and-hers graveyards.

Bill Berkey, 66, takes care of the Jewish cemetery, Oheb Shalom, on the north side of the 6100 block of O'Donnell Street. Margaret Berkey, 68, is caretaker for the First German United Evangelical Church cemetery on the south side of the block.

The Berkeys eat meals together and trade chit-chat and cemetery chores during the day. When bedtime comes, they retire to homes adjoining their respective graveyards.

It's a marital arrangement, said Mrs. Berkey, that works just fine.

"I go over there every morning at 5 o'clock to open the gates and wash and iron and make coffee and feed the birds and feed the squirrels," she said. "And he comes over here for supper and then we say good night and he walks back across the street."

In between the domestic routine comes the life work of Margaret Berkey, the daughter of a graveyard caretaker, born in a room above the stone arch of the cemetery's gateway; a woman who celebrated her wedding reception on the rolling lawn of the graveyard and reared a son there who grew up to be a mortician; a woman whose tombstone is already chiseled with her name and standing amid the rows of granite and marble markers.

Listen to Mrs. Berkey describe her job: "People don't realize what we go through. The undertaker orders the burial and he tells you the lot number but you have to look it up in the book, look for the lot and where it's located. Then you call the man that digs it, then the vault man puts in the vault and the boards and the lowering device, then you put in the fake grass and set up the chairs, then you have to take the flowers out of the flower wagon and put it on the dirt pile and make it look real pretty.

"You have to make sure the coffin goes up to the head of the grave, get the death permit and the check and be sure so much goes to the church.

"After everything is over, you take the chairs off, fold up the fake grass, take the lowering device off and take the flowers off the dirt pile and put them where they won't be in the digger's way. The funeral director stays to make sure the vault lid is put on right and then the dirt digger can do his work — I get a boy to come and cover it up for $25 — but you have to wait for the family to leave before you can do any of that. I'm telling you, there's a lot to do at a funeral that people don't realize."

In between funerals, the caretakers sod new graves, cut grass nonstop in the summer, shovel snow in the winter, trim bushes, rake leaves, direct people to the graves of friends and relatives, and think up new ways to quell vandalism.

"It's just a lot of work," said Mr. Berkey, who in March will celebrate his 30th year with Oheb Shalom, where he is revered as a caretaker of uncommon concern for detail. "In the summer all you do is cut grass, and you never know how busy you're going to be. You can go two months without a funeral and then you get three and four in a week."

Mrs. Berkey remembers growing up in the graveyard after the end of World War I, before the O'Donnell Heights housing projects were built. On farmland adjoining the old church cemetery were blueberries to be picked, she recalls.

"There used to be a bell in the arch, but one of the church men took it years ago," she said. "There wasn't any bathroom in the house back then, and no heat. My mother cooked on a big black wood-and-coal stove and she used to heat bricks in the oven to keep our feet warm at night."

Her father, an Eastern Shore native named Cyrus Stewart, started out as a gravedigger at the seven-acre cemetery, one of many along the eastern end of O'Donnell Street. He served as caretaker from 1918 until his death in 1971. Along the way, many relatives found their final place of rest on the other side of the black stone arch.

"There's my brother over there, and my cousin there, and my sister's little baby over there," said Mrs. Berkey, who became caretaker when her father died. "My cousin's little baby is there and my grandfather is over there, he's buried between his two wives. And I'm going to get buried here," she said with pride. "Here's my stone."

There are some perks to taking care of a graveyard. In addition to the free room and board, good deals pop up, like the discount Mrs. Berkey and her husband got on their headstone because a mistake prompted the original family to reject it.

It costs $325 to buy a plot at First German, and $475 to go six feet deep at Oheb Shalom. Jacob Blaustein, the founder of the American Oil Co., was buried at Oheb Shalom in 1970. No particularly well-known people are buried at First German across the street, but stories are attached to several of the graves, like the tombstone sculpted in the shape of fire captain's helmet No. 12

to honor William George Schulte, killed in the Pratt Street fire of Aug. 4, 1887.

One tall marker lists the names of five seamen who lost their lives in the Patapsco River during the great hailstorm of May 1, 1917. The gravestone was erected by the dead men's employer, the Furness Shipping and Agency Co. of Rotterdam, the Netherlands.

Margaret Berkey left the graveyard for health reasons in 1984 and lived across the street with her husband.

But it pained her to see how poorly the new man was taking care of the place, to see how her childhood home was deteriorating.

It didn't take much persuading last year from the elders at First German United Evangelical Church on Eastern Avenue near Broadway to get her to come back.

"My heart broke," she said. "The guy was letting weeds grow up into wild trees and all the dirt piles from the graves were still standing all around and the grass was knee-high deep. They got me back because they know I love it. I know it belongs to the church, but it's like my own."

Today, Mrs. Berkey said, the place is looking so good that it's almost on a par with her husband's graveyard, which is immaculate.

"A lady wrote me a letter and said she had a plot but didn't want to get buried in here because it was looking so bad, and I told her I didn't want to get buried in here either when the other guy had it," said Mrs. Berkey.

"But now it's looking good again, and it makes me feel proud," she said. "A lady told me the other day it's the best it's looked in years, and I kissed her!"

November 11, 1990

Capping off a tradition

IN THE DAYS WHEN THE HIPPODROME THEATER BOOKED LIVE ENTERTAINMENT on Eutaw Street, Lou Boulmetis' grandfather cleaned hats for such famous Americans as Red Skelton, Bob Hope and the Three Stooges.

Mr. Boulmetis has followed in the old hatter's footsteps by providing customized lids, 5,000 of them, for the followers of George Bush and Dan Quayle.

At Hippodrome Hatters, the dying trade of cleaning, blocking, and making hats lingers toward the end of the millennium. But this Sunday the world will see a bit of its work as delegates to the Republican convention don Bush/Quayle painters' caps from the old family business.

"The Republicans just called me up out of the yellow pages one day in January, asked for a price on 250,000 embroidered baseball caps or 350,000 painters' caps," said Mr. Boulmetis.

"Most people who call up with an order like that are serious."

But so far the Republicans need only 5,000 caps, embossed with Bush/Quayle on their crowns to better catch the eye of television. They were delivered yesterday to the convention site in Houston.

"It's worth many thousands of dollars," said Mr. Boulmetis, 40, who runs the business with his wife, Judy.

A contract for a quarter-of-a-million painters caps — which could come through if campaign offices around the country want them after the convention — would be worth about a million dollars before expenses.

Such high-profile jobs show up now and then at 15 N. Eutaw St., where Mr. Boulmetis' grandfather moved the business in 1930 after spending 14 years at the St. Louis Cleaners on The Block.

Mr. Boulmetis has made, altered, and cleaned hats for the Barry Levinson movies "Tin Men" and "Avalon," and he gets work from theaters and people who re-enact battles from the Civil War.

And, although he has never met the man, he has sold Sherlock Holmes "deer stalker" hats that found their way to the dome-like pate of Gov. William Donald Schaefer.

"He's a very big size," said Mr. Boulmetis. "A seven and five-eighths."

Had he been born in the 19th century, Mr. Boulmetis could have done good work for another well-known politician who liked to shield his skull.

25

"My specialty is top hats from the 1800s," he said. "I can make a hat look like Abe Lincoln just took it off his head."

But he and his wife mostly clean chapeaus for the common man.

Hordes of hats come in from dry cleaners in Pennsylvania, New Jersey, New York, Virginia and right off the street, some of them hanging together with duct tape.

"Two days ago, a man came in with a hat that was falling apart. He said it was his lucky hat and he was pleading with us to clean it," said Mrs. Boulmetis.

"It was a 1940s fedora, Goodwill wouldn't have taken it, but it was this man's best friend," said Mr. Boulmetis.

"It was a religious object to this man, so we cleaned it for him," said his wife.

Another time, a man came in with a hat that was run over by an 18-wheel tractor trailer.

Said Mrs. Boulmetis, brimming with pride: "Lou brought it back to life."

Just the way he brought Hippodrome Hatters back to life.

In 1983, Mr. Boulmetis was a regional manager for the General Mills Corp. with a master's degree in business administration from the University of Baltimore.

Down on Eutaw Street, his namesake grandfather, who had jumped ship in Baltimore during World War I as a 15-year-old cabin boy on a Greek freighter, was spending his days cleaning hats.

Mr. Boulmetis had helped the old guy over the years, picking up the trade on odd afternoons of his childhood, and when his grandfather died at age 85 in December 1984, he took over the business.

"It started when I was a kid," Mr. Boulmetis said.

"I'd see my uncle altering suits, my father dry-cleaning and my grandfather doing the only thing that looked worthwhile to me — cleaning hats."

He committed himself to the vocation on Christmas Eve of that year when, going through some of the old man's stuff, he found a picture of his beloved Papou cleaning hats in a photo dated Christmas Eve, 1946.

He still uses his grandfather's tools, most of them wooden and no longer made.

"Even though most people don't know a crown from a brim, I could train someone to do this in an hour," he said.

"But it takes a lifetime to master."

August 14, 1992

Ex-stripper's days are now quiet ones

IT ISN'T RIGHT FOR JEAN HONUS TO BE ALL ALONE ON BARNEY STREET.

The house is quiet; hours are long.

And there's no action.

Not like the days when men gave her diamond watches just because they liked the way she moved.

When strangers by the hundreds whooped and hollered and whistled as she sashayed her knockout figure across a stage.

Back when Jean Honus did the striptease on Baltimore's Block in the glory days of burlesque.

The theaters and musicians, the bookies, the barkers, the wise guys, the prizefighters and the straight men, all gone.

At age 74, the woman born to a coal-mining family in Shenandoah, Pa., accepts that time has reduced the art of burlesque to stark nudity and robot music.

But it's not right, she says, that she outlived almost all of her friends from her burlesque days.

"I'm very lonely," says Miss Honus, cooking up a big pot of rigatoni and hot sausage, grateful for the chance to entertain a new visitor to her South Baltimore rowhouse, eager to fill a fresh ear with her stories. "I go out every day now and sit with friends, but people don't want to hear too much of your troubles. You try to hide from loneliness, but it's so hard. I don't know what to do with myself so I just get up and get out of here. I go down to the market even if I don't have to buy anything."

Fast living and hard liquor, she says, killed most of her colleagues years ago.

"I have no friends because they drank themselves to death," she says, tears coming to her eyes. "Drink ruined my girlfriends, girls that should be here today with me. I took care of myself and I'm here. They drank morning, noon and night — they thought they were having fun, but they weren't happy. Sometimes I'd take two days off from work just not to drink, to get some sleep and take care of myself. I had a lot of fun, but it all just came and went."

Miss Honus, who dyed her hair platinum blond in the early 1940s and promoted herself as the Jean Harlow of The Block, started as a burlesque chorus girl — a "pony" — at age 13.

She wound up stripping for the next 40 years, performing her last bump and grind at Blaze Starr's 2 O'Clock Club when she was 56.

"I got a very good hand that night. Even when I was 50 I got a better applause than a lot of the young ones," she says. "I loved my work, I loved my audience. If the audience didn't want you, the boss didn't want you. If they didn't applaud, I'd stomp my feet until they did. But this one night, I just felt that I wanted to quit."

Miss Honus' career started in New York City, where her mother searched for work during the Depression and used to leave young Jean alone in their one-room apartment off Broadway.

"I wasn't even in school, and no one questioned it," she said. "One day, I went to the Gayety on 47th and Broadway with an older girl who wanted a job in burlesque and the man saw me and said: 'Do you know your right from your left?' That's how I got my first job."

The burlesque circuit and an entourage called the "Bothwell Brown Revue" took the teen-ager from New York to Atlantic City and eventually Baltimore, once famed in seaports the world over for the nightlife of The Block; a good town, Miss Honus remembers, where a good-looking girl with a nice figure could always get a job and make her money go a long way.

"I knew I could make Baltimore my home port, support my Mom here and still go on the road," she says. "And that's what I did."

Baltimore Street had a community of home-grown characters beyond the imagination of Damon Runyon, guys named Shykie and Shimkie and Abie; Jewish theater owners who remained kosher while selling tickets to the girlie shows; a place where you could work with strippers named Sapphire and Electra and then meet Boris Karloff backstage without recognizing him because he wasn't in his Frankenstein costume.

This street was where the most famous theater in town was the Oasis because it advertised "The World's Worst Show" and the entertainment lived up to its billing.

Miss Honus, who liked stripping to the swing of "Little Coquette," didn't have to play there.

"The pay was small; if you got $100, that was good; the bosses never told anyone what the girls' salaries were and you had to fight for your raise," she says. "If I didn't get mine, I'd just go on the road. The most I ever made was $250 a week in the '60s. That was pretty good back then."

Miss Honus was confronted more than once by jealous wives, whom she advised to take care of their problems at home, and her hotel room was showered with sulfuric acid by a man who had courted her in vain.

An entire industry surrounded burlesque then, says Miss Honus, including tailors who specialized in custom-made gowns for strippers.

"Today they just come out with nothing on, but in my day, if you didn't have a beautiful wardrobe, you didn't work," she recalls, noting that she sometimes spent half a $200 paycheck on a gown. "I had maybe two dozen gowns at a time. I'd fill up a trunk when we went on the road. I still have a beautiful fringe gown that I kept — red velvet with one breast cut out and covered with lace. I won't give it up."

She might, however, donate her treasures — the newspaper clippings and the photos and the costumes and trinkets — to a museum of burlesque if one existed, especially if it happened to exist on The Block.

"I always felt that I knew my work," she says. "I can't say I learned it. I went out there and did it — nothing was stopping me. But today, here I am."

Here on Barney Street in a house crowded with baby dolls and stuffed animals, an old trunk in the basement stuffed with memories.

Married at 15 and widowed at 25 when her husband died of leukemia, Miss Honus never remarried. She has no children. She goes on bus trips once in a while, or out to the track when she feels up to it.

But it's not the same.

Her dogs kept her company for years, but they died, and now Miss Honus keeps radios playing day and night, upstairs and down, for the company of a human voice.

"Some people knock burlesque terribly, but I don't take any stuff from them. I tell 'em: 'I'm better than you'll be any day'," she says.

February 2, 1993

29

The shoe man can still put
the leather to the road

IT MAY BE THE SHOE MAN'S LAST WALK UP HARFORD ROAD: A SLOW, AFTERNOON trudge through the heart of Hamilton — in and out of the doughnut shop, the cleaners, the pizza joint, the video store and the gas station with the simple pitch: "Anybody need shoes today?"

He says: "You never know when you might sell a pair of shoes, so I just go right down the line."

Edward Angell has gone right down the line to the end of the line.

After more than 30 years of pedestrian sojourns from one end of Baltimore to the other — selling thousands of pairs of shoes and Christmas cards in season — old age and fragile health will deliver him to a retirement home at the end of this month.

"Things are starting to come to an end," says Mr. Angell, 78, who moves with a loping limp because of an artificial hip. "It's sad, but people say it's in my best interest. It's not that I can't work. I can still work."

Just the other day, he went about proving it.

At noon, Mr. Angell leaves his small apartment next to the Pyle Fence Co. and crosses Harford Road to wait for the No. 19 bus in front of Alessi's Citgo at Southern Avenue. Without a driver's license, he depends instead on transit buses to make sales calls along Harford Road, York Road, Reisterstown Road and as far away as Hunt Valley.

"My gosh, I'd like to know how many miles Eddie's walked in his life," says Jean Hammond, a sales clerk at the Towson Bootery and a friend for 35 years. "People come up and say: 'Guess where I saw Eddie Angell?' It could be anywhere. He's always on the road."

From Mr. Angell's left wrist hangs his office — a blue canvas bag with his catalog, order forms, and a "Brannock Device" for measuring feet. His right hand is deep in his pocket, jiggling change.

The bus comes, and he takes it just five blocks north to Echodale Avenue on the edge of the Hamilton shopping district. "I don't like to start walking until I get on the job, but then I get going pretty good," he says. "I know the spots, mostly businesses where people are too busy to get out to the store."

He walks into the Dunkin' Donuts, a glad hand extended in front of him, announcing: "Edward Angell. I sell Mason Shoes — all leather, arch support and cushioned insoles." People look up from their coffee, stare as he opens the tattered catalog on the counter, and pass. He asks the woman behind the counter: "Hon, you need a pair of shoes?" She doesn't. Only Jim Sinnott, who bought a pair of white bucks from Mr. Angell four years ago, gives the shoe man the time of day. With admiration, he says: "You can't sell shoes door-to-door without being a hustler, particularly in this day and age when most people buy shoes at the dime store."

Warehouse discount stores, two-career families where no one is home during the day, fear of strangers, and cheap, disposable footwear have steadily pushed door-to-door shoe salesmen toward the exit sign.

"It was the Edward Angells that made this company what it is," says Rich Johnson, an officer with the 90-year-old Mason Shoe Co. of Chippewa Falls, Wis., which had direct sales of about 2 million pairs of shoes last year. "Almost all of our customers order out of the catalog for themselves. The true, door-to-door guy like Mr. Angell is a dinosaur."

The dinosaur lumbers from the Dunkin' Donuts to the Harford Cleaners to the Amoco station to the Goodyear store in search of a 20 percent commission on wingtips, loafers, running shoes, pumps and work boots, all without luck.

"I just keep going," he says. "Sooner or later, there'll be a break. It's not everywhere you go they're going to buy a pair of shoes. It's not an item you need everyday."

At the Jiffy Lube, Mr. Angell walks into a service bay calling out: "Anybody need any shoes?"

The men just stare at him until one of them points to a co-worker and laughs: "He needs a new brain."

"I don't sell brains," says Mr. Angell, turning his back on them for Harford Road and an afternoon that bears no fruit for a man used to selling eight pairs of shoes a week.

Edward C. Angell was born and raised on Bolton Street before spending more than 50 years on Bosley Avenue in Towson, where he lived until about five years ago. His father was a Metropolitan Life insurance salesman who lived to be 97.

Before Mr. Angell hit the streets — where he has been bitten by dogs, robbed and even had the police called on him — he had a civilian job at the old Edgewood Arsenal and Fort Detrick. Before that, he worked for local dairies and ice cream plants.

Never married, he lives alone with a portrait of himself as a young man painted by his late mother, Irma. His one great love is the water, as the members of Hillcrest Swimming Pool know. In the afternoons, he might unwind at the Enoch Pratt Free Library and the evenings often find him in the company of a few beers. Most of his meals are taken at the Golden Key Restaurant, a Greek diner on Harford Road where everybody knows Mr.

Angell and more than a few have bought shoes from him.

Says waitress Gerri Parks, serving him a big bowl of pea soup and a ham and cheese sandwich: "That man walks and walks and walks."

Mr. Angell stares into his pea soup, considering the feat he has accomplished and the fate that awaits him this month at Towson's Presbyterian Home.

"Physically, it's been tough, being on the street and all," he says. "But I've made a fair and decent living. I guess it's for the best."

June 11, 1994

Chapter 3

Icons

Skee-Ball is still queen of beach arcades

OCEAN CITY — SHE IS THE AGING BUT ALWAYS ALLURING ATTRACTION OF THE arcade.

Seventy-five years old this summer, she is a mechanical maiden who has been a cheery opponent to generations of fun-seekers here by the sea and throughout the United States.

Her name is Skee-Ball.

Along with a tub of Thrasher's french fries and a stop at Second Street and the beach to marvel at Ranoa Hofman's magnificent sand sculptures, a few games of Skee-Ball are among the handful of "must-do" items for people who return to this resort year after year.

"We call it our 'two-to-toothless bread and butter machine,'" said Sam Gaffin, who has been trading idle amusement for loose change at Marty's Playland on the Boardwalk since 1948. "It has appeal for everyone in the family."

"I play a half-dozen games every time I come down the ocean," said a man in his late 20s during a recent stroll down the boards. "It always makes me feel like I'm 5 years old again."

Invented by a Philadelphia piano maker named J. B. Estes in 1909, the lasting beauty of Skee-Ball, like the beauty of a sugar cookie, is its simplicity.

The player rolls a wooden ball down a cork-lined alley, the ball hops over a curved lip about 14 feet away and is supposed to pop into one of five rubber cups numbered 10 to 50. In Skee-Ball, like in life, gutter balls score zero.

For a dime (remember the dime?) a player gets to roll nine balls, aiming for the elusive perfect score of 450 points. The average game hovers somewhere around 200 points, with any score over 100 earning one-third of a coupon toward the typical arcade prizes like plastic cowboys, rubber dinosaurs, and flimsy beach chairs.

"Generally, girls are better at it than the boys," said Mr. Gaffin, speaking from 36 years of overseeing fun and games on the Boardwalk. "They don't throw the ball as hard and it rolls up into the cups instead of banging around up there and falling in the gutter."

Like most everything else in this country, time and technology have altered the appearance of Skee-Ball (the new games — which cost up to $2,450, score points digitally, and some have computers that talk and whirr). But progress hasn't by-passed the heart of the game, rolling a ball into a cup.

"The original games were 35 feet long," said Samuel H. High, III, president of the Skee-Ball company, a corporate offshoot of the Philadelphia Toboggan Company, a roller coaster manufacturer that bought the rights to the game just before the end of World War II.

Mr. High said the first machines took up a lot of floor space, and when the Great Depression sucker-punched America in the bread-basket, large arcades began going out of business, and were replaced by smaller buildings.

The machine was shortened from 35 feet to 14 feet by Maurice Piesen, a New York law clerk who bought the rights to Skee-Ball from Morris Goldberg, a Coney Island amusement huckster who had purchased them from originator Estes in 1920.

"Those 35-footers were real brutes," said Mr. High, age 50. "The change in size made it easy for just about anybody to play, especially kids."

In 1930, the game was sold to the Wurlitzer company, and Mr. High reports that the maker of the famous pianos and organs "produced a tremendous quantity, over 5,000 in one year, which in those days was a lot, and flooded the market.

"It almost killed the game," Mr. High said. "And then the war came along, and war kills everything."

When the Philadelphia Toboggan company bought out Wurlitzer in 1944, they introduced an angle that Mr. High says resurrected Skee-Ball — coupons to be traded in for prizes. "It just took off from there," he said.

Older games — which originally cost 5 cents to play — had a lever one had to pull to release the balls. Some of these games can still be found on the Boardwalk. Today, the balls drop automatically. While many arcades have held the line at a dime per game, some charge a quarter, but offer a full coupon per wining game instead of a third of a coupon.

The next big innovation in Skee-Ball came in 1968, with the introduction of automatic coupon dispensers. "It's increased each game's capacity by 50 percent," said Mr. High. "The player didn't have to wait around for someone to hand them the coupon."

More importantly, according to Lloyd (Ed) Jester, Jr., owner of Jester's Sportland Arcade, one of the oldest game rooms in Ocean City, the automatic dispensers "don't stand around and talk to girls instead of working."

All of the arcade owners pointed to the machine's durability and lasting popularity with all age groups as Skee-Ball's greatest attributes.

"For the beating they take, they hold up pretty well," said Mr. Jester. "I'll never take 'em out, I don't care what kind of video games they come up with.

"This is a game even handicapped people can play. We get 'em in wheelchairs in here all the time. They roll right up to the Skee-Ball alleys and start rolling them balls."

And who rolls best?

The Guinness Book of World Records doesn't appear to have a category listing the hottest dead-eye Skee-Ballers of all-time, but Sam High says he once witnessed an exhibition he's yet to see duplicated.

According to Mr. High, the unofficial world record belongs to 84-year-old Noel Janotta, a special projects employee for his firm.

"Back in '64 at an [amusements] convention, it was late in the afternoon and there wasn't many people around our booth. So one of our oldtimers [Mr. Janotta] began to play to pass the time.

"He starts off with a perfect 450 game," said Mr. High. "Then he rolls another, then another, and another. By now he's got a crowd around him, and before it was all over, he'd rolled 13 perfect games in a row. I've never seen anything like it before or since."

Anyone who can document a greater feat of Skee-Ball prowess is invited to give Mr. High a call at the Philadelphia Toboggan company in Lansing, Pa.

For a dime, you can't beat it.

August 3, 1984

Where the landmarks are a church and a water tower with 24 pillars

ISSAC BASHEVIS SINGER, THE GREAT STORYTELLER, SAID: "GOD GAVE US SO many emotions, and such strong ones. Every human being, even if he is an idiot, is a millionaire in emotions."

I spent a good ten or twenty grand of my emotional bankroll the first time I saw the Curtis Bay water tank high atop Baltimore and the harbor channel that gives the peninsula neighborhood its name.

And every time I return to the corner of Prudence and Filbert Streets to stand in its magnificent shadow I drop another piece of change.

Not even an idiot could look at this strange and fantastic landmark, one of the most powerful icons in a city peppered with them, and not react to it.

"It has a major presence all to itself," said a woman who paints the streetscapes of Baltimore for a living. "It looks like it landed here from another planet." It landed in Curtis Bay, old waterfront dairy land and strawberry fields turned to heavy industry, from the mind of Frank O. Heyder in 1930.

The principal draftsman for the Bureau of Plans and Surveys through the middle of the century, Mr. Heyder lived in an Elmley Avenue rowhouse near Herring Run Park that was crowded with 3,500 books on the architecture of the 16th, 17th and 18th centuries.

Newspaper stories from the early 1930s describe Mr. Heyder as a man "fascinated by cathedrals and domes and complicated structures," and it was this fascination and $44,989 in public money that saw the tank erected between 1931 and 1932.

A squat and simple tank made of iron was already on the hill, having replaced a large black water tower built in 1893 by the Monarch Engineering Company, and what Mr. Heyder designed for the city was a masonry skirt to adorn it.

The skirt is made of colored gravel mixed with poured and highly polished concrete that appears as a blue-gray granite. Above this base is dark brown brick and above that run sections of hand-picked bricks that change color 20 times before fading to light tan at the top, where they are laid in herring bone fashion. A series of 24 pillars and 24 panels runs around the building with the wall color reversed inside of the panels.

"The first time I saw it, I thought it was a synagogue," said Brendan T. Carr, the neighborhood priest.

Frank Heyder also experimented with the terra cotta cornice, whose original clay brown was fired with other colors.

"Neither the coloring in the base or the cornice has ever been tried before," said Mr. Heyder, who died March 18, 1973.

His experiments were carried out splendidly by bricklayers working for the Mullan Construction Company, although two young workers, Otto Polo and Ricco Grosso, lost their lives in falls from the tank 16 days apart in February of 1932.

When the work was done a few months later, Frank Heyder's vision for the high hill over Stonehouse Cove was called "the most beautiful structure ever built under supervision of the Public Improvement Commission."

But the old Polish woman who trudges up Filbert Street just before 7 o'clock every morning doesn't pay it much mind as she crosses in front of it.

Like most of the folks who live near the tank, she wishes the city would paint the rusting iron dome, but it's a minor concern as she makes her way to a more significant landmark just south of the tank: St. Athanasius Roman Catholic Church, now in its 100th year, where Brendan Carr is the first non-Polish pastor since 1895. A small woman with a kind face and strong memories of hard work and good fun, she doesn't want to give her name. Except for a brief stay in Highlandtown, all of her 85 years have been passed in Curtis Bay.

The neighborhood was once a stronghold of Baltimore's Polish community rivaling Canton, and it remains the hilltop residence of the Polish Home Hall, a big brick house famous for polka-driven wedding receptions and oyster roasts.

Curtis Bay is now a community made up of various ethnic groups, but in the first decades of the century it was thick with families fresh from Poland as the old woman's was.

"It was all Polish through the early Fifties," said a woman from Kentucky whose front door faces the water tank. "When I moved here in 1952, I was a foreigner."

The old Polish woman makes the steep walk up Filbert Street from her home on Fairhaven Avenue every day and twice on Sunday for Mass at the parish where she was baptized and celebrated the sacraments of First Communion, Confirmation and Holy Matrimony; the church from which her husband was buried five years and ten days after their marriage in 1925.

The old church building, now closed to the public and awaiting renovation, was replaced by a new one in 1957. Sitting in the rectory at St. Athanasius, willing to talk of the old days as long as she doesn't have to suffer the embarrassment of seeing her name in the paper, she told the story of the neighborhood: "One family came and then the others followed, a lot of the men worked at the old wheel foundry on Curtis Avenue. From Pennington Avenue to Curtis

Avenue was nothing but woods, and when we had to go over to Holy Cross cemetery we walked through the woods. All around everywhere were string-beans and strawberries and everybody raising chickens and cattle."

Her father, Konstanti Aleksalza, helped raise money to build the Polish Home Hall, where English and Polish were taught in days gone by. He played the organ, and the family home was filled with Polish youngsters from around the city who came to practice for the church choir.

"It was the happiest days when the young boys and girls used to come to learn how to sing in our house," she said, remembering her mother making big pots of duck's blood soup, a Polish delicacy known as czarnina, for the 14 children who lived in their house. "We had a happy life. It was a wonderful living, each one was good to another.

"Today I wake up at 5 o'clock on the dot every morning, cross myself with holy water I keep near the bed, and thank God for making it through the night. I take pain pills for my arthritis, eat a little pound cake with coffee and then I walk up that hill to Mass and I feel so relieved when I get to church. I thank God that I'm here."

Here, in Curtis Bay.

September 1, 1991

The quest for Bawlmer's treasures

DEAN KRIMMEL IS LOOKING FOR A SIGN THAT SAYS "STEAMED MALES."

Mr. Krimmel does not belong to an encounter group for frustrated men, he is a City Life Museums curator building an exhibit of objects unique to this town, the stuff "that makes Baltimore Bawlmer."

Near the top of the list, with the harbor waters where they once spawned by the millions, are crabs.

It doesn't take an anthropologist to come up with a few mallets and a vintage can of Old Bay seasoning to put on display for folks who've been using these things all their lives. But Mr. Krimmel is convinced that rarer treasures — like a crab house sign advertising "Steamed Males" — surely are collecting dust in a garage somewhere between Essex and Baltimore Highlands.

And he'd love to have them.

"We have until the end of May to [collect] and we're lacking things," said Mr. Krimmel. "We need some more crab material, a great visual from something that's really known like Connelly's [restaurant] or a picnic table where families ate crabs together. We have a Colts football but not any Orioles stuff from the fans' point of view. We'd like a piece of Memorial Stadium."

For almost a year, area residents have been asked to donate everyday items for the "Collecting Baltimore" project, with special days set aside for people to drop off icons at the Peale Museum on Holliday Street.

The curators cried: Bring us your Baltimore!

Precious little surfaced: a scrub brush with bristles worn down by repeated workouts on white marble steps; a bucket to go with the brush; municipal knickknacks and such curiosities as a certificate from the Baltimore Gas and Electric Co. congratulating a Highlandtown family for insulating its house with Formstone.

"We want more brushes and pails, but we want more than that," said Mr. Krimmel. "This exhibit is supposed to be about the heart and soul of Baltimore. How do we see ourselves?"

How Baltimoreans see themselves may have hindered donations.

"A lot of lifelong Baltimoreans didn't get the point," he said. "They may have wondered what they had to offer. . . . The last thing we want is for people to be intimidated. This is about everyday Baltimore."

An unscientific survey conducted for the exhibit asked 500 locals what immediately came to mind when they thought about their hometown. The most frequent answer was the harbor and crabs. Orioles baseball was third, followed by rowhouses, neighborhoods and city markets.

"The lowest symbol on the totem pole was The Block," Mr. Krimmel said.

When asked what made Baltimore different from other U.S. cities, those polled cited down-to-earth, friendly people — living examples of the city's small-town warmth.

The one consistent negative was crime and violence, along with a general feeling of decline and a lack of care between neighbors.

More than a few residents regretted not only that many of the things that made Baltimore are gone, but also that Baltimore has been lost along with them. A big part of that loss was the beloved Baltimore Colts, taken from the city a dozen years ago by team owner Robert Irsay. Mr. Irsay will be represented in the exhibit by a door from the Golden Arm, the restaurant once owned by the fabled quarterback Johnny Unitas.

It is the door to the men's room.

"Unitas put a handwritten sign on the door that said 'the Bob Irsay room' the night the team moved," said Bill Grauel, the current owner. "The sign has been stolen 25 or 30 times, so we keep a good supply on hand."

Much of what's already been gathered is on display at the Peale: painted window screens, flower planters made from old tires, a pony cart used by hucksters known as "a-rabbers," a Styrofoam grave decoration that says "HON" and scenes of city life painted by Tom Miller.

Next year, the project will move into the city's new, 30,000 square foot Morton K. Blaustein Exhibition Center at Lombard and Front streets, and it's going to take a lot more stuff to fill out the exhibit.

There's a lot of Baltimore right under your nose. That round, maroon teapot at the back of the china closet may only represent an heirloom your grandmother used to entertain her lady friends. But turn the pot over, and chances are that the name of local spice king McCormick will be written across the bottom.

That was everyday Baltimore.

Carolyn A. Anderson has lived every day of her 49 years in the same city rowhouse, up on Cornwall Street near the city line on the eastside. Her contribution to the exhibit is the hard shell of a single steamed male.

"I get the shells from Don's Crabs on Joppa Road," said Ms. Anderson. whose name was Jendrusiak until her father changed it to appear more American. "I clean out the shells, boil them in bleach water and spray-paint them gold with sparkles and holiday scenes on the inside."

One sad day, such contrivances may be the only vestige of crabs in Baltimore, a memory along with the Esskay slaughterhouse and the Schaefer Brewery. Ms. Anderson thinks the city may have already waited too long to start collecting.

"Each generation loses a little bit; each generation a little more gets lost," she said. "My grandmother and mother made their own kielbasa. I don't. My mother did a lot of crocheting, they could have some of that in the exhibit. I love the old Baltimore, but some people might be thinking: 'Ah, what do they want to see that for?'"

March 23, 1995

Dominant symbol

IT SPELLS "DOMINO SUGARS," BUT IT SAYS BALTIMORE.

And from its angled perch some 16 stories above the water, it speaks with an accent that is pure Bawlmer. No one even pronounces the final, 10-foot-tall "s."

" I can see it from my kitchen window. When I'm sitting down eating dinner, I can see it," says Liz Hartlove, who runs a family bar on Fort Avenue and has spent all her 52 years in South Baltimore. "When you see that sign, you know you're home."

That sign is the second-largest field of neon on the East Coast; a 120-by-70-foot neon Polaris that has cast its blood-orange radiance across the upriver waters of the Patapsco since April 25, 1951 — 650 neon tubes searing a 760-amps-per-hour image into the psyche of Charm City.

All from the roof of a building known along the waterfront simply as "the sugar house."

"I love the red glow," says Dickie Gammerman, who lives on a boat in Fells Point. "And there's always this steam rising from it."

From nightfall until the time the bars close, the glow burns with enough energy to keep 15 households running, costing Domino about $70,000 a year to power and maintain it.

"It's our lighthouse," says Jenifer Ganzer, a local artist who has photographed the sign many times. "Whether you're looking at it from the front or back, it doesn't matter because it means the same thing — Baltimore."

Even though the Domino Sugar Corp. plant generates its own power, the sign was turned off as a good-faith gesture in 1974 during the United States' energy crisis. By the time it returned in 1983, the Inner Harbor had been sugarcoated as a tourist attraction, and the icon gained thousands of new fans.

No one was more pleased than the folks who grew up with it in Locust Point.

Says Fort Avenue bar owner Larry Gross: "Day in and day out, it warms your heart."

A little bigger than a basketball court, the landmark assures the homesick they are near a place they love; the star by which intoxicated boaters navigate out of the Inner Harbor; and the incandescent soul of a city built not on pleasure — as the modern waterfront's marinas might suggest — but the kind of hard work that takes place in the refinery whose product the sign represents.

"It's a symbol of the fact that Baltimore has been importing raw materials and processing them into useful products for a long time," says Dennis Zembala, director of the Baltimore Museum of Industry on Key Highway, just around the bend from the sugar plant. "I can look right at it out of my office window. The red — like heat, like sugar, which is energy — gives the harbor a warm glow. I stare over there all the time."

A simple joy, gazing at such monochromatic brilliance.

"One warm summer night I was playing at a club in Locust Point and got lost," remembers Dave Giegerich, pedal steel guitarist for the Hula Monsters. "I turned down some street and WHOA! There it was, towering over me like an Edward Hopper painting."

Or better yet, a massive silk-screen by Andy Warhol, whose adopted home of New York has a smaller version at a Domino refinery on the East River. The company has closed plants in Philadelphia and Boston and maintains a third in New Orleans.

Baltimore's Domino sign is big enough that anyone cruising through town on Interstate 95 can see it, and foreigners who have been here but a few days recognize it as more than an advertisement for sugar.

"I was drawn to it," said visiting Russian artist Sergei Daniel in the fall of 1995, his easel atop Federal Hill and the sign's 32-foot high "D" in his sights.

High winds play havoc with the small glass posts and the copper wire that ties the neon tubes to the letters' metal housing. The letters are coated with porcelain enamel and glass that has cracked in places, letting in rain and causing rust.

Birds nest in the letters; unluckier ones break tubes by crashing into them, and bees overdose on the sticky residue that settles on the sign from the stacks of the refinery that has processed sugar on Key Highway since 1922.

Generations have known the romance of strolling near the sign on a summer night's date, but only a few have experienced the thrill of looking out over the city from it.

A lucky few, such as 32-year-old Gary Brent.

"Pick a day in May when it's 75 degrees and get on top [of] the sign, and there's no better place in the world to be," says Brent, whose company — Installations Your Way — has the contract to maintain the sign.

Gorgeous from the ground — even if it's just a scarlet hint glimpsed from the crest of Caroline Street or the roof of the Broadway Recreation Pier — the sign reveals itself on close inspection as a cold metal skeleton for hundreds of feet of 15-millimeter-gauge glass tubing.

Sometimes a side of the rectangular border goes out, rarely an entire letter. Each of the dozen letters has four strokes of neon so that even if, for example, three go out in the intricate, 18-foot-tall, lowercase "g," it will remain visible.

Brent says he is "perpetually replacing" failed tubes and their transformers, yet on the best nights only 90 percent of the tubes are lighted.

To get the color, red neon gas is forced through clear green tubing coated inside with phosphorus. The gas interacts with the coating for a strong orange hue, but as the phosphorus ages, the orange takes on a pinkish tint, which appears reddish from the ground.

"We're climbing that sign once a week, going behind the letters and inside the letters to fix the wiring and transformers," says Brent. "I've pulled transformers out of there from the '50s that still work even though their casings have completely rusted away."

And the same sticky residue that drives bees wild adheres to the neon tubes, which turn black with airborne soot. "The neon shines through all of that," he says.

As it does through the bedroom window of Harvey Street's Alan Romefelt — "It's my own personal nightlight," he says — and blazes in the imagination of Pasadena glassblower John Stopkowski.

"Every time I go down to the harbor now, I tell people: 'Hey, I service that sign,'" says Stopkowski, 29, whose Absolute Neon company was subcontracted by Brent to repair, replace and repump tubes for Domino. "The 0 is so big that when I replace one of its tubes, there's hardly a curve in it."

When the Domino Sugars sign was first turned on, Julius and Ethel Rosenberg had just been sentenced to death for espionage; Gen. Douglas MacArthur was fired by President Harry S. Truman; and the city was beginning to fund construction of the Jones Falls Expressway.

The sign was built by 99-year-old Artkraft Strauss Co. of New York — which has made nearly all the spectacular Times Square neon since the Great Depression — and installed by Triangle Sign Co., a local business.

"There aren't many classic neon signs left in the country outside of Times Square," says Ed Hayman, a publicist with Artkraft Strauss. "The ones in Times Square are solid neon, but in terms of square feet, they're smaller. The only one bigger we know of is the Newport cigarette sign on the Cross Bronx Parkway, which measures 150 feet by 63-and-a-half."

Today, people ask Domino's chief engineer Mickey Seither to turn it on at odd hours for all kinds of reasons. One man asked that it be switched on during the day in honor of his son's bar mitzvah.

Says Seither: "We have no intention of doing anything with this sign except keeping it lit."

September 22, 1996

A city is crying in its beer

MR. BOH LEAVING THE LAND OF PLEASANT LIVING AFTER 111 YEARS?

Unthinkable and insulting. The notion that National Bohemian beer will no longer be brewed along the shores of the Chesapeake Bay is such an affront to Baltimore's civic integrity that Patrick "Scunny" McCusker is convinced only one man could be behind such a plot.

"Irsay!" he declares.

Though no doubt capable of such a deed, the man who sneaked the Colts out of Baltimore isn't responsible for the latest bit of egg on the city's face.

The decision to close the metro area's last major brewery — announced by the Stroh Brewing Co. on Thursday with the news that 430 jobs will be lost — was simple corporate pragmatism. A necessary move, says Stroh's, to remain competitive in today's tough market.

That's what you hear every time a conglomerate kills off a little piece of a community's heart while putting people out of work. And while Boh sells poorly in the town of its birth, the logic behind the decision doesn't make it feel any better.

"It's like somebody coming in to take away all the duckpin bowling alleys," says McCusker, whose Nacho Mama's restaurant in Canton is a shrine to National beer and Mr. Boh, the one-eyed little man with the mustache whose status here over the years has evolved from mascot to icon.

Says McCusker: "We're going to have to wear black armbands."

While Stroh's affirmed yesterday that it plans to continue brewing "Natty Boh" — albeit at a plant near Lehigh Valley, Pa. — it was hard for some to bear that Mr. Boh will lose its local roots.

And who can say how long a beer with a fraction of the market will survive?

Didn't they already kill off Boh's highfalutin sibling, National Premium?

This is a product that loses customers when the price of a case goes up from $7 to $7.50, whose supporters tend to be guys in their early 20s mining a retro vein of hip for a cheap buzz, old-timers who were drinking it when Truman was president and street drunks able to scrape up a $1.59 for a 40-ounce bottle.

One local woman says she can't testify to the taste but swears by it as a fine way to kill garden slugs.

"It's terrible," says Tony Della Rose, whose family owns a pub by the same name on Belair Road. "I think they should have did something to make it the No. 1 beer like it used to be."

Used to be is a long time gone for National Boh, which enjoyed a golden age in the 1950s and '60s when it was the standard beverage at baseball games, football games and crab feasts, accounting for about half of all beer consumed in the Baltimore area.

The 100,000 barrels a year now distributed locally is almost nothing compared with giants like Coors and Budweiser, which would not give out sales figures.

"This stinks," says Hugh J. Sisson, who runs the Clipper City microbrewery less than a mile from the 36-year-old Halethorpe plant that Stroh's will close a week before Christmas.

"I'm a native Baltimorean and I'd like to be the biggest brewery in Baltimore, but I didn't want to get there this way," says Sisson, whose plant has the capacity to brew more than 50,000 barrels. "It's sad because Boh is the original local beer, and I remember when it was the dominant local beer."

A glimpse of the brand's faded glory can be seen on the side of a Fallsway building just south of Gay Street where a mural of the National logo peels away from the bricks under the legend: "I love it!"

Mark Tewey owns Brimstone Brewing, a microbrewery that operates out of National Boh's original bottling plant off the corner of Conkling and O'Donnell streets in Canton.

Once crowded with beer meisters, the area used to be known as Brewer's Hill. Now, Tewey runs a 2,000-barrel-a-year operation while a demolition company guts the huge brick plant next door where National was brewed through the 1970s.

Tewey asserts that what is now passed off as the Boh enjoyed by Baltimoreans after World War II — a fine elixir by all accounts — is "bogus." The only thing that differentiates one industrial brand from another, he says, is a label and the amount of water added to the mix.

And if bad comes to worse and Stroh's decides it can no longer afford to keep Mr. Boh on tap, Tewey has a plan.

"I'd love to get a movement together to save National Boh for Baltimore as a microbrewery," he says.

"People laugh because micro-brews are so expensive, but you could do it if you brought back the original formula and put the old red and black label on it. I know a lot of people who remember it as a good beer."

October 19, 1996

J

Era fades, step by step

ARE THESE STEPS CLEAN?

The question is asked of Shirley Horner in front of her East Baltimore rowhouse on South Robinson Street. The sun shines, and the three slabs of white marble gleam, apparently spotless until Horner leans down, licks her thumb and rubs it against a smudge.

"See that?" she says as the spot disappears. "They can be cleaner."

The century in which thousands of tons of marble were laid in front of rowhouses throughout the city is about to end. And those fabled steps, tiny marble altars to hard work upon which thousands knelt with scrub brush in hand, could use an army of Shirley Horners today.

"When I was growing up, everybody got out and scrubbed," says the 64-year-old. "They were white marble, and you kept them clean. It was the thing you did."

Not only is that "thing you did" not done so much anymore, but the city's shame isn't even a secret: Visitors to the Baltimore City Life Museums are greeted by a display of marble steps that says: "Scrubbing is a rare sight today."

Gone are the days when sidewalks were crowded on Saturday mornings with women and children and their buckets, brushes, cleanser and pumice stones. And grown into middle age is the last generation of kids who would bang on doors and offer a scrub job for a quarter or half a buck.

"As a young girl, I would scrub them to make money. In those days, if your steps weren't clean, your house wasn't clean," remembers Rosalyn Gaines, who grew up on North Augusta Avenue in the early 1960s. "My girl-friends and I would go all up and down carrying everything we needed. We did good business, mostly with people who were getting up in age."

People still scrub, but you have to look hard to find them. When you do hear that whisking sound that comes from taking a stiff brush to smooth, wet stone, chances are it's being made by folks getting up in age.

"There's only about 10 of us left around here scrubbing," says 82-year-old Agnes Emery, her knees on a mat as she scours her milky-white steps in the 2800 block of Orleans St.

Not only are Emery's steps clean, they're smooth to the touch, in contrast to the coarseness of neglected marble. One way to keep them smooth is to rub hard with a pumice stone such as the crumbling one a white-haired woman on South Dean Street has been using for 52 years.

"The stone wears down the bumps, like popping a pimple," she says, willing to share tips on maintenance but not her name. "You can get them real pretty."

The Bon Ami Co. of Kansas City, Mo., still makes scrubbing "cakes" of 94 percent feldspar and 6 percent soap, but folks in Baltimore say they haven't seen pure pumice stones since the 1960s.

"You'd take that stone, wet the steps down real good and start scrubbing," says Jackie Cornish of the Druid Heights neighborhood north of Bolton Hill. "You rub it right up on the marble, and it gets the marks out. The younger generation has not picked up on this tradition."

Household cleanser has emerged as the preferred cleaning agent by default, but Cornish disdains it because, she says, "the chlorine goes down into the stone and yellows in the sun."

Over the years, people have sworn by a variety of methods: steaming hot water; high pressure power washing; cold water and scouring powder; any good white laundry soap; any good yellow laundry soap; lard and boiling water; lemon juice and hot water; and muriatic acid.

The Horner steps on Robinson Street get the acid treatment about twice a year. "You can actually see the dirt coming up out of the marble," says James Horner, Shirley Horner's husband.

Michael DiMenna, the owner of Schumann Hardware, a Depression-era store in a sea of white marble steps at Monument Street and Kenwood Avenue, says people come in for information that was once common knowledge.

"They want to know how to get their steps clean," DiMenna says. "I tell them, 'Scrub them every day for 30 years.'"

As Emery's neighborhood north of Patterson Park continues a 30-year slide away from tidiness and homeownership, the lifelong resident of Orleans Street makes herself feel better by scrubbing her steps two or three times a week.

Her risers are bright because she cares. But they are creamy because they are new, an oddity among the miles of steps that began appearing in great numbers in the first years of the 20th century.

"Two years ago, a drunk come down Orleans Street in his car and took mine down," Emery says as she heaves her bucket of dirty water into the gutter. "I took the $1,500 in insurance money and bought new ones from a monument place in Towson."

A call to the city's department of surplus property could have gotten her a set of originals for about $500.

In an out-of-the-way spot in Druid Hill Park stands a pile of vine-covered marble from demolished rowhouses. The dismembered steps are the legacy of Cal Buikema, the recently retired city parks chief, who rescued tons of valuable stone from demolition crews headed for landfills. Depending on size, the slabs sell for $120 to $300 each. But few people take advantage of the surplus because few people know about it.

In the first years of this century, marble from the Beaver Dam quarry near Cockeysville sold for about $4 a cubic foot. It was among the purest, whitest marble ever mined in the United States and was the first used for the city's marble steps and for monuments to George Washington in Baltimore and Washington.

"I've seen some beautifully maintained and others degraded, but it's the diagonal the steps make that intrigues me," says John Wood, an artist from Massachusetts who has documented Baltimore rowhouses. "You see that jagged line of steps in every American city, but only in Baltimore are they marble."

By the end of World War II, after local builders turned to less-expensive marble from Georgia, marble steps had given way to red-brick and concrete ones. With prosperity came big wooden porches instead of steps that led straight to the sidewalk.

Marble costs about $45 a cubic foot today, far too expensive for the average house.

Yet that little touch of elegance is one that made Baltimore unique among American cities in the first half of this century. And if it was your chore to do the steps, you weren't done until you cleaned the marble facing that ran from the ground up to the parlor sill.

"I do them once a week, generally Saturdays if the weather is nice," says 77-year-old Carol Lawrence of the 3700 block of Foster Ave. in Highlandtown. "I taught my girl how to do it years ago when she was young, but none of my kids live in the city no more."

October 27, 1996

Ocean City resident made stadium letter perfect

THERE WERE 317 STAINLESS STEEL LETTERS ON THE GREAT STONE FACE OF Memorial Stadium.

Chuck Yealdhall made every one of them by hand.

"It wasn't a matter of 'Can you do it?'" said Mr. Yealdhall, who did the work for the Belsinger Sign Co. "It was: 'Here, do it!'"

The big letters, along with four numbers that say "1954," make up the dedication to America's dead in the world wars that is bolted, letter by letter, to the front of the stadium.

And when the sun sparkles across the polished steel script, it is the most beautiful part of the building in which little apparent thought was given to beauty.

"When you get far away from it and look up at it, maybe the ordinary person doesn't appreciate it," said Mr. Yealdhall, shielding his eyes to stare up at an achievement once believed to be the largest display of stainless steel in the world.

"It was very impressive doing them, when you're right next to them and they're so big," he said. "Then you can see the work in them."

It would be hard to miss the work in 10-foot-high, three-dimensional letters of steel like the ones that crown the ballpark with the legend: "MEMORIAL STADIUM."

Few things appeared more odd to Baltimoreans of 1954 than the exotically modern letters on the front of their new sports stadium. "They were ahead of their time," said Mr. Yealdhall. "The architect must have dreamed them up. If you had a book of every [typeface], I don't believe you'd find it." And you wouldn't, according to the designer, a Polish architect named Francis J. Tarlowski.

"It is not an imitation of anything, and it has no precedent," Mr. Tarlowski told a reporter in 1954. "It took a little courage to do certain things... I was personally very pleased."

"Somebody said it looked like Russian hieroglyphics," said Donald Belsinger, one of the five Belsinger brothers who inherited the company from its founder, Harry Belsinger Sr.

The sans-serif, monotype letters are indeed very strange — the M's are actually N's with an extra stroke slashing down through each of them; the E's are tall and thin with the center bar nearly touching the bottom; and long S's tilt so far to the right that they look like tildes, the wavy Spanish accent marks.

"This kind of M I've never seen before except here. If you tell me it's a letter, I know it's an M, but if you just put that shape on the wall and said, 'What is it?' I wouldn't know. We're definitely looking at somebody who took the opportunity to express their personal artistic bent in letter form," said Stephen Heaver Jr., an instructor in the Maryland Institute of Art Department of Design and an expert on typefaces.

"I don't have a lot of sympathy for this kind of thing; it's not made for easy reading," said Mr. Heaver. "But I suspect he was sincerely trying to interpret the mood of the building, and perhaps because people stop to study [the oddity] they take the time to stand long enough to read the dedication."

Said Donna Beth Joy Shapiro, president of the Baltimore Art Deco Society: "So what if they stray too far from standards? That's how different typefaces evolve. I think it's nifty that this memorial was so important that they designed a whole system of lettering just for this building."

When Mr. Yealdhall began slicing the first letter out of big sheets of 20-gauge stainless steel in a sign shop on North Payson Street in 1953, he was still a young man: a World War II veteran several years out of the Army Air Forces, living in a Brooklyn Park apartment with his English war bride and their young son.

He is 68 years old now, white-haired and retired in Ocean City.

As the last major league season at Memorial Stadium rolls toward its goodbye summer, Mr. Yealdhall ponders the job he did 38 years ago for the Belsinger company.

He wonders what will become of his work once the old brick ball yard is abandoned.

"I'm very proud of it," he said of the gleaming inscription: "...a memorial to all who so valiantly fought and served in the World Wars...with eternal gratitude to those who make the supreme sacrifice...Time will not dim the glory of their deeds..."

Beneath that poetry have streamed tens of millions of fans to cheer and boo and marvel at some of the 20th century's greatest athletes: Ted Williams, Johnny Unitas, Pele, Brooks Robinson, Jim Brown, Jackie Robinson and Warren Spahn.

The massive dedication was shepherded from design to reality by Mr. Yealdhall between late 1953 and April 15, 1954, when he worked for the Belsinger company. Major league baseball had just returned to Baltimore after being gone for a half-century.

He remembers it as six months of careful, deliberate work — though once, in the middle of the job, somebody caught one of the Belsinger kids using one of the giant A's for a sliding board.

"I guess I put in about 1,000 man-hours on them," said Mr. Yealdhall. "There was no continuity, you didn't do 'em in the order of the words. You just did 'em. Maybe one day I'd do all the C's or all the E's. You'd cut 10 or 12 of them at a time.

"The skill involves the knowledge of how to bend the steel," said Donald Belsinger. "You have to analyze it and know what you need to do to shape odd pieces, to achieve what the architect and designer wants."

Mr. Yealdhall said it went like this:

- First, a co-worker traced full-sized patterns of each letter on brown paper.
- Then carbon paper was laid on the sheets of steel, the brown paper pattern of the letters was put atop the carbon, and the letters were traced by hand, leaving an outline of the shapes to be cut.
- The steel was placed on a 1946 state-of-the-art "Do-All Zephyr" band saw at Belsinger's, and the blade's 4,000 revolutions per minute carved out the letters with friction. Every letter was made on the Zephyr at the Payson Street shop except the ones 10 feet tall, which Mr. Yealdhall made at a shop with a bigger saw.
- All burrs and imperfections were filed down by hand.
- With hand shears, Mr. Yealdhall snipped strips of metal to be welded around the edges of the flat letters to give them depth.
- Inside the hollow backs of the letters, the edges of the sheared strips were soldered for strength.
- Threaded bolts were then fastened to the back of the letters for mounting on the stadium.
- The last step before mounting was to go over each letter with dry Bon Ami polishing cleanser.

As Ms. Shapiro said, pretty nifty.

Mr. Yealdhall thinks so, too.

Looking up at the letters, he shielded his eyes from the shimmering glare and tried to conjure the memory of seeing them in place for the first time. He couldn't, the memory lost somewhere in the last 38 years.

But with the future of the stadium in doubt — although many people believe the dedication will be preserved in some form — Mr. Yealdhall had no trouble expressing how he felt about the letters today.

"It's a memorial and should be kept as one," he said. "Maybe people will appreciate it more after they tear it down."

May 14, 1991

Christmas vigil in field of memories

CHRISTMAS DAWN BROKE COLD AND SILENT OVER 53,371 EMPTY SEATS ON 33rd Street yesterday.

As the children of Baltimore rose to greet wishes delivered and desires unmet, Larry Wilson walked the vacant aisles of Memorial Stadium, a lone set of eyes standing watch over an obsolete coliseum — a Christian security guard pulling the midnight-to-eight shift on the anniversary of his savior's birth.

"It's my regular work day and Christmas fell on it," said Mr. Wilson, 38.

For the effort, he earned $9 an hour, time-and-a-half holiday pay.

At 6 a.m., the temperature was 20 degrees and Mr. Wilson was two hours away from driving home to Woodlawn to be with his wife, Miriam, and their 15-month old daughter, Nabiera.

Hardly a car passed on 33rd Street, darkness covered the fabled infield where Brooks Robinson turned ground balls into outs, and Bugs Bunny played on a black-and-white TV atop an ancient refrigerator in a small, heated ticket booth where Mr. Wilson passed most of his shift.

"I don't really celebrate Christmas like the masses," he said. "I know that it means Jesus Christ was born, so I celebrate by praying. I did some praying after I got here, a little after midnight. I thanked God for Jesus and then I talked to Jesus about the problems of the world — the hunger, people out of work, how there should be more peace. I thanked him for the help he's given us and the help he will be giving us."

Mr. Wilson also got up from his folding chair every half-hour or so to make a round.

"I walk every bit of a couple miles each night," he said. "I watch out for vandalism and trespassing. I look for anything suspicious, make sure everything is locked up and secure."

Built in 1954, the year Mr. Wilson was born, the stadium is dedicated to all Americans who died in World Wars I and II. An urn sits in a glass case across the hall from Mr. Wilson's post, and in it resides a spoonful of earth from every American military cemetery in the world. Bronze plaques on the walls herald the achievements of businessmen and politicians who worked to get the stadium built, along with athletes who performed better than others who competed here.

Once in a while, when it's warmer, Mr. Wilson will stop to stare at the field where the Baltimore Orioles and the Baltimore Colts won fame and championships. "I come out just to look," he said of the eerie, empty bowl. "I think of the crowds and the ballplayers and what it must be like to be a star. Nobody wants this stadium to be torn down."

It's all dusty history now, part of a Baltimore that existed before the Colts moved to Indianapolis in 1984 and the Orioles left for Camden Yards in 1991.

And for eight hours a day — be it Christmas morning, just another Friday, or the Fourth of July — it is a memory Mr. Wilson is entrusted to protect.

"Kids like to hang around outside sometimes," he says. "They run around in the flower beds out front and want me to let them use the bathrooms." No one was hanging around yesterday when it was 19 degrees at 7 a.m. and dawn splintered flinty and gray over the right field bleachers.

Despite the cold, Mr. Wilson gulped ice water from a jug he keeps in the refrigerator.

"It keeps me alert," he said.

Loose cords banged against flag poles ringing the top of the horseshoe-shaped stadium; beyond the center field fence, pine trees stood unadorned.

Wild cats, Mr. Wilson said, now breed in the stadium, and once a nearby Waverly resident called the police to report a break-in.

Officers found two women huddling in the Orioles dugout. "We're not sure what they were doing," said Mr. Wilson.

As wide swaths of daylight turned the cloudy sky a pale blue and made the aluminum seats in the upper deck gleam, Mr. Wilson remembered a favorite childhood Christmas from his days in northeast Washington.

"One year I got this big red car," he said, his kind, round face beaming. "It was called the Crusader 101 and it had remote control. My eyes were big as apples when I saw it. That topped it all. It was huge and waiting for me right under the tree."

There was no tree waiting for Mr. Wilson when he got off work yesterday morning. No Christmas lights and few gifts.

He gave all of that up six years ago when he married a Muslim who celebrates Kwanzaa, the African-American holiday.

"I sort of miss the traditional stuff," he said. "I know that the tree and all isn't the real meaning of Christmas, but it's a good reminder... a nice complement."

December 26, 1992

Chapter 4

Cityscapes

At Sis's in South Baltimore,
try pinochle in the corner with Bucky

SIS'S HOLE ISN'T EXACTLY A BAR. IT'S MORE LIKE A CLUB BASEMENT WITH a liquor license.

Two things are constant in "the Hole" — Miss Sis behind the bar and Wednesday night pinochle games.

To get in you scoot down three black metal steps just off the corner of Cross and William streets in South Baltimore, and, if you're taller than the average man, duck to keep from rustling several hundred Christmas balls that hang from snippets of string tacked into a low ceiling.

Margurietta Clark Fischer — "No one even knows my real name, I'm just Sis" — will be behind the bar, sipping on a small bottle of Pabst, popping the tops off of cans of Bud and Coors, and pitching wisecracks back at the regulars.

"I run into your grandmother the other day," says Sis to one guy. "She didn't have anything good to say about you."

Oldies play on the radio... "so sad to see good love go bad," sing the Everly Brothers... and the jukebox is always turned off. It's about 38 feet from the front door to the men's room at the back, and the baby blue wall that runs down the side is hung with framed photos of young women modeling just about everything but outerwear.

The place is clean, like a private home, and most of the people who frequent Sis's consider each other family — both good eggs and bad apples — and regard South Baltimore as a village where the neighborhood's dead are as familiar as those who still drop in for a cold one.

"This," says Jay Crossney, a Fort Avenue barber, "is the most neighborhood bar in town."

Miss Sis had two crockpots going last Wednesday night, one on the bar filled with layers of thick potato pancakes, and one on a ledge behind the bar where hot dogs float in a bubbling bath of baked beans.

The big Wednesday night pinochle game, which takes place on a corner of the gray Formica bar worn thin by the passing of years and cards, begins while Sis is still "making up plates" for regulars — some of whom can eat eight hot dogs in a sitting, 11 when they're hungry.

The game "down the Hole" has been going on for years with a variety of players but it orbits around Charles "Bucky" Lynch, a local boy of 57 who made good in a chain of Lucky's Convenience Stores and with them has earned a legend for generosity.

"Bucky used to throw change out of the front door of his first store across the street when we were kids," says Mr. Crossney, "and we'd run around and pick it up and go back in and spend it."

Mr. Lynch sits in a corner with his right arm cushioned by foam rubber, a note pad to keep score, and Sis's bar phone where the entrepreneur's endless business and personal calls are routed on Wednesday nights.

In between calls he says how he can still see the vision "of my drunken, bald-headed grandfather sitting down here, you know, the one who used to push that cart around and collect wood and junk," and tells how one too many 10-cent Gunther beers in this very bar led to Bucky Lynch's marriage of 28 years to the former Judy Bradley.

"We were all sittin' around down here laughin' and drinkin' and Judy says to me, 'Let's get married,' and I said, 'You're crazy.' Then someone went and called the preacher and said we couldn't get married until noon the next day. Being a smart guy, I called up the preacher and says, 'I got $40 says we can get married tonight,' and the preacher says, 'Give me 15 minutes to get ready.'"

The young lovers had to wait until the bar closed because the owners, Joe and Rose Muir, were standing as witnesses.

"So we staggered down Charles Street to Fort Avenue to the preacher's house — there was a dog layin' in the front room where he married us, that didn't seem too appropriate — and when he asked for the ring, I says, 'So long,' but then Rose says, 'Judy, I'll lend you my ring' and that was it. We went back to Rose's apartment and about 4:30 in the morning we staggered home."

At the bar, to Mr. Lynch's left, sits Joseph "Guv" Randall, one of his store managers. Next to Guv is Bill Beall, a Lucky's warehouseman. Some people come to Sis's on Wednesdays just to watch Mr. Beall eat.

Rounding out the game is Mr. Crossney, known in the clique as "Pinochle Jay" because he has sacrificed considerable pride and the last several years of his life to apprentice himself to the peculiar game.

He still keeps his crib sheet hidden under a pile of napkins behind the bar when he forgets the fundamentals.

"You can't pick the game up overnight," says Mr. Lynch. "But any dummy can play it."

And every Wednesday night, and frequently on Saturday afternoons, the boys down at Sis's prove it.

Mr. Beall and Mr. Lynch, the best players, regularly team up against Mr. Randall and Mr. Crossney, spotting the weaker players 40 points in a game that runs to 100.

The longer you play, the better you get, and Mr. Lynch credits the all-night pinochle games he and his siblings played growing up on Webber Street.

"I'd go up Holy Cross Church where it said pay what you can for your candles," he says. "So I'd put a nickel in and take a box of 72 candles home, and we'd play pinochle by candlelight under a tent made out of a blanket and Mom thought we were sleeping."

It's a game — played with 48 cards from the nine to the ace — of memory, skill, intuition and curious jargon. Throughout the night, in between the phone calls and the potato pancakes and reminiscences, runs a chorus of bids and bumps, tricks and trumps, meld and marriage.

After the cards are dealt, players speculate or bid on how many points they can win during each hand.

If the total isn't reached — through combinations such as the "marriage" of same-suit kings and queens and "a run" of 10 through ace of the same suit — the number of points bid is deducted.

Even with a 40-point handicap, Mr. Lynch and Mr. Beall, historically, fare poorly.

"We beat 'em," declares Mr. Lynch after several hands have been dealt. "104 to 70."

Miss Sis is down the other end of the bar by this time, giving away food to friends, telling stories about house parties she used to have just for winos — "they'd leave crawlin' down the street with an ear of corn in their mouth and a bottle of wine in their back pocket" — and explaining how she came to her life's work.

"I had a bunch of kids at home, nine of 'em," she says, "and I had to work."

She got her first barmaid's job in the basement bar, formerly a Democratic club, back in 1957 when Joe and Rose Muir owned it. Now a widow, Rose Muir still lives upstairs from the Hole.

Miss Sis opens every day at about 4 p.m. If you see a white cardboard sign announcing "Bar Open" affixed to the bricks outside with masking tape, you know the bar is serving. She rips the sign down every night and tapes it back up the next day.

If she likes you, you'll know.

If she really likes you, and it's Wednesday night, a pile of home cooking on a plastic plate will be shoved toward you across the Formica bar, and when you try to pay for your drinks she'll tell you it's on the tab of a fat man at the end of the bar with a phone in his ear and pinochle cards in his hand.

December 11, 1989

With good times to spare

BERNIE AND VERA RUZIN HAVE RUN THE OLD DUCKPIN BOWLING ALLEY ON Eastern Avenue nearly all of their lives and they love it the way some people love their families.

Which means they've hung in for almost a half-century at Patterson Bowling because the good times outweigh the aggravation.

When your family numbers more than 400 people — 14 leagues of bowlers whooping it up under one roof — that's saying something.

"These are good people," said Vera, 69, on a typical night at Baltimore's oldest continuously operating alley and maybe the only one with stuffed animals in the window.

"If I'm running errands to the bank or the post office, the customers watch the place until I get back," she said. "I've never showed up and said: 'I wish I wasn't working today.'"

Bernie, 73, met Vera at the bowling alley back when his father, a shrewd man from Krakow, Poland, ran the place. Vera was walking down Eastern Avenue and Bernie was looking out the front window, watching the world go by. He asked if he could walk her home, and before she knew it, Vera was a bowler's girl. That was 1945.

Since then, the game that can be traced back to the Stone Age when rocks were rolled at sheep bones, has taken care of them.

Income from the 12 lanes off the corner of Eastern Avenue and Chester Street — six lanes downstairs, six upstairs — helped Bern and Vera pay a mortgage and raise a family.

Through the 1960s, he also was a champion, winning in 1962 the prestigious *Evening Sun* tournament trophy, which stands above the alley's front door. On the final night of his 30-game, 3,984-pin victory. Bernie told the press: "It's a shame everybody can't win to know how it feels."

For $1.50 a game — compared to the $2.40 to $3.25 nonleague bowlers pay at big-chain alleys — anybody can walk into the Patterson and know how it feels to knock down some pins under a tin ceiling.

Kids bowl for $1.25 and shoes rent for 50 cents.

"Or nothin' at all. Miss Vera is so kind," said a member of the Wednesday night Sacred Heart of Jesus ladies league. The league moved to the Patterson last year after the Conkling Street church closed its basement alley.

Said league leader Sue Frankowski: "A couple of weeks ago we were laying on the floor carrying on, we were having such a good time."

The place is open seven days a week. Here, a codfish cake sells for 65 cents.

A pot of free coffee sits next to a wooden phone booth and the good-timers and wisenheimers go out of their way to tell Bernie how good it is while sending out for convenience-store java.

Johnny Unitas still throws Memorial Stadium bombs from pictures on the wall, not too far from a big "Honor Roll" board that lists the local aces: Berends, Mrowczynski, Kulacki and Filipowski.

Bernie and Vera have watched many of their customers grow up and grow old.

"You're 52 already?" said Bernie to a guy named Jerry. "You're getting old, man."

Bernie knows old.

"I remember when they were putting the lanes in, I was 6 years old," said Bernie, who maintains a 110 average, down about 25 pins from his heyday. "It's the same wood, except for the patches. We had pin boys until about 1960; that's when we put the machines in."

The benches are also made of wood, like the ones in church, and from these pews, the faithful clang cowbells every time someone rolls a strike, the secret of which once hung from a sign that said: "A SLOW, ACCURATE BALL IS BETTER THAN A FAST WILD ONE."

They are words that teams like the Bums R Back and the No Threat Four live and die by, the credo of folks with gray heads and young hearts, people who love bowling but can't quite explain why.

It's a night out of the house.

But a lifetime of these nights has Bernie and Vera ready to roll their last frame.

"I want to retire. I want to travel or do something, take it easy for a while. I'm 73 years old," said Bernie. "I want to get out."

For three years he has tried to unload the lanes his father built inside an old broom factory in 1927, and for three years — to the comfort of his customers — Bernie has failed to close a deal.

He has listed the property with three different Realtors, with an asking price of $190,000 for the building and $225,000 with the business thrown in. Nobody is biting.

"I'm close to boarding it up," says Bernie. "I thought somebody would want the building at least... I loved the bowling game. All these people in here, they're all friends of mine."

And what will happen to all these friends when the lights over the pins go dark for the last time?

"They'll bowl other places," he said.

April 2, 1995

An unusual spin, but elevating art

IT'S THE BIGGEST TOY IN BALTIMORE, AND A GOOD EYE IS ALL YOU NEED TO PLAY.

Rising 55 feet on a candy-striped pole where Covington Street meets Key Highway is a 3-ton whirligig: a tower of intricate magnificence tricked out with bicycle wheels, oil filters, a duck with whirring wings, the figure of a man pumping a unicycle, aluminum blades that mirror the sun's sparkle, stainless steel milkshake cups, an airplane, an angel and more doohickeys than one paragraph can hold.

Planted in a public courtyard behind the American Visionary Arts Museum, it doesn't seem to do much more than spin and swivel in the wind.

Yet it has the power to turn wheels in the imagination like almost nothing else in the city.

"It's a kind of a wing-ding Ferris wheel," said Keith Hill, Jr., a Southern High School student playing basketball across from the sculpture on a recent sunny day.

Even the wing-ding's shadow, projected against the side of the museum when the sun begins to drop, is captivating.

"It makes you do something," said John Lau, an architect visiting Baltimore from Chicago. "It makes you think."

Of what?

Most folks say it conjures memories of carnivals and pinwheels and a strong but undefined joy. Specific responses are as varied as the person looking at it.

"It brings the buildings alive; it brings the light alive," said Ben Wilson, a sculptor who has found himself alongside the giant gizmo for months while building an outside wedding altar for the museum.

"When I'm working in the garden, it's like someone is looking at me," he said. "It's like a person I've gotten to know — sometimes it goes really slow and quiet, and other times it's fast and banging."

The whirligig is visible from the slopes of Federal Hill and some of the houses atop it, from cars on Key Highway, high-rise condos on the South Baltimore waterfront, the balcony of the museum — where you can almost reach out and touch it — and harbor boats plying just the right course.

"There's so much to look at, you have to just stand there awhile," said Betty Haynie, a Baltimore Zoo keeper. "It's childlike."

It was installed with a crane in September of 1995, and people who stumble upon it for the first time usually react the way Ms. Haynie did: "Whoa! What is that?"

School buses drop off students at the Visionary Arts Museum park on Covington Street: and when the children move toward the museum doors, their necks crane to the sky.

You simply cannot pass by this thing without looking, and if you are close enough, you can hear it hum, creak, clank and whir.

"It's cool — all the spinners up on top," said Jarrid Miller, a 13-year-old student from McDonogh School on a field trip last week.

One of Jarrid's classmates wanted to know if the contraption was called "Vollis Simpson," a name painted in red on a white metal plate that hangs from the cross beam. Next to it hangs a green sign that says: "Lucama."

They are the names of the whirligig's 77-year-old creator and his hometown in North Carolina, where more than two dozen homemade whirlies and windmills catch the breeze in an old mule pasture behind his home.

On the day it was installed, Mr. Simpson said: "It's a little tight right now, but it'll go to town when it loosens up. On a windy day it'll have a ball."

Mr. Simpson built Baltimore's whirligig at the request of Rebecca Hoffberger, director of the Visionary Arts Museum.

"It's going to be lit at night and because of the mirrors, it will send out light," said Mrs. Hoffberger.

You would have to be some kind of full-time Scrooge to find fault with something that makes people happy for free, but Mrs. Hoffberger remembers a meeting with neighbors about three years ago when a man shouted: "We don't want your whirlies and twirlies in our neighborhood."

Compromises were worked out to keep the museum roof free of sculpture, and no one seems to mind a whirly-twirly in the neighborhood now.

"To have something that whimsical right in your midst so beautiful and fantastic" is a gift of living in the city, something you can't get in the suburbs, said Richard Leitch, president of the Federal Hill Neighborhood Association.

Alisa Anderson, a South Baltimore artist who sews for theaters and costume shops, has strolled by Vollis Simpson's obsession many, many times.

Staring up at it through sunglasses the other day, she tried to describe how the sculpture made her feel. The wind blew, the crossbeam swayed on greased bearings, and the whole thing came alive.

Ms. Anderson never did find the right words, but she walked down the road smiling.

April 16, 1996

Vital limbs of the city

AL CAPONE'S WEEPING CHERRY TREE DRAPES A STUNNING CANOPY OF PINK IN front of Union Memorial Hospital each spring, attracting arbor ardor from all who see it in bloom.

Less celebrated, but no less spectacular, is a monument almost no one sees: a mammoth "Tree of Heaven" behind a derelict rowhouse in the 200 block of South Carey Street, one of those wild junk trees that sprout between cracks in concrete and push up through the floors of abandoned houses. It's a giant Ailanthus soaring nearly 60 feet on a trunk more than 15 feet around, according to its entry in the city's 1995 Notable Tree Commission registry.

But whether the tree be gangster Capone's gift to the hospital that treated his terminal syphilis in 1939 or a weedy alley rascal that grew into a state champion, Marion Bedingfield has a place in his heart for each of them.

Not to mention the 300,000 or so other trees that line the streets and median strips of Baltimore and are now blooming — like the gorgeous Kwanzan cherries at City College and lavender-hued "red buds" on Roland Avenue — from Dickeyville to Dundalk.

"When leaves start coming on the trees, I get extremely busy," said Mr. Bedingfield, a tree specialist with the city's forestry division. "I don't want to go up and hug 'em, but I like them. I'll get about 100 calls in the spring from people asking: 'What's that beautiful tree I saw on Charles Street? I want one.'"

If you live in Baltimore and want a tree planted in front of your house, write a letter to the forestry division. Plantings can follow requests by up to a year. With staff at a modern-day low of 37 (down from more than 100 in the early 1970s), no one will promise when it will arrive or if the one you liked so much in the median of Gwynns Falls Parkway is suited to a residential neighborhood.

Chances are it will be a red maple, the No. 1 tree planted in Baltimore because it's so hardy. If it's a white blossoming gingko — a native of China whose roots go back to the Jurassic era — the odds are 50-50 that you'll be holding your nose when it blooms every April.

"The stink is the fruit from the female," said Mr. Bedingfield, a city tree man for the past 20 years. "When we get them, the nursery tells us they're all males, but you can't tell until they're old enough to bear fruit."

While a lot of the division's time is spent removing dead and damaged trees, Mr. Bedingfield is always looking for neighbors who are willing to help him green the city. And the squeaky wheel tends to get the tree.

"I asked for one in front of the bar after a windstorm took the old one down," said Carole Santmyer, the barmaid at Barnacle's in South Baltimore. "The old one was big, almost to the top of the building."

"Some people complain about the bird mess, but the birds got to live, too, and trees make a street look better," said Albert Babka, who owns the bar. "It's tax money well spent."

Baltimore spent $100,000 on new trees this past fiscal year, with plantings in the spring and fall. Each year, about 2,000 trees are taken down or die (many from vandalism) and 2,500 more, a variety of 30 different species, go into the ground.

The ones planted downtown tend to live between seven and 13 years before they croak under the stress of urban life. In residential neighborhoods, a tree can last longer than most people.

"We try not to make the mistakes we made in the past, like the silver maples from 1915," said Mr. Bedingfield. "Washington, D.C., said they had 1,500 of them, all we had to do was take them. But it's a brittle wood, and it used to be our No. 1 storm damage tree until they started coming down."

A survivor of the curse of the silver maples stands off the corner of Kirk and Bonaparte avenues in Northeast Baltimore. "It has a yellow fall color and that's nice if you like yellow," Mr. Bedingfield said. "I like reds and oranges."

Those are the fall colors that can be seen in what Mr. Bedingfield calls "our most recent mistake, the Bradford pear. It's a gorgeous tree with a 30-foot spread and the leaves turn red in the fall," he said. "But after it gets so big, it splits into two stems. I'm always getting calls at 3 a.m. for a Bradford that's split."

Among trees of strange and historical note in Baltimore are the "watermelon red" crepe myrtle at St. Paul and Saratoga streets, donated in the early 1970s by the singer who calls himself Tiny Tim; an English elm in Fort McHenry said to be grown from a cutting taken off the tree that shaded George Washington as he took command of the Continental Army at Boston in 1775; and the weirdly twisted Osage orange near the Reptile House in Druid Hill Park, a tree whose circumference of 17 feet 2 inches is so oddly shaped that a street through the park was built to curve around it. The more spectacular trees get the attention they need, but the average rowhouse shade tree tends to suffer neglect.

"We can't do the basic maintenance like mulching that would allow them to grow stronger in the long run," said Jim Dicker, the city arborist who heads forestry and its annual $2.5 million budget. "To really care for trees, we'd need 70 or 80 people. We don't do routine pruning of every tree, only about 10,000 a year. At that rate, it would take 30 years to get around to all of them."

Yet, to Marion Bedingfield, even a row of unpruned trees is better than nothing but concrete. He's convinced that there's less violence on streets with trees.

"They make you feel better," he said. "That's a given."

April 29, 1996

Chapter 5

The
Waterfront

Derelict dreamboat sinking in hot water

SHE WAS GRAND ONCE, THE VIVACIOUS TOY OF MILLIONAIRES FROM THE Roaring '20s.

Today she is old and so beaten that many think her life of almost seven decades ought to end on the muddy shores of Cherry Hill where she has been mired for two years.

Except for a determined young dreamer from Poland named Andrew Wawrzecko who is dedicated to refloating and restoring the derelict luxury yacht called the Odyssey.

"I want to see her up one day," said Mr. Wawrzecko, speaking alongside his project on a cold winter afternoon, hip-high in harbor water with tools in his hands. "These days people are not making these kinds of boats.... Art is what can be rebuilt and handed down from generation to generation to show people things from a long time ago."

Built in New Jersey by the world-renowned Mathis-Trumpy Co. in 1923, the Odyssey hosted movie moguls and kings during its heyday. The Mathis-Trumpy Co., which folded in Annapolis in 1973, was known as the birth-place of the most elegant wooden power boats afloat. It had built custom-made yachts for U.S. businessmen with names like Armour and DuPont and for a politician from Independence, Mo., named Harry Truman.

For all of his dedication — now more than two years of most of his time and money on the 61½-foot boat that is a sister to the presidential yacht Sequoia — it seems likely Mr. Wawrzecko will see the Odyssey destroyed before he sees it floating.

Since early June, the machinist-welder in his early 30s has been receiving letters from various city and state agencies ordering him to move the boat. And after repeated complaints from a nearby marina about the rotten-hulled vessel, the Maryland Department of Natural Resources has given Mr. Wawrzecko until Jan. 25 to move the Odyssey or be charged with abandoning a boat in state waters.

As of now, he can't even float it, much less move it. And he doesn't have the tens of thousands of dollars it would take to have a boat yard even attempt the risky job.

"I went down and talked to him and said, 'Look, this is it. This is your last chance,'" said Cpl. Gregory K. Kirkpatrick of the DNR police. "Unless he does something soon, he has until Jan. 25, when I'll cite him for abandoning it. If he's found guilty in court, it's no longer his boat, and we put out bids to contractors to have it removed."

The maximum fine for abandonment of a boat is $1,000 plus removal costs.

Asked why he continues the struggle despite the fact that the keel and ribs of the boat are rotten, Mr. Wawrzecko has an explanation. Reminded that he has a deadline of less than two weeks to move a huge vessel that drained the hope of previous owners with far more money, Mr. Wawrzecko has an explanation. Told that he is wasting his time, Mr. Wawrzecko has an explanation.

And all of them are the same.

"I need good hearts to understand my situation," said Mr. Wawrzecko, who works for an Anne Arundel County machine shop and says he doesn't have much money to spare. "All I have to do is seal the last side of my boat, get the water out of it and get it to break off the mud and float. I need understanding. I'm really going to move this boat away."

His nemesis, Middle Branch Moorings manager Debbie H. Valencia, doesn't believe it.

"I know this boat. It's junk, it's disgusting, and there's no way it can be saved," said Ms. Valencia, who has been trying since last spring to force the Odyssey's removal and now worries that a wood-burning stove Mr. Wawrzecko uses on board might cause a fire that would ignite her marina's fuel tanks. "If you raise it, it'll collapse. The only thing you can do is destroy it."

Ms. Valencia says the Odyssey is an eyesore that robs her Waterview Avenue marina of potential business. Mr. Wawrzecko says that forcing the issue before he can finish his work will rob him of his biggest dream since he left Warsaw for the United States of America six years ago.

"Everything that you're working on that you care about likes time," he said. "Some people would like to see that boat crashed right there. They just don't wish me good luck. I've spent too much of my time and money to have them come and tear it away.

"It's not a piece of junk to me."

Before the Odyssey was Mr. Wawrzecko's dream, it was a desire that almost consumed a telephone service man named Robert E. Marx. Before Mr. Marx, all its former owners were reportedly millionaires.

"It's going to take about $40,000 to $50,000 for the bottom alone, just to get it into a floating state," said Mr. Marx, who had to keep bilge pumps running constantly to keep the Odyssey from sinking — which eventually happened when electric cords to the pumps pulled away from a pier outlet.

"It's like a never-ending process. You can't pull it up just anywhere. You can't pull it up with a lift because it weighs 51 tons. If you pull it up on a cradle, it'll break in half. It has to be taken up on a rail, and I think there's only two rails in the Baltimore area where it could even be attempted. That's costly, and then it has to stay on the rail for months and months while the guy replaces the ribs and all the bottom planks.

"Three years of my life," Mr. Marx said, "went down on that thing in one night."

After the vessel almost broke, Mr. Marx — who couldn't sell it because surveyors would always tell potential buyers that the bottom was rotten — donated it to a maritime training school. By the time Mr. Wawrzecko spied it while looking for a crabbing boat at the old Tower Marina in South Baltimore sometime in 1986, it could stay afloat only with the aid of pumps.

He, too, lost electricity one night. And the Odyssey went down again.

Now her bottom-deck salon is filled with murky green water, a U.S. flag flies from a bent television antenna, and in the wheelhouse is the captain's bunk — rusty bed springs covered with foam rubber and an old sheet.

Mr. Wawrzecko claims to be living on board, arguing that the Odyssey can't be abandoned if it's his home.

Ms. Valencia, who keeps a sharp eye out for any activity on the boat, disagrees.

"I haven't seen him over there in days," she said recently. "It has no water, no heat, no electric and no bathroom."

She just doesn't understand, says Mr. Wawrzecko.

"I'm doing my work when I can, but it's hell," he said. "I don't know why everybody is pushing me so hard to move it right away."

January 16, 1989

Sea dog hopes to keep a love alive

CHESTER LOVES GERTRUDE.

He is a 61-year-old harbor hound born across from the Eastside docks, a wanderer who has played and worked on the waterfront since he was a young boy on his father's crabbing boats. She is a wooden hulled freight ferry built in a forgotten Baltimore boatyard in 1915, a durable workhorse that began hauling supplies to countless ships when Woodrow Wilson was president.

They have been together almost 10 years now, and the old beau is looking for a way to save his favorite girl, who has seen better days.

Chester and Gertrude belong to the old Baltimore, a port city whose commerce was not tourists but cargo; a town where work on the waterfront was plentiful, especially for a kid like Chester Rakowski, who picked beans to buy school clothes and grew up in Fells Point when the neighborhood was simply known as Broadway.

"My whole life has been boats, nothin' but boats," he said, sitting on Gertrude's deck with a beer one recent sunny Saturday in Marley Creek before sailing her upriver to dock near the Hanover Street Bridge for the winter.

"My Dad's name was Chester and he worked for a smelting and refining company over on Clinton Street and my mother worked in packing houses — she come to this country from Warsaw. We lived in a corner house at Fleet and Castle, they tore it down to build Will's Dairy," he said. "My father and his friends were crabbers who worked out of Fort Howard and Miller's Island. They'd come in with barrels of crabs and sell 'em for a dollar a dozen on the street. I come to traveling with him. Growing up like that, you learn from the water, how to tie and throw lines."

As young Chester worked around the harbor — dropping out of the old Holy Rosary parish school on Eastern Avenue in the seventh grade and taking his first real job as a 13-year-old deckhand for the old Rogers Towing Co. that would "hire anybody who could walk or crawl" — the Gertrude was hauling every thing from lubricating oil to grain around the upper Patapsco and between the Inner Harbor and Eastern Shore.

"She had a twin built just like her called the Little Charlie," said Walter

Tokarski, 64, an employee with the Marine Launch Co., now owned by Vane Brothers, and a deckhand on the Gertrude in the 1930s.

"She would haul manure over to the Eastern Shore and bring back watermelons and tomatoes. My father [William] ran her for a while, and when war broke out she used to carry ammunition and stores to ships. At one time there were hundreds of boats like her around Baltimore."

"I always liked running her," said Paul Thomas, another Vane Brothers employee. "She's a good handling, solid boat. You didn't have to worry about banging her against anything."

As far as Chester Rakowski and his waterfront buddies know, the Gertrude is the last of the wooden-hulled harbor supply boats built just after the turn of the century. She almost faded like the rest about a dozen years ago or so when a group of drunken sailors shanghaied her to get back to their ship. They got lost and ran Gertie aground.

A 95-horsepower diesel vessel converted from gas, she is 49 feet long, weighs 27 gross tons, and her decks of long-grain Canadian fir once carried up to 105 barrels of oil at a time. Her heavy wheel is wooden and was patterned after a Conestoga wagon wheel.

The Marine Launch company sold her to Mr. Rakowski in late 1980 when he still operated the Waterview Marina in South Baltimore. She was replaced by a sturdy pair of steel-hulled boats — the Carlyn and the Willkate — with more power and deck space.

"She's a good strong boat — big, old and slow," remembered Al Lennon, another former Marine Launch employee who was a childhood friend of Mr. Rakowski and ex-skipper of the Gertrude. "And we did whatever we could with her to earn money."

Which is just about what Mr. Rakowski has done on the water.

He shipped out in the merchant marine during World War II at age 17, "to the South Pacific on the John W. Medrom in '43," he said. And in 1945 — after trips to the Admiralty Islands and the Philippines — he left the high seas and took a job with Curtis Bay Towing and, later, Triangle Towing and the defunct Baker-Whitely Towing Co. In between, he ran a launch called the Good Hughes.

About the time he went to work for Baker-Whitely in the mid-1950s, he built a 28-foot cabin cruiser from scratch, laying out her ribs in the South Baltimore row house on East Gittings Street where he has lived for 35 years.

"After I made her ribs, I set her up in the yard of the old Adams Coal company near Canton around Fleet and Essex streets," he said. "The neighborhood gang and my friends from the tugs would come down and help me out. One day four or five of us lined up all our beer bottles to see how much we drank and it run a ring from stern to bow and down both sides."

No stranger to a glass of cold beer, he says, "I've been in more gin mills than I've seen lighthouses, and I've seen many a lighthouse."

It was on tugboats that he advanced his cooking talent, improving on old family goodies from Poland like duck's blood soup and stuffed cabbage called "galabki," complementing his menus with Baltimore favorites like sour beef and dumplings.

In the last several years, since the city voided his lease on the haggard Waterview Marina in a Middle Branch Park cleanup effort, cooking has brought Chester some income through catering private parties with pit beef and steamed crabs.

Cooking and working as a deckhand on the water, he'd regularly pass the Gertrude, which was docked at Thames and Ann streets for years, as she supplied such vessels as the hospital ship Hope.

And he never forgot her.

Originally picked up from Marine Launch to do odd jobs around Mr. Rakowski's marina, the Gertrude re-emerged as a craft for uniquely Baltimore pleasures — floating Fourth of July picnics to watch fireworks off Fort McHenry and an annual autumn "Pumpkin Ride" for neighborhood kids from South Baltimore.

But lately Chester and Gertrude, like many lovers, have begun to resemble one another. They sag a bit, aren't as strong as they used to be and show signs of age.

Chester, a gifted handyman with a huge laugh that creases his face and brings tears to his eyes, is the kind of guy who will surely find help for his boat before taking care of himself.

He's hoping a non-profit group like the Lady Maryland Foundation or his friends at the Fells Point Yacht Club might take an interest in the Gertrude and make her the kind of vessel suited for repair at the Maryland Maritime Institute, a shipbuilding school proposed for the foot of Caroline Street.

"She's in rough shape, but I'd like to get her fixed up as a showpiece for the people of Baltimore," he said of "ole Gertie," who tooted a welcome alongside the queen Elizabeth II when the luxury liner last visited Baltimore. "All the folks who used to take Sunday afternoon rides keep asking when the Gertrude is gonna get running so we can go back to the fun days we used to have."

As for himself, Chester Rakowski has no complaints.

"Aww yeah, as far as I'm concerned I've enjoyed my life," he said. "It's been a good life, boats, and ships and travel and experiences. What I did or didn't do in life, I think it panned out pretty good. I'll be around boats till I die."

November 28, 1988

Rusting away in harbor,
ship remains vessel of dreams

MORE THAN 15,000 TONS OF HOPE SIT DEAD IN THE WATER ALONG A SPOOKY stretch of South Baltimore harbor known as Fairfield.

Lashed to bollards down at the gray and battered end of Childs Street is the Sanctuary, an old American hospital ship that was one the first vessels to visit the nightmare of Nagasaki, Japan, after the atomic bomb. A generation later it was a workhorse of the Vietnam War, treating more than 25,000 casualties over four years.

Now it just sits in the Patapsco, 522 feet of potential good will.

In the mind of veteran good-deed-doer the Rev. Robert M. Meyers — the Presbyterian minister who persuaded Congress to sell him the decommissioned ship in 1988 for $15 and a promise it would be used for "humanitarian purposes" — the Sanctuary is a vision of health care and education for citizens of the Third World.

"We've been there almost two years and nothing has happened, but I'm an optimist," said Mr. Meyers, the 63-year-old president of Life International, a non-profit charity organization in Silver Spring trying to put the project together. "I'm an eternal optimist."

But optimism meets the real world down in Fairfield, where, visible to the right of motorists southbound out of the Harbor Tunnel, the Sanctuary is a rusting dream in need of at least 7 million scarce, recession dollars before it can go anywhere.

Mr. Meyers, who has scores of volunteers and a half-million dollars in donated medical equipment on standby, says he is looking under every rug for loose change to get the Sanctuary back to sea.

"I went to Venezuela and told them that if they gave me $7 million in oil, we'd sell it, fix up the ship, and send the Sanctuary to their country for a year," he said.

The Venezuelans said they'd get back to him.

Mr. Meyers said that Gov. William Donald Schaefer told him the same thing more than a year ago, and he's still waiting to hear back from the governor, relying on a faith that allowed him to endure the 15 years that he waited for Congress to give him the ship.

What he wants from Mr. Schaefer is a powerful corporate leader to chair the fund-raising efforts for the ship, but with powerful corporate types scrambling to keep businesses together, that hasn't been easy.

A spokesman for the governor said that Mr. Schaefer has put out requests to the business community on behalf of the Sanctuary but has found no one even remotely willing to take on the ambitious project. The task is made more difficult because the mission of the Sanctuary, however virtuous, is directed overseas.

"It's a ship we shouldn't abandon. It can be [Baltimore's] goodwill ambassador and serve humanity, but the big problem in this economic downturn is how it's going to get paid for," said Rep. Helen Delich Bentley, R-Md.-2nd. "The American people are hungry, and they're hurting, and they're not very happy about any foreign aid. Repeatedly, I'm hit with people saying let's keep our money here."

Mr. Meyers, who docks the ship for free with the blessing of the Maryland Port Authority and has come up with enough cash so far to pay insurance and utilities, said he is open to local alternatives for the vessel if the money can't be found to get the Sanctuary under sail.

But the picture of a vintage hospital ship with the word "LIFE" painted huge across a bright white hull as it steams into the Horn of Africa to heal unfortunates is just a bit more romantic than the image of poor Baltimoreans trudging down to Fairfield to have their teeth fixed and blood pressure checked.

"It could be a hospital here for low-income people. We could provide medical service to those who can't afford it," said Mr. Meyers. "But if the money can't be raised, and I don't think the recession should be an excuse, we could tow the ship to the Third World and save money that way."

Much of the ship's Vietnam-era medical gear, such as operating rooms, an X-ray department and dental clinic, remains in fairly good condition. Mr. Meyers said finding doctors and sailors willing to donate their time is not a problem, either.

Life International said it also has the money and volunteer labor to begin chipping and painting the Sanctuary hospital white, but it can't begin because the ship's free berth is right next to thousands of new Toyota cars parked on the dock and waiting to be moved to dealers.

The car company fears that the paint will blow over and mar the new vehicles, and Mr. Meyers is seeking a temporary berth away from the Toyota dock to paint the Sanctuary. It is one of the five sister ships of the almost legendary hospital ship Hope, which delivered medical care to developing nations around the world from 1958 to 1974.

Its mission, if realized, will differ from the Hope by delivering long term service up to two years per country and by bringing in people for medical training. And with only six years of use on its 47-year-old boilers, two complete overhauls up through Vietnam and the rest of the time spent in mothballs, the folks at Life International think they can get good use out of the Sanctuary well into the 21st century.

"We want to get into much more of the sociology and anthropology than just medicine," said Robert Mead. a Baltimore publicist who has worked as a volunteer on the project. "If we know enough about the local taboos, maybe we can bring in some of the medicine men and make them paramedics."

January 12, 1992

The little tugboat that could — and still can

THE INNER HARBOR HAS BEEN A SHOPPING MALL FOR MORE THAN A DECADE; private marinas have taken over the waterfront from Key Highway to Canton; and fewer and fewer adults remember when watermelon barges from the Eastern Shore docked at Pratt Street.

Sometimes it's easy to forget that Baltimore is still a working port. The tugboat Athena is a dirty little reminder.

Old, tough and battered, it is the harbor equivalent of a junkyard wrecker that will not die, a floating tub of welded steel named for the Greek goddess of wisdom.

Below the Athena's rust-pitted deck churns a second-hand generator that once powered a circus, an 820-horsepower diesel engine considered a weakling alongside the 5,000-horsepower modern tugs and an electrical panel that looks as if Dr. Frankenstein used it to jump-start his monster.

Behind the tug's stack flies a U.S. flag that looks like a survivor of the bombardment of Fort McHenry.

And on board are a trio of sea dogs from Denmark, South Baltimore and Liverpool, England: Capt. Kai Erik Hansen, 52, from the island of Fyn; his first mate, Mark Rooney, 29, born on Covington Street; and engineer Gary Cowin, 37, who grew up about a mile from the Cavern Club where the Beatles got their start.

On a crisp, cloudless autumn Sunday night, the Athena waits for its crew at a rotting wooden pier on South Clinton Street.

After most people have finished dinner, Captain Hansen, his mate and his engineer board the tug in old work clothes for a simple trip they have made many times.

With an empty barge lashed to its bow, the Athena will sail north through the C&D Canal to Marcus Hook, N.J. The barge will be filled with 5,000 barrels of sodium hydroxide, also known as caustic soda, and hauled back to a chemical plant in Curtis Bay.

There, the W. R. Grace & Co. will convert the caustic soda into chemicals used in the processing of gasoline, heating oil and diesel fuel, and sell them.

When Mr. Cowin cranks the Athena's engine, the whole boat vibrates.

"The Athena is a thing of the past," Captain Hansen says. "The only reason she's still around is she was built to last."

As the lights of downtown fade behind the stern, the skipper's Danish accent announces over a marine radio for all harbor craft to hear: "Security call, security call. Tug Athena pulling out from Clinton Street with a light chemical barge on the nose. Turning around and heading up the canal. The tug Athena."

The son of a shipbuilder, Captain Hansen was born in a house built with brick from a 12th-century Danish fortress.

He ran away to sea at 16 and sailed around the world before landing at the foot of Baltimore's Broadway in 1958. Back then, the Broadway Market was a wooden shed that sold live chickens and almost every business in the neighborhood was tied to the waterfront. Captain Hansen sailed in the U.S. merchant marine during the Vietnam War, worked on local tugs when the war ended and bought the Athena in 1986.

Mr. Rooney, the first mate, is convinced that his love of ships saved him from street-corner foolishness and neighborhood crime during a South Baltimore childhood.

"I had no interest in just hanging around my neighborhood," he says. "I wanted to do things. I wanted to work on boats."

Mr. Cowin arrived in the United States nine years ago and lives in Canton. The son of a retired marine engineer, he says that unemployment is so bad in his English hometown that someone sawed the arm off a statue of the Beatles' fabled "Eleanor Rigby" to sell as scrap metal.

"Kai hasn't been that busy lately," says Mr. Cowin. "But if I were back in England I'd have no job. I'd be on the dole."

These are all men who are happiest when earning their living as sailors, men who would be happier if there were more opportunity to do it in Baltimore. In all of September, the Athena did not leave her berth on Clinton Street once.

"For five weeks we didn't have one job," says Captain Hansen. "There's so little work on the waterfront and so many people out there trying to get it."

A few dozen harbor tugs in Baltimore dock ships, push barges and tow cranes and derricks. Some of them are independent, like the Athena; others are owned by railroads and other corporations.

While cargo tonnage and ships making calls in Baltimore have risen over the last year and a half after three failing years, no one expects the port to return to its glory days of the 1960s and 1970s.

At least the Athena can count on its monthly trip to New Jersey when W. R. Grace contracts with the Vulcan chemical company of Birmingham, Ala., for 5,000 barrels of caustic soda.

Vulcan ships "the caustic" from its plant south of Baton Rouge, Louisiana, up the east coast to New Jersey on the Chilbar. For the past five years, the

Athena has been the mule in the middle of the deal.

The Athena arrives in the Delaware River early Monday morning, expecting the Chilbar and its belly full of caustic soda to be ready at 8 a.m., an event that shows no sign of happening any time soon.

The sun is rising on the tug's right, over the Delaware side of the river; on the New Jersey side, rush-hour traffic and a speeding Amtrak Metroliner hug Interstate 495.

"We've been running as fast as we could go all night to get here on time, and now it's sit and wait," the captain says.

There is nothing to do but find a spot to "hang on" in the river until the ship is ready.

"You always want to carry an extra can of coffee with you in case somebody wants to throw you out," Captain Hansen says. "If the watchman asks what you're doing there and you say: 'Oh, we got a steering problem or an electrical problem, we'll be right out of here. By the way, do you need a can of coffee?' Then they tell you to stay as long as you want."

For the rest of the afternoon, as jets taking off from Philadelphia fly overhead, Captain Hansen mostly stays in his room; Mr. Rooney casts a line over the stern of the Athena to snag "the big rockfish" he swears is always just one cast away; and Mr. Cowin pops into the galley to make a cup of tea and eat a sandwich.

The galley refrigerator is stuffed with provisions for three days away from land: pizza, lunch meat, cheese, ground beef, gallons of milk and apple cider, eggs, breakfast sausage and bacon, fresh bread, Entenmann's sticky buns, Little Debbie lunch cakes and bags of bite-size Hershey chocolates.

Before the Athena left home, coffee began brewing in a big aluminum percolator, and the crew drinks it constantly from a weird collection of mugs.

During the long hours of waiting, Captain Hansen says: "The longer it takes, the more money we make."

Mr. Rooney makes $150 a day when working on the Athena and Mr. Cowin $10 more.

When the boat is running, the Athena's rate is $125 an hour, which drops to $85 when it is waiting for the ship to discharge the cargo.

Captain Hansen charges a flat rate of $350 to pump the caustic soda off the ship and into the barge.

Killing time at 10 a.m., Mr. Rooney reads aloud to Mr. Cowin from a book called "Ship Handling with Tugs."

"In the old days," he says, "a pilot charged with the loss of a vessel was often beheaded on the spot."

It isn't until Tuesday afternoon that the Athena passes under the Key Bridge on its way home.

Once again, Captain Hansen addresses harbor traffic over the marine radio.

"Security call, security call," he says as the Lady Maryland passes the

Dundalk Marine Terminal under full sail on a brilliant day. "Tug Athena on Fort Carroll bound for Grace chemical in Curtis Bay with a chemical barge."

By the time they return to Clinton Street, 66 hours have passed since they left Baltimore, the Athena's fuel tanks are lighter by 1,000 gallons, most of the food is gone and the barge of caustic soda has been docked on time at W. R. Grace in Curtis Bay.

If no other jobs come their way, it will be another month on shore before they leave again for Marcus Hook.

"I've been around boats so long," says Mr. Rooney, "that when I'm home I go a little stir crazy."

December 14, 1992

Couple's renovated tugboat
has comforts of home

IT HAS TO BE THE ONLY TUGBOAT IN BALTIMORE WITH A CLOTHES DRYER VENT rigged up to the smokestack.

The Wildflower, a 55-year-old work tug that started moving barges around the Patapsco after World War II, is now docked among fancy yachts and sailboats on the Canton waterfront. It belongs to a dreamer named Brad Pumphrey and his wife, Jennifer, who have made it their home for about half the price of a modest Owings Mills townhouse.

"It's got a lot of character and it's going to last forever," said Mr. Pumphrey, 26, who fell under the spell of shipboard living on childhood fishing trips with his father. He pays the bills with a digital imaging job at the University of Baltimore library and runs a harbor taxi on weekends.

"No one thought it was doable," he said of the unlikely transformation of a squat tub of double-plated steel into a custom home paneled with Honduran mahogany. "But it's easier to take an empty shell and build an interior than try to upgrade an interior you don't like. This isn't your average tugboat anymore."

Not quite.

The Wildflower sports a full bath with standard tub.

A laundry room.

All but one of the old steel hatches are now Plexiglas windows with miniblinds.

The master bedroom slopes up under the bow, the top deck will soon bloom with a bed of plants and flowers, and there's a Jenn-Aire range and espresso machine in the galley.

Mrs. Pumphrey, a 27-year-old social worker for the city, said the Wildflower was her husband's vision, but one she never doubted. The Pumphreys, who wanted to keep private what they paid for the tug and its renovations, bought the boat in July and moved aboard in February.

"Brad's the dreamy type, I'm more practical," said Mrs. Pumphrey, who laid the kitchen and bath tile. "But I saw it as realistic because he works hard, and when he starts a project he finishes it."

Mr. Pumphrey is, in fact, obsessive about his passions.

It's not enough that he did most of the renovations himself — he's putting

81

together a World Wide Web page about the Wildflower so folks out in cyber-space can tour the tug from anywhere in the world.

"There are people who have done the exact thing we have," he reckons. "We just don't know who they are."

Built for the Navy by the Avondale shipyard in New Orleans, the vessel was launched Dec. 27, 1940. After six years of government service, the tug began plying the Patapsco River as the A. J. Harper, guiding coal barges to Bethlehem Steel in Sparrows Point until 1971.

A local ship chandlery, the next owner, changed the tug's name to Martom and used it to ferry supplies to anchored ships. Kai Hansen, a Baltimore captain who ran away to sea from his native Denmark as a teen-ager, bought the Martom in 1990, renaming it the Wildflower in honor of his wife's work with the species.

The Wildflower's last voyage was a short one, a few blocks north from Clinton Street to the Anchorage marina, where Boston and O'Donnell streets meet at the mouth of Harris Creek. The Wildflower had to be towed there and won't be up and running for at least a year.

Mr. Pumphrey took out the original steering gear because it would have run straight through the kitchen and living room, which were built above the engine. When he and his wife get enough money — a constant theme in their project — Mr. Pumphrey will install hydraulic steering.

To make living quarters in a boat designed as a floating engine, Mr. Pumphrey had thousands of pounds of metal burned out by welders. making him a favorite among scrap metal scavengers who comb the waterfront. So much steel came out that some was mixed with 30,000 pounds of concrete and poured back into the hold to keep the tug from riding too high in the water.

Mr. Pumphrey acknowledges he doesn't know much about the tug's 400-horsepower Detroit diesel engine. But he got a pair of fat operating manuals in the deal with Mr. Hansen and intends to pore over them the way he studied pilot books to earn his captain's license for inland waterways.

"This is a slow boat, she can do 9 knots," he said. "But I wanted a boat we could travel in and this thing is solid."

Mr. Pumphrey bought his first houseboat in 1990 for $7,000. In fixing it up, he said he discovered talents in yacht carpentry and marine repair. He sold the boat for $11,000, repaired yachts for a Pasadena boatyard, and lived with Jennifer for awhile on the yacht of a wealthy man too busy to enjoy it.

He and Jennifer have known each other since they were 14, and after their 1992 marriage they lived in a rowhouse near Patterson Park. "I was miserable on land," Mr. Pumphrey said.

In the Wildflower, he sees a life in which he'll only have to join the landlubbers for as long as it takes to make enough money to keep his family afloat.

"Our work will never be done, but it's livable," he said. "After a long hard day in cyberspace, you want to come home and touch wood. You want to be on the water."

April 25, 1995

Seaborn bottle yields
its message, vintage '80s

THIS IS THE STORY OF A ROMANTIC NOTION AND ITS JOURNEY FROM ANTIGUA to Inagua to Alaska to Pimlico.

Fifteen years ago, Jessica Harrison's name and address began bobbing along the edge of the Sargasso Sea in a whiskey bottle. The note promised a $5 reward to anyone who found the bottle and wrote to the Harrison family on West Rogers Avenue to tell of the discovery.

Last month, a letter arrived from Petersburg, Alaska. "This completes the cycle," said Marlene Ezrine Harrison, Jessica's mother. "It took a little while."

On Aug. 5, 1980, on a trip from Fortaleza, Brazil, to New York City, Joan Gayle Brinch threw the bottle over the side of the freighter Mormacsaga about 375 miles northeast of Antigua.

The wife of the ship's captain, Mrs. Brinch often accompanied her husband on his voyages. Once at sea, she would slip notes into bottles, seal their caps with wax and toss them overboard.

"Long before I married my husband, I read a lot of romantic novels," said Mrs. Brinch, who lives in Harrisburg, Pa. "I always had a love affair with the sea, and sending a message in a bottle always seemed like a romantic thing to do."

To a seasoned sea dog such as Soren Brinch, the son of a captain and the grandson of captains on both sides of the family, the practice seemed a little silly. But, because Mrs. Brinch entertained the dozen or so passengers on board the freighters with her bottle-tossing, her husband humored her by going along with the stunts and lending them dignity by marking the exact latitude and longitude.

"On the way home from a trip, we always had a bottle party with cocktails," remembered Mrs. Brinch, who was widowed in 1986. "Everyone would get their bottles and seal them with wax, and before dinner we'd throw them off the side, always in deep water.

"I have four nieces, and I'd throw a bottle for each one of them on every voyage," said Mrs. Brinch, who has no children. "There were 10 voyages, so

I threw 40 bottles. Within a couple of years, a bottle was found for three of the girls. But poor Jessica, her bottles never got found."

Until February of 1992, that is, when Alaskan fishery executive and wandering adventurer Patrick Wilson was combing the beaches of Great Inagua, the southernmost island of the Bahamas.

"I used to dive for treasure down there. I like to beachcomb and camp and enjoy the sun," said Mr. Wilson, who has been visiting Inagua for 20 years. "I was camping on the unpopulated side of the island; very few people ever go there. On that side, the current sweeps the island and deposits massive amounts of debris — boats, wreckage, bales of dope, torpedoes, parts of aircraft and all kinds of garbage."

Amid the flotsam and jetsam, Mr. Wilson "came across this clear bottle that had a typed note in it and the cap still on. The cap says 'James Burrough, Ltd. Distillers.' The paper inside was rolled so I could read the message. It was a little faded and crusty, but no water got in."

Judging by the coordinates where the bottle was tossed, the southern Bahamas is the most likely spot for the bottle to have landed, said W. Doug Wilson, oceanographer for the National Oceanic and Atmospheric Administration in Miami.

"An Antilles current may have taken it. It flows northward along the island arc outside the Inagua. Or the North Equatorial current may have taken it. That's a general westward flow through the southern Bahama area," Mr. Wilson said.

"On the other hand, it could just as easily have gone into the Caribbean and come back out. Or it could have gone around the whole North Atlantic once or twice. Did it take 12 years to reach Inagua, or was it sitting on the beach for 10?"

After flying home to Alaska with the bottle, Mr. Wilson let it languish at the back of his closet for three years because of his ambivalence toward people who send messages in bottles.

He had been thrilled by finding a commemorative Guinness Stout bottle thrown overboard by the Irish brewery on its bicentennial in 1959, and he took pains to dry the soggy contents: a booklet about the Dublin brewery, an ad for Ovaltine and a scroll from King Neptune.

And years ago, on the same side of Inagua, he found a bottled message written in five languages by an Israeli crossing the Atlantic from Tel Aviv. "It was so weathered and crumpled and broken into pieces that I couldn't figure out what it said. I wrote to the guy but never heard anything back," Mr. Wilson said.

The silence from Tel Aviv and other nautical dead-ends persuaded Mr. Wilson not to write the Harrison family.

The bottle sat in the dark until Brenda Kleinfelder began putting together an exhibit of ocean debris for Earth Day this year. A research assistant for the Marine Advisory Program in Petersburg, a town of about 3,500, Ms.

Kleinfelder decorated an office window with things found on Alaskan beaches.

One day, after happening by the exhibit, Patrick Wilson walked into Ms. Kleinfelder's office "and dropped his bottle on my desk," she said. When friends learned that he hadn't written to the Harrisons, they pestered him until he did.

His letter left Petersburg May 13 and arrived on West Rogers Avenue May 18.

Jessica Harrison, a "free spirit" who has done a lot of traveling, gets junk mail from around the world. When she isn't home to open it, her mother files the excess in the trash.

"But right by the garbage can I decided to open this one," said Mrs. Harrison. "It blew my mind."

And, with a quick call to Alaska, the bottle's 15-year odyssey was nearly complete.

Joan Gayle Brinch was grateful that a bottle had been found for each of her nieces. Patrick Wilson's faith in people who drop notes into the sea was restored. The Mormacsaga sits in the James River as part of the government's ready reserve fleet. And Marlene Harrison is trying to figure out how much interest to pay on a $5 reward offered when Jimmy Carter was president.

But the person whose name is in the whiskey bottle was unaware of it all.

As the connections were being made, 20-year-old Jessica Harrison was camping in the Pacific Northwest with friends, having too much fun to spare a minute to call her family.

When she finally checked in over the Memorial Day weekend, her mother told her to sit down, that she had some news.

"I had just been telling a friend about the bottle as we were crossing over the [Willamette] river to get to downtown Portland. There were ships in the river that looked like the ones my uncle used to work on," said Jessica. "I don't think he believed a word I was saying."

June 6, 1995

Chapter 6

Food
for the
Spirit

Chorizo is link to Spanish family past

THERE LIVES IN BALTIMORE A MAN WHO GRINDS OUT WORLD-CLASS CHORIZO for close friends, family, and a belly — his own — that hungers for Spain's sausage staple.

Charlie Vega says he was forced into it. After being spoiled as a child with endless links of homemade chorizo, from breakfast through dinner, he moved to Baltimore and went without.

Like others whose palates have been seduced by the Mack Truck robustness of authentic chorizo, Mr. Vega rarely found store-bought or restaurant chorizo here that equaled the sausage of his youth.

"When I was growing up it was just there all the time," said Mr. Vega, a Mechanicsville, N. Y. native who moved to Baltimore 15 years ago to study guitar at the Peabody Institute. "And it was always my grandmother who made it."

Mr. Vega attributes the scarcity of quality local chorizo to Baltimore's small Spanish community — minor compared to the tens of thousands of Poles who market wonderful rings of homemade kielbasa. But the ease with which he mastered his family's recipe leaves him puzzled by the commercial chorizo void.

"There's really nothing to it," he said on a recent Sunday evening, his Butcher's Hill apartment lively with the aroma of chorizo hanging to dry. "It's just a matter of throwing it all together."

Charlie Vega only wonders why he didn't decide to throw it all together sooner, saving himself the disappointment of domestic and imported chorizo, often expensive, that was too bland, greasy, or stiff for his tastes.

Six years ago he searched out the recipe of his late Spanish grandmother, Maria Vega.

Two years ago he mustered the effort to put the family secret into action, and just the other day he was up to his elbows again in ground port butts, preparing to suffuse the sweet meat with red wine, garlic, paprika and several other hand-ground spices before guiding the mix into casings.

"I got the recipe from my father," said Mr. Vega, 38, an ophthalmological instrument maker at Johns Hopkins Hospital who drifted into the medical field after realizing he "wouldn't be the next Segovia" of classical guitar. "My old man got it from his mother [Maria] who wrote it down somewhere along the line."

The line the recipe has traveled is a long one: it blossomed in the southern Spanish city of Seville, where Maria Vega was born; moved to Madrid where she was raised; journeyed to the exotic New World locale of Luke in Western Maryland, where Maria and her husband Valentine settled before World War I; moved north to Mechanicsville, N. Y., where Charlie's father worked for the Boston and Maine Railroad; and finally surfaced in Baltimore after Charlie tracked it down.

The Vega recipe is just one interpretation of the versatile sausage used in meals from one end of Iberia to the other, with hybrid versions — like chorizo lunchmeat — sold throughout the Spanish-speaking world.

Chorizo is fried with eggs, simmered in stews, and baked with both fish and fowl; nibbled as an appetizer and sliced for pot pies and paella. Only bread and wine are more of a constant on the tables of Spain.

"Chorizo is made differently all over Spain," said Mr. Vega. "In the south, around Seville where my grandmother's people are from, the chorizos are more pungent, more garlicky, spicier."

There are small villages, like Jabugo, throughout the southern Andalusian region of Spain where women work in cooperative chorizo mills, mixing the meat and spices and stuffing the casings by hand before the sausage is hung to dry for two weeks, slowly cured with the smoke from smoldering evergreen oak.

Because Mr. Vega's chorizo are not smoked, the result is a link that is pliant and colored deep purple, not blood red and hard like most. They also tend to be leaner than commercial chorizo, and free of the lard that adheres to those imported in cans.

Chorizo is almost always made of pork, but veal is used, and local Spanish chefs talk of casings stuffed with venison and even pigeon in poorer parts of their homeland.

While paprika and red wine are the mainstay ingredients of chorizo, Mr. Vega says it is garlic that separates chorizos from sissy sausages.

"You see all those old guys around the Mediterranean — it's the olive oil, the wine, and garlic that keeps them in good shape. My grandfather [Valentine] lived until he was 98. He quit smoking when he was 90 when he decided it was bad for him, but he still drank a bottle of wine a day."

Mr. Vega's one regret, a result of his sitting on the recipe for four years before trying it out, is that Valentine never got a chance to sample his grandson's chorizo.

Charlie Vega's chorizo leaps over a generation or so of sausage tamed by his aunts for the milder American taste, and zaps the tongue straight back to the south of Spain.

"I think Grandpa would have approved," he said with a smile. "They're pretty close to Grandmom's."

February 19, 1986

Crabs crawl from Bay to belly in less than a day

FIFTEEN HOURS AND TWO MINUTES FROM BAY TO BELLY.

That's how long it took a dozen Chesapeake Bay blue crabs to journey roughly 45 miles along a commercial route — a price on their stiff backs every step of the way — after being plucked from the upper bay.

They were taken early in the morning out of cool waters off the shores of northern Kent county, landed on the deck of a workboat named "Bad Boy's Toy," and were trucked to a roadside crab stand in Baltimore before hitting the destination that makes sense of it all: the tummies of a local family gathered around their kitchen table.

Along the way, five people turned a buck, and a living, from the summertime demand for hard shell crabs.

Essex waterman Danny Beck, a third-generation crabber, is the guy who caught the crustaceans and a little more than 60 bushels of their relatives last week.

Mr. Beck, one of about 100 commercial crabbers based out of bayside creeks along eastern Baltimore County, almost never meets the thousands of folks who consume his product.

Likewise, the average crab eater usually has no idea exactly where the delicate devils come from — as long as they're Chesapeake Bay crabs, it's pedigree enough.

Ralph Marston is the man in between. A roadside crab huckster and classic middleman, Mr. Marston knows the work habits of the crabbers he buys from and is regularly on hand to greet the people who pay him for the privilege of devouring local treasures from the Land of Pleasant Living.

The journey of these particular crabs — from the Bay, to Danny Beck, through Ralph's Crabs, and finally into a steam pot and the anxious mouths of Rodney Sewell's family in the 1600 block of Northgate Road — begins near dawn on a Wednesday morning.

Leaving the dock at his home on Browns Creek with a three-man crew at 4:30 a.m., Mr. Beck and his rig reach the waters near Worton Point, northeast of Pooles Island, before full daybreak.

The crabs that end up on Rodney Sewell's newspaper-covered kitchen table in Northeast Baltimore are some of the first caught this morning, which breaks hazy and gray.

Using an electric spotlight to locate plastic foam floats that mark his 1,250 crab pots, Mr. Beck, 37, snares the float with a pole hook, and pulls the rope attached to the float within reach of Chuckie Mizell, his 27-year-old right-hand man.

Mr. Mizell, who has worked the water since he was 12 and hopes to operate his own rig next summer, uses a motorized pulley to haul the crab pot at the end of the line aboard "Bad Boy's Toy."

He shakes the crabs caught in the square wire "pot" onto the stern where Fred Mizell, his 64-year-old father, and a third crewman, Darren "Jim" Hallock, 21, sort through the catch by hand and with tongs.

Chuckie Mizell re-baits the pots with alewives and heaves the traps back into the light-olive water as the crabs are separated into classes.

The big sellers are "No. 1 Jimmies" — heavy males at least $5\frac{3}{4}$ inches wide that sell dockside for $30 to $35 a bushel in mid-summer and eventually bring between $12 and $20 a dozen in restaurants.

Mr. Beck says when all his seasonal expenses are tallied — from 6,000 gallons of fuel to $50 a day for each crewman — it costs him just under $18 to catch a bushel of crabs.

When they're scarce, early and late in the season, he might command $50 a bushel wholesale for the No. 1. When they're plentiful, which, he says, they've yet to be this year, the top price can drop to $18 or $20 a bushel.

The second class, which Mr. Marston has an eye for, are "No. 2s," males between 5 and $5\frac{3}{4}$ inches. They sell for $12 to $18 a bushel wholesale, and wind up as $7 a dozen crabs at Ralph's roadside stand.

The other "keepers" are females, rarely used by restaurants, good for soup, and said to be sweeter than males, and "whiteys" — paper-shell males that carry little meat because they've recently shed old shells for new.

Dead crabs turn up from every category, maybe three out of every dozen caught, and Fred and Jim casually toss them overboard along with live ones under the five inches, the state's legal limit.

Mr. Beck, bearded, pot bellied, and candid, eats soft crab sandwiches, butter-baked chicken wings, and double-stuffed Oreo cookies — washing it all down with bottles of Coke — as he pilots the boat between points where he's dropped pots.

He says the season is slow this year, and curses his luck — even on this reasonably good day — saying that if he could more easily stand people and telephones he might just pack it all in for a crab house of his own.

The crew works mostly in silence amid the loud, jarring noise of the boat's engine, and continues from Worton Point to Howell Point on up to Grove Point, just above the mouth of the Sassafras River. They pick nearly 600 pots clean before Mr. Beck turns the boat toward home about 2 p.m.

It's a little less than an hour and a half south through the bay to his Browns Creek pier. The men stack most of the bushels in the back of Mr. Beck's delivery truck, and the rest are put in cold storage to complement delivery of the next day's catch.

At 4:45 p.m., Mr. Beck drives his red Ford pickup with a white, unrefrigerated plywood storage box in back down a dusty gravel road from the Essex waterfront to two nearby crab houses — Al's Seafood, an Eastern Boulevard branch of the original Fells Point business, and Schultz's Crab House at 1732 Old Eastern Ave.

Each restaurant buys about a dozen bushels — mostly No. 1s and some No. 2s — and then it's off to see Mr. Marston, who has a young man selling crabs while waiting for Mr. Beck alongside the Big B Supermarket, on Chinquapin parkway, just off the Alameda.

Mr. Beck gets there a little before 6 p.m. and unloads a few dozen bushels of No. 2s and some whiteys when Mr. Marston shows up, a beeper on his belt so his suppliers can always reach him.

The two men settle their deal on the hood of Mr. Beck's truck, discuss the difference in supply between the Eastern Shore watermen and those who work the upper Bay.

Mr. Marston complains about crab house owners who call the police to shoo him and his workers — even though they hold the proper health department and city vendor licenses — from spots along several East Baltimore corners.

He's convinced that his customers, who steam crabs at home, and those who eat them in restaurants are two distinct markets. The crab house people believe that Mr. Marston nibbles into their profits by offering live crabs anywhere from $5 to $12 a dozen cheaper than they do.

It's an argument, says Mr. Marston, and Mr. Beck who says he agrees with him, that never ends.

His long day of work complete, Mr. Beck drives home to Essex for a short night's sleep before it's time to leave the docks again.

A steady stream of cars pulls up to Mr. Marston, who separates his crabs into bushels selling for $4, $5 and $6 a dozen. He cracks open a fresh bushel of Mr. Beck's No. 2s and announces that he now has $7-a-dozen crabs.

Many customers, thrilled when the captive crabs snap up at them when the baskets are jostled, seem to have made the decision to buy crabs on the spur of the moment.

Mr. Marston, 47 years old and itching for a crab house of his own, is friendly to everyone.

"Why don't you go back across the street, and I'll throw them to you," he tells one middle-aged woman who buys a dozen. "Then you can tell your friends that you caught them."

It's 6:30 p.m. and Vanessa L. Timmons, 23, and her young son, Dennard, park across the street from Ralph's Crabs.

"My man Ralph here is the only man we get crabs from," she says as Mr. Marston fills a brown paper sack with 14 of the $7-a-dozen crabs from Mr. Beck. "On the days Ralph don't show up, my mama has me riding all around town for crabs."

Mr. Marston turns from his customers and confides: "I don't put no dead crabs in there. And I always put in some extra, 13-14 a dozen. And we don't hold onto no crabs that are barely living and will be dead when they got home…

"You take care of the customer," he says confidently, "and the customer will take care of you in the long run."

Vanessa Timmons puts her son and the bag of crabs in her silver sports car and drives less than a mile to her family's home on Northgate road. She arrives about 7:15 p.m. and discovers that a relative has not returned a crab steaming pot that they borrowed.

She sets the bag of crabs on the kitchen counter, and with a younger brother heads back out to buy a new pot. Nothing, she says, will stand in the way of the supper her family has looked forward to all day.

Rodney Sewell, her stepfather, waits in the living room as Mrs. Timmons returns with a large, stainless steel pot. He helps her season the crabs — vinegar and mixed spices they bought from Mr. Marston — and sits at the kitchen table as the flame is lit beneath the pot just after 8 p.m.

Sharing space atop the stove with the crabs is a pan of oil for french fries, a skillet of ground beef to make sloppy joes, and a frying pan that waits for fillets of fish.

But all tastebuds are primed for the contents of the shiny steam pot.

"I eat crabs almost every day," says Mr. Sewell, a 46-year-old truck driver for a local metal products company. "I'm a crab lover, been one all my life."

He waits for the 20-to-25 minute cooking time to pass and reminisces about the beginning of his love affair with Maryland blue crabs.

"I grew up crabbing in Cherry Hill off the Hanover Street Bridge in the early 50s," he says. "We caught them the old-fashioned way with a string and a fish head or a chicken neck, and a buddy would scoop them up with a net. We'd sell a bushel for $3 or $4, which was a lot of money, and go back and catch some more for ourselves."

Turning his eyes and mind back to the crabs that wait, Mr. Sewell adds: "Once you cook them and eat them, you don't even think about the traveling that crab has done. You put them boys in the pot and if they're kicking and snapping, they're good crabs and that's all that matters."

The time is 8:27 p.m. when Mrs. Timmons removes the stainless steel bowl she used to cover the pot and places steaming hot crabs, no longer olive and blue but orange with white bottoms, in the bowl.

She sets the bowl before Mr. Sewell, who chooses one to his liking, holds it aloft by a back fin like a prize, and yanks a claw from the body.

A stream of hot juice — a combination of bay water, some vinegar, and the moisture of the seasoned crab — flows from the broken joint.

The juice is a welcome sign of freshness, and Mr. Sewell sucks the spot from where it ran. He cracks the claw with his hands for the first taste of the meat.

It's 8:32 p.m., a light rain falls, thunder booms, the Orioles are playing ball a mile or so away at Memorial Stadium — Danny Beck and Ralph Marston are finally off duty — and everything is right in the gastronomic world of Rodney G. Sewell, crab lover.

"Mmmmmmmmmm," he says, as Mrs. Timmons and her brother dig in for crabs of their own. "Mmmmmmmmmmmmmmm, mmmmmmmmmmmmmmm."

Fifteen hours and two minutes from bay to belly.

August 10, 1986

For all their blessings,
24 in Patterson Park family give thanks

THE SUN BREAKS OVER PATTERSON PARK JUST BEFORE 7 A.M., SENDING Thanksgiving's first light into a large brick town house, darkness thinning into gray as Eleanore Rybczynski fills a 26.17-pound turkey with handfuls of bread stuffing.

Her husband, attorney Edward B. Rybczynski — pronounced Rib-chin-ski — sits at the kitchen table in his robe, sipping coffee and eating toast as a stereo fills the house with the voices of a choir.

From time to time his wife gently calls his name and Mr. Rybczynski rises and moves next to her, his wife indicating that the huge bird needs to be turned this way or that.

The three-story house just above Eastern Avenue on Patterson Park Avenue, a former Spanish consulate built two years after the Civil War, is calm as dawn spreads into foggy daylight over East Baltimore.

At 7:36 a.m., Mrs. Rybczynski opens the oven door and her husband slides the turkey into a dark hole heated to 325 degrees.

Eight hours later the bird will feed 24 people — all of them Rybczynski family members.

"This is when I get the most done, before the kids come," said Mrs. Rybczynski, taking off her apron as she gets ready to change for 9 a.m. Mass at Holy Rosary Catholic Church.

"The kids" are seven boys and three girls that began arriving after Edward and Eleanore married in 1954, starting with the birth of Paul in 1956 and continuing through David, born in 1969.

Mr. and Mrs. Rybczynski are each the children of corner grocers and grew up on the city's east side during the Great Depression and World War II. They met as young adults at a Polish social club and worked hard to raise 10 children in the city when most of their contemporaries were fleeing for the suburbs.

Their children and grandchildren are the family, the point on which all things are focused.

Said Mr. Rybczynski: "We look for excuses to get the kids together."

Grabbing a bag filled with canned goods, he and his wife leave the turkey roasting a few minutes before 9 a.m. and make the short walk to Holy Rosary.

Mr. Rybczynski, sporting a red bow tie, is the lector for the service, at which most worshippers will drop off food for the poor.

Mrs. Rybczynski sings in the choir with three of her sons and daughter-in-law Mary Veronica. Mary's 10-week-old daughter, Emma, looks up at the singers from a carry-cradle on the balcony floor of the ornate Polish church.

Down below, at the end of a long aisle down which Mr. and Mrs. Rybczynski and all but one of their married children walked to exchange vows, the Rev. Chester Mieczkowski celebrates Mass.

"Let us give thanks to the Lord," he says.

The congregation responds: "It is right to give Him thanks and praise."

The service ends with "America the Beautiful" as Mr. and Mrs. Rybczynski file out onto Chester Street for the short walk home.

It is barely 10 a.m. and already the sweet smell of countless roasting turkeys is wafting through the narrow streets and alleys around Patterson Park.

Back home, Mrs. Rybczynski cooks scrambled eggs and home fries for bachelor sons Mark, 25, and David, 20. All her children took piano lessons growing up, but Mark, who plays keyboard in a wedding band, and David, who studies saxophone at the Berklee College of Music, hope to build careers in music.

As they eat their eggs, the brothers trade opinions on jazz. Mr. Rybczynski listens closely as they talk. Later, he admits that he cares little for jazz but would travel anywhere in the country to hear his children play.

As morning drifts into afternoon, the family pulls together all the odds and ends needed to accommodate a sit-down dinner for 24, a feast supported by two tables stretching 17 feet between the dining room and kitchen. A piano bench is pulled in from a baby grand in the front room to make sure there are enough seats for everybody.

The doorbell starts to ring and the house fills. Son Tom and his wife, Mary Veronica, bring a couple of dozen oysters from Broadway Market and a tureen of oyster and spinach stew; daughter Carol and husband David Dieter arrive with pork and sauerkraut soup; Paul and wife Sara bring squash — "an American vegetable" — and newlywed son John and wife Irma show up with homemade French bread and a casserole of vegetables shaped like a birthday cake.

The Poly football team beats up on the team from City College — Mr. Rybczynski's alma mater — on cable television as Tom shucks oysters and the turkey cools in a shaft of autumn sunlight next to him.

The kids, all grown, tease each other over who will get the biggest piece of brown and crispy turkey skin, just as when they were little.

David Dieter polishes silver as his relatives walk from room to room sipping beer from long-necked brown bottles or wine from crystal; his 2½-

year-old son, Joey, runs through the house with his cousins, falls, and bangs his nose on Uncle Paul's knee, crying until Mommy kisses it and makes it better; and Mr. Rybczynski sets out crystal around each table setting as Mary Veronica folds linen napkins.

Daughter Carol Dieter takes the sweet potatoes and peels them by hand on a sheet of newspaper. She looks up at her family and laughs. "Don't I look like June Cleaver? I'm wearing my pearls."

The 83-year-old matriarch, great-grandmother Marie Nowak, is dressed in regal purple and shares the spotlight with all the youngsters. Her smile fills the kitchen as she is squeezed, kissed and hugged by all of her grandchildren, among them a chemist, a choir director, a Realtor and an electrician.

Crystal pitchers are filled with ice water and fresh cider, and for a few seconds, Mr. Rybczynski stands in silence at the head of the table.

It is clear. It is time.

The family bows their heads and Mr. Rybczynski begins: "Dear Lord," he says, "We have so much to be thankful for..."

November 23, 1990

A Meal with two vegetables and good portions for $5

DON'T BE FOOLED BY THE MAUVE MOLDING AROUND THE CEILING, THE NEW gray and lavender Formica, or the life-is-a-middle-class-breeze wallpaper that looks like it was stripped from the breakfast nook of an Owings Mills town house.

You'll know you're in the right place because the slabs of raw meat are still piled one atop the other in a glass chill box under the cash register, a still life in bloody brown with heads of lettuce.

You'll know because behind the counter, flipping eggs and directing the show, will be George Basil, a living, spatula-wielding legend at the corner of Boston and Van Lill Streets on the Canton waterfront.

You will know that you are in the newly remodeled Sip & Bite, perhaps the most fabled Baltimore diner of the last quarter-century.

"They make the best liver and onions in the city," said Steve Boone, the former bass player for the Lovin' Spoonful who ate all-hours breakfasts there throughout the 1980s. "And the stories are legion."

Such stories, said Jerry Kelly, who owns the X-rated Earle Theater on Belair Road and knows a few things about burlesque in real life.

"I'll never forget," he said, "the night the lady lost her teeth, fell right out of her mouth while she was eating."

But George Basil asks you, please, to forget all that: close your eyes to the 2 a.m. floor show of cops and robbers, Realtors and hookers, preppies and transvestites; car-phone yups, surf-whipped sea dogs and dreamers dying of loneliness; bums, nuts and losers; fat cats, politicians, history professors and people who were born along the Baltimore docks when cargo ships still sailed from here to there on the wind.

Close your eyes and open your mouth, says the man who just spent $135,000 to improve the facilities and 24-hour-a-day ambience of the Sip & Bite.

Raising a finger in the air, George declares: "I haven't raised my prices one penny, not one penny! Where you going to go to eat a meal with two vegetables and good portions for $5? No place!"

And no place is where they are coming in by the dozens every day, from

12:01 a.m. to 11:59 p.m., more now than before.

"Somebody was telling me it was remodeled," said a man the other night while ordering hot roast beef with gravy at 1:30 in the morning. "But I didn't believe it."

Mr. Boone once shared a stage with the Beatles. He has re-habbed many a Baltimore rowhouse and has eaten runny eggs around the world. He would believe anything about the Sip & Bite.

"It's a landmark in the same way the old Ambassador Restaurant was [at Pratt and Eutaw]. Man, back in '73 or '74 that place was Damon Runyon land with every wall-eyed freak in Baltimore," he said. "But the Sip & Bite was always a cut above because the food was better."

When George closed the restaurant for two weeks in January for renovation, many of his customers and a few of his employees were forced out onto Boston Street to find food and work at other cafes.

None of them liked it very much. "I went across the street for the duration," said a guy named Bill, a big man with a pony-tail. "It just doesn't taste as good."

When George re-opened the regulars came back to find the waitresses the same but the restrooms, of which the employees are proud, brand-new. "Have you seen the bathrooms yet?" asks Louise Smith, perhaps the skinniest waitress in town.

The old counter stools were preserved and George kept the lone green office chair by the meat case for parties who can't all crowd into one booth, but the floor is new ceramic tile.

The char-broil grill and the handicap-access ramp are new, but the enlarged write-ups from newspapers prosperous and defunct still hang on the wall, attesting in adjectives stolen from detective novels about the food, the characters and the mystique of the Sip & Bite.

This is a crabcake and Greek salad joint so deep in the peculiar romance of Baltimore that, according to an old packinghouse lady, a young woman once made a waitress give her the heavy porcelain coffee cup she was drinking out of to better remember the man who seduced her over scrambled eggs in a booth.

Most likely George was behind the counter at the time, calling out orders the same way he's been doing since 1968.

"When I first come to this country I worked for my uncle for a few years and then I never work for anybody but myself — 60 hours a week in here," he said. "Anybody who works hard in this country can make it. You can become anything."

Like a spatula-wielding legend in the most fabled diner in Baltimore.

March 22, 1992

Last bread baker in Little Italy

THE SPIRIT OF A HORSE-DRAWN BREAD WAGON BANGS AROUND BALTIMORE inside a dented Dodge van with "M. Marinelli & Son" hung in the window.

Behind the wheel sits the "son" — 81-year-old Anthony Marinelli, last of the old-time Little Italy bakers still making bread at his house. Just about the same age as his business, Tony Marinelli's entire life has been mixed up like flour and water in golden loaves of "pane."

"There were four or five Italian bakers around here in the old days," says Mr. Marinelli, whose earliest memory is hanging on his father's bread wagon when deliveries were made door-to-door. "I'm the only one left."

At the turn of the century, when nearly half the families in America had stopped making bread regularly at home, bakers began landing at the head of the Patapsco River on waves of German, Italian, Jewish and Polish immigration.

In rowhouses, storefronts, backyards and basements throughout the city, the newcomers made bread reminiscent of the old country with some concession to American tastes. Dependent on their own neighborhoods for business, Baltimore's ethnic bakers ventured out along cobbled streets for new markets, wagons piled with loaves.

By World War I, when it was still a sin to have bread sliced at the store, at least five families in Little Italy were turning out bread from brick ovens in their homes: Marinelli, Scelsi, Giordano, Maranto and Impallaria.

Scelsi, convinced that wood heat blessed the bread with exquisite texture, burned wood in brick ovens long after others had switched to oil. Maranto threw stale bread in the oven when fuel ran low and delivered door-to-door from wicker baskets.

Pasquale "Joe" Impallaria moved his wife and 11 children into second-floor bedrooms above the ovens every winter to save money on heat. During the Depression, his wife, Polisetta, gave cotton flour sacks to homemakers who sewed them into sheets, pillowcases and clothes for their children.

And, according to Anthony Giordano, 67, when the family bakery closed for four days after his father Sam burned his hand, "people thought it was the end of the world."

He marvels: "People still stop me on the street and ask: 'When you gonna make that good bread?'"

Having tried in vain to duplicate Giordano bread in the Magic Chef oven at his Tunlaw Street home, he just smiles and shakes his head. "It's not the recipe, there's not much to dough. It's the oven that makes the bread."

The brick-oven bakery that his grandfather, Giovanni, ran closed in the mid-1960s. In 1961, the Scelsis went out of business. And the ovens that operated for most of the century under the names Impallaria and Gramigna went cold in 1981, at a time when a loaf sold for 45 cents.

Maranto still bakes 14,000 loaves a week — supplying small accounts like Apicella's Grocery as well as Giant supermarkets. But it moved to West Baltimore in 1916.

Only Tony Marinelli and his Thai bakery crew are still making wholesale commercial bread in Baltimore's original Italian neighborhood.

He is Little Italy's last direct link to the old-country bread men who started bakeries right off the boat. Never married, Mr. Marinelli dotes instead on his seven-day-a-week business. None of his six sisters or their college-educated children is interested in taking over.

"He said he was going to sell the business to me a couple of times, but always he change his mind. He just can't let go of it," says baker Niwattra "Nina" Rukki, 43, a Bangkok university graduate who has worked for Mr. Marinelli since 1976. "I'm looking at other [prospects]. It might take him forever to sell to me. And I don't want to be baking bread when I'm as old as Tony."

Without the bakery, counters the stubborn Mr. Marinelli, he wouldn't have lived this long.

"You gotta do something. Ain't no use hanging on the corner like all the retired guys, worried about when you're gonna die," he says.

About 800 loaves a day roll out of the cinder-block bakery behind the Central Avenue rowhouse where Mr. Marinelli eats, sleeps, and labors to sustain the business his father started a few years after arriving in Baltimore from Italy in 1910.

"It ain't a hell of a lot," he says of production. "People think it's a lot, but it ain't."

Compared with the 370,000 rolls an hour that pop out of H&S Bakery's $450-million-a-year operation in nearby Fells Point, Mr. Marinelli's bakery is a quaint way to pay the bills.

"He's still around, huh? When I was young, he was already old," said H&S chief John Paterakis, 64, who started out as a boy on his father Isidore's bread truck. "Tony's still making it by hand? Nobody makes it by hand anymore."

Yes, essentially by hand.

"With the big guys, it's all push-buttons, and the bread comes out soggy-like," says Mr. Marinelli. Customers from all over town seem to agree, making their way to 321 S. Central Ave. for a fresh, crusty, 80-cent loaf, which

Tony promotes as "cheaper than wholesale."

"He's got the best," said Morrell Park's Lester White, trading a handful of coins for a bag of Marinelli bread. "Whenever we have spaghetti, I come down here, about 20 years now. His bread's got that old-time flavor — crisp on the outside, like velvet inside. It's a dying art."

Hardly.

The metropolitan Yellow Pages lists six columns of retail bakeries. From the Greek Town Bakery on Eastern Avenue to Brown's Caribbean Bakery on Park Heights Avenue, many ovens still produce fresh bread.

But in Little Italy, only Anthony Marinelli continues.

"You can see him running around delivering bread in that little van at all hours," says Nick Vaccaro, who runs a neighborhood pastry business. "He's working day and night."

Mr. Marinelli delivers to about 20 restaurants around town.

He sells day-old loaves cheap for garlic bread; helps St. Leo's when the Roman Catholic church puts on spaghetti dinners; and sells his childhood parish hundreds of pounds of raw dough that is deep-fried and sprinkled with powdered sugar at the St. Gabriel festival.

But that's just crumbs compared with the bread traffic along streets named Stiles, Exeter, Fawn, Trinity, Albemarle and High in the days when Mary Scelsi DeNitti's father sold his business to Anthony Marinelli's dad.

"My father, Salvatore, and his three brothers started baking bread on President Street when they came over from Italy in 1906," said Mrs. DeNitti, 89, the daughter of bakers and a baker's widow. "They had two wagons on the street with the horse, selling bread. They used to ship it to restaurants and grocery stores in burlap bags and hand-deliver it to doorsteps from baskets."

By 1913, the Scelsi brothers took a separate path to prosperity.

Believing more money was to be made selling bread in the growing town of Pittsfield, Mass., Joseph Scelsi left the family's President Street home.

Up in Pittsfield, Joseph Scelsi made good and soon sent for his brother Salvatore.

"That's when we sold to Marinelli. Tony was just a couple of years old when we sold to his father," recalls Mrs. DeNitti. "His father said: 'I don't know nothin' about bread,' and my father told him, 'I'll teach you.'"

As Salvatore Scelsi taught Michael Marinelli, Michael taught his son Anthony, and Anthony has taught Sombut "Nick" Poosiri, Pichayut "Too" Vickyanont, and Ms. Rukki, who live in a house Mr. Marinelli owns next to the bakery.

"Tony's a good guy, he still serves most of the restaurants down here, but his bread today is not the bread my father taught his father," says Mrs. DeNitti. "It's not like years ago. Times change."

In an art dating back to crude cakes baked in the Stone Age, times change.

While Anthony Marinelli manages his business from the house where he has lived nearly all his life, makes deliveries, and sells loaves at the front door, he doesn't really make the bread that bears his family name anymore.

The fingernails with dough beneath them belong to Mr. Poosiri, Mr. Vickyanont and Ms. Rukki.

Whether a baker has landed among the potholes and railroad tracks of Central Avenue by way of Sicily or Bangkok, they still get up before dawn to make the dough.

The first shift of Mr. Poosiri and Mr. Vickyanont moves through a silent, flour-dusted choreography in a room the size of a suburban kitchen.

Dented trash cans filled with sugar and salt stand in a corner. A refrigerator with glass doors holds Fleischmann's yeast and Esskay lard. Stacked against one wall are 100-pound sacks of Con-Agra flour.

In front of the wall that separates Mr. Marinelli's bakery from his kitchen stands an automatic mixer made in the 1940s by the U. H. Day Co. of Cincinnati, a white metal monster caked with dried dough. "You grease it and oil it every couple weeks, you got a dough mixer for life," says Mr. Marinelli.

Mr. Poosiri pours buckets of water into the machine's gaping jaw to moisten the flour, yeast, lard, salt, and sugar already inside. He hand cranks the jaw shut, hits a button, and the mixing begins.

Later, the machine spits back 300 pounds of dough that rises from the hopper like a frozen white wave.

One man chops 16 clumps of fist-sized dough per minute from a large mound on the work table; the other rolls the 1-pound clumps on the table and tosses them into wooden trays. The clumps are "punched" two or three times to get air into the dough. After they are fed into a machine that shapes them into loaves, the dough is arranged on baking trays sprinkled with corn starch.

By the time the sun is breaking, an electric oven set between 325 and 350 degrees is turning dough into the staff of life. The oven, which has six revolving trays, turns out more than 200 loaves every 50 minutes.

Just up is Anthony Marinelli. Shirtless after washing — a blue towel over his shoulder and a religious medal hanging from his neck — he walks a few steps from home to bakery to see how the day is shaping up.

He says: "I gotta make sure they make the bread right, like I tell 'em to."

Replies Ms. Rukki: "It would be easier if he had better equipment."

Such a legacy might have passed Tony Marinelli by, if he hadn't hurt his back at Bethlehem Steel Corp. in 1945.

"I started riding on the truck full time then, running bread in and out of the restaurants," he says. "My father left me the business when he died in 1979. He was 95 and walked with two canes, but he kept going. He used to dunk 2-day-old bread into a big glass of wine in the morning, and that was breakfast. He came to this house from President Street in 1914 with a horse and wagon. We used to sell all over the city in them days."

The good old days of Scelsi, Marinelli, Giordano, and Impallaria.

Some crust was thicker than others, some more tan than brown. Each bakery tapered its loaves a special way. And individual marks — a long part near the side or four lines across the top — were cut into each loaf for identity; richer in character than "American bread" sold in grocery stores.

"Fresh hot bread with good Italian oil, salt and pepper, and grated cheese! We waited for it like it was steak. You always had a piece of bread to eat," recalls Jenny Impallaria Cremen, 67. Such simple treats made the Depression pass more easily for her family than others.

And, of course, an Impallaria loaf was the best in Little Italy.

Unless you ask Anthony Giordano, whose grandfather would sit down in front of the oven after making the day's last loaf, break out a jug of wine and his clarinet and play Italian songs for hours.

"This ain't just me saying this," says Mr. Giordano, "but ours was the best."

Unless you ask Mary DeNitti, whose mother, Maria Scelsi, worked the oven for nearly 30 years after her husband died in 1934.

"The older ones down here, they were all raised on my mother's bread," says Mrs. DeNitti. "You ask any of them — it was good."

Good, but not quite as good as Marinelli bread, according to Anthony Marinelli.

"Everybody knows our bread is good — delicious, like my father made it," he says. "You make the bread right, it's good."

January 16, 1994

Special place at the table

GETTING TO THE CHRISTMAS TABLE WAS A FANTASTIC JOURNEY FOR THE Zannino family — all the way from Highlandtown to The Alameda in a 1964 Ford Country Squire station wagon on a route through Clifton Park.

"We didn't see a lot of trees in Highlandtown so when we drove through the park we'd start singing: 'Over the river and through the woods to grandmother's house we go,'" recalls Mimi Zannino, one of eight children packed into the wagon.

At Grandma Felicia Glorioso's, the air was fragrant with pasta and eggplant; trays of biscotti, made with love and a recipe carried from Sicily in 1909, beckoned; and holiday linen covered the tables — one for the adults and another for the children.

"Card tables were put together for all the cousins to sit at — it extended the dining room table and spilled into the living room," says Zannino, 38. "They also used the Formica table in the kitchen with the piano bench. Everybody wanted to sit on the bench — the girls with their girl cousins, and the boys wanted to sit with the boys. There was a heck of a lot more laughing when we all sat together. Christmas was the magic day when you didn't get reprimanded for acting up a little bit."

Thinking back to those twinkling Christmases now 30 years gone, Zannino says: "We wanted to sit away from our parents. It was like a club."

A magical club where it didn't matter that all the chairs were different, the card table wobbled when you cut your food, and the big table was often in another room completely; nothing mattered because you were with children your own age, peers with whom you shared a heritage but didn't see that much.

And it was Christmas.

A generation removed from the charm of Grandma Felicia's house, Zannino's godson can sum up the magnificence of the children's table at the tender age of 10.

"We get to talk about kids' things without grown-ups asking a lot of questions," says Valentine Marziale, top dog of nine Zannino cousins seated together at his grandparents' Christmas Eve table. "Parents don't know what we're talking about because we're only kids."

What Valentine knows instinctively, academics have studied for years.

"So much depends on how large the extended family is and how varied the ages," says Robert Dicker, a child and adolescent psychiatrist at Long Island Jewish Medical Center. "If you grow up with cousins in the same age group, then adolescents tend to be very happy in this exclusive club, sneaking away from the table together. There wouldn't be a rush to get to the older table."

Of his own 1950s childhood, Dicker says: "On one side of my family, the patriarch was so strict with rituals that I wish there'd been a kids' table. If the real meaning of the holiday is carried out, it doesn't matter where one is sitting."

It's distance that matters, says Alice Sterling Honig, professor emerita of child development at Syracuse University — a distance that cannot be measured by a length of table.

"There are families where children are given the clear feeling that the adults don't want them at the main table," says Honig. "From that distance, a child can see with their own eyes where the good Christmas is."

Which was not the case with the Rattini family of Rosedale.

"All the cousins sat at our own table when I was a kid, and we didn't care, it was fun," says Louisa Rattini-Reich, 42. "Before we could eat, a relative came around with palm fronds to shake holy water on us. We ate the same food as everybody else, spaghetti with squid and baked eel."

In those days, the local Rattinis traveled to Syracuse, N.Y., to celebrate Christ's birth with relatives. Now, the traditional feast is held at Rattini-Reich's mother's house near Golden Ring Mall, where a custom-made wooden table — "big enough to feed an army," says Rattini-Reich — has made a children's table unnecessary.

Children were sprinkled among the adults at the holiday table when 68-year-old Clementina Bombaci Rattini was growing up in Syracuse, and her new wooden table will make that possible again.

In the Lichtenberg family of Pikesville, where holidays meant Passover, Rosh Hashana and Yom Kippur, not only did the children's table linger in near perpetuity, but no one ever graduated from it.

"The kids were me and my brother and sister, my two cousins and this friend of the family named Barry, who was older than us and wasn't married so they sat him with the kids," remembers Marc Lichtenberg, a 34-year-old accountant.

"There weren't any more children born until we got married and had kids so we stayed at the card table with the cloth over it in the living room until we were 25."

With families expanding and people living longer, convenience tends to supplant custom, and in many American homes, grown-up and children's tables have given way to the holiday buffet.

"Chaotic but happy," is how local publicist Dave Belz remembers the buffet Christmases of his Northwood childhood. "A big party of 40 people with turkey and ham and kids wandering between people's legs."

That was not the custom off Charles Street and Cold Spring Lane when Steve Martel was growing up, but that is what it has become.

"I was at the kids' table with eight or 10 cousins until I got into college. It wasn't until I started to listen to what the adults were talking about that I got interested in the big table," says Martel, 33, who teaches social studies at the Odyssey School in Roland Park.

"My father and my uncles would go at it over history and politics, always history and politics. Moving up to the adult table to participate in that and understand the Irish wit was important to me."

Now, it's different. Not any better or worse, just different.

"We all sit around in the living room," says Martel. "And everybody gets to talk to whoever they want."

December 26, 1996

Baker's recipe for success

If YOUR TASTE BUDS ITCH FOR TRULY SOUTHERN BAKING, THEN YOU'VE GOT to scratch 'em on the goodies at Tina Paul's West Baltimore sugar shack.

For Paul — a former forklift operator who began selling baked goods at flea markets — "from scratch" is a family tradition: Many of her signature specialties have been passed down from Florence "Puddiny" Johnson, her 91-year-old grandmother.

"Everybody says they bake from scratch, but most of them are talking about something that came out of a box," says Paul, owner of the Truly Scratch Bakery at 1103 W. Baltimore St. "Baking by taste and touch is the true measure of scratch. We do it without recipes, and nothing is ever the same. We measure things out in the pit of our hands."

From the pit of Paul's hand to the bottom of your stomach go butter pound-cakes, sweet potato and blackberry pies with distinctive hand-fluted crusts, homemade dinner rolls, butter-pecan cookies, cornbread, peach cobbler, coconut cookies and rice pudding. Dinners include chicken and dumplings, and crab cakes with collard greens and yams on the side.

Nearly all of the ingredients used at the tin-ceilinged, former beauty-supply store near Arlington Avenue come from the Hollins Street Market a few blocks away.

"Everybody's eaten my food, even Tipper Gore when she was here," says the 50-year-old Paul, who runs the seven-day-a-week business with her mother, Elaine Paul, and her son, Thomas Pendleton. "The very rich and the very poor come here."

Though folks go bananas over the sweet potato pie — "I use a lot of butter and pay no attention to health when it comes to sweet potato pie," says the licensed nutritionist — Paul's calling cards are dinner rolls so good that neighborhood youths who have never tasted homemade bread prefer them to candy.

The rolls, made from dough that rises three times, are another legacy of her grandmother's kitchen, although vegetable shortening has been substituted for the bacon fat grandmother used.

"It costs me a cent and a half per roll to make them, and I charge 50 cents a roll. They're the most expensive dinner rolls in the city. $6 a dozen and it's not open for discussion," she says, pinching out balls of dough before dawn yesterday morning at the start of a typical 15-hour day. "But I'm charging for the labor, for the wear and tear on my hands. The pennies that come into this place are the glue that holds my family together."

Paul is a Christian — a chalkboard next to a bubble-gum machine lists folks who need prayers, and gospel music fills the store — but many of her friends and customers are Nation of Islam Muslims. In deference to their beliefs, Paul not only sells no pork but has cut pig meat out of her diet so that the hands that bake from scratch never touch swine.

Paul, a 1965 graduate of Douglass High School, decided to start her own business after several companies she worked for, including the medical-supply company where she drove a forklift, folded.

Friends had raved about her cooking — she had good luck trying it out on the public at the annual Heritage Festival in Essex — "and I thought, I can do better taking care of myself," she says.

To test the market, she began baking at home and selling goods at the sprawling flea market on North Point Road in 1991. Sales were discouraging the first weekend, but her customers came back and told their friends.

The family has sold baked goods from several locations since then, including a month-long stint at Harborplace, before buying the current building about six months ago.

She gave up a longtime home in eastern Baltimore County to come back to North Fulton Street, near a house where she grew up.

When Paul gets discouraged by profits that don't stretch as nicely as her piecrust and the lack of skilled labor — even from the local culinary college — to duplicate her family's secrets, she turns to the Lord and her baking buddy, Ron Peluso.

Peluso, a baker for Geresbeck's market in Middle River who once owned Herchowski's Bakery in Canton, befriended Paul when she would come into his store to buy cakes and ask his advice.

"I helped her out by lending her some equipment to get her started," says Peluso. "She only uses the best ingredients, but her only detriment is she can't do everything herself and still keep up with demand.

"Her biggest challenge is to build customers, but she doesn't have any advertising budget because she's always using one day's receipts to pay the next day's bills. But she won't give up."

How can you give up, asks Paul, when someone bites into a buttermilk biscuit that brings tears to his eyes?

"It's not all about money. It pays off in feeling good about yourself," she says. "People look at me and say, 'Oh, Lord, this reminds me of my mother. My mama is gone, but you brought her back.'"

September 19, 1998

Chapter 7

Keeping
Faith

A flicker of hope in darkest hour

THE IMPOSSIBLE, THE DESPERATE, THE LOST CAUSES — HE IS THE PATRON saint of them all.

And nowhere, except maybe in heaven, is St. Jude bigger than in Baltimore.

"He's one powerful saint," said Carmen Protera, a believer, pointing to a statue of the martyr at St. John the Baptist Roman Catholic Church. "Man, if anybody can help you, he's the man who can."

With that in mind, the hopeful come by the thousands, particularly during Lent, to a small shrine in the church at the corner of Paca and Saratoga streets, near Lexington Market.

They come on foot, on lunch hours and on bus tours, from around the Beltway and across the nation, to pray to St. Jude Thaddeus, apostle, cousin of Christ, and one very popular saint.

Danny DeVito made a trip to the shrine to pray and light candles to St. Jude while he was in town filming "Tin Men"; a woman from Chicago flew in a few years back just to lay her daughter's bridal bouquet at the statue's feet; and out-of-town flight crews from Baltimore-Washington International Airport have come on Christmas Eve to pray.

"He endures," said the Rev. Nelson Agilla, director of the shrine, "because he brings hope to hopeless situations."

There have been formal devotions to St. Jude at St. John the Baptist since December 1941, when they began as a small prayer service, most likely to enlist his help in America's new war.

"The story goes like this," said Mary J. Protera, 75, a member of St. John the Baptist church since she was 9 and a secretary in the rectory since 1957. "During wartime, Father Henry Iannone got permission to start a novena [prayers of special intention] and advertised for anyone with a loved one in the service to come, and he gave everyone that showed up a little American flag and it started to grow that way. The parents were praying for their boys to come back safe.

"At the time, we only had a picture of St. Jude in the front of the church. We put an honor roll [of worshippers] in the back of the church, and people just started to flock to us. After about three years, a woman donated a beautiful statue of St. Jude to us, and it began to grow and grow some more."

Eventually, a shrine decorated with mosaic tile was built to house the statue, and hundreds of votive candles were put before it.

Today the shrine is the national center for St. Jude devotions — so popular that four novena services attracting hundreds of believers are held every Wednesday.

Susan Givigian has been in the act of one perpetual novena since the afternoon of Jan. 15.

Her daughter Francoise, an 18-year-old Washington College student known as Fra, was severely injured in a car crash that day, an accident that damaged her brain stem and left her in a deep coma.

Seeking deliverance from the tragedy through faith, the Locust, N.J., resident asked Maryland Shock Trauma Center officials for names of local churches. After hearing St. Jude was nearby, she looked no further.

For weeks, every day without fail, she made the walk from the Shock Trauma Center at University Hospital up the street to St. Jude's, where she has attended Mass and prayed for the miracle of a complete recovery.

"When you can't communicate with your daughter, and the doctors aren't telling you what you want to hear, then your faith is all you have, and you turn to St. Jude in your despair," said Mrs. Gavigian, who got to know the staff at the shrine so well that she occasionally took naps in the church rectory.

"This is my greatest source of comfort," she said. "This is the only place I want to be. Faith has the ability to do what the doctors can't do. You can't intellectualize it."

While at St. John's, she sees the flowers of gratitude laid at the shrine, the notes of thanks mailed from around the country, and she is encouraged to remain resolute in her request for a miracle of full recovery.

"I believe people like St. Jude have God's ear. I hope I do," she said, "but if not, I hope he does."

Authorities at the Archdiocese of Baltimore aren't sure how St. Jude became the saint for problems without evident solutions — the big problems of life and death, not things like losing your house key, for which St. Anthony is the saint to call on.

A little pamphlet circulated at the shrine says St. Jude's legend began by word of mouth.

"When one person had successfully implored help from St. Jude in some intimate problem which apparently defied solution, he would pass the wonderful news on to a friend who was experiencing troubles," the pamphlet says.

Through the news, more believers are brought into the flock, the saint's legend is perpetuated, and the shrine at Paca and Saratoga streets prospers better than many of Baltimore's Catholic parishes.

The wonderful news is often made public, through thank-yous placed in newspaper classifieds or by more dramatic acts, as when pro golfer Bobby Nichols donated $3,500 of his earnings for winning the 1964 Pro Golfers Association tournament to establish a St. Jude shrine in his native Louisville, Ky.

"I wanted to do it because I figured this was an impossible tournament to win," Mr. Nichols told skeptical reporters after his three stroke-triumph in 1964 over Jack Nicklaus and Arnold Palmer.

"I'm not superstitious," said Mr. Nichols, who still calls on St. Jude. "There's a difference between being superstitious and having faith. I have a lot of faith."

March 16, 1990

Good eggs and nice memories of Easter

AT THIS TIME OF YEAR, BACK IN THE OLD DAYS, THE EASTER CRY SAILED through the alleys of Baltimore.

"Who's got an egg?
Who's got an egg?
Chicken with a wooden leg!
Who's got a guinea-ghi?
Who's gonna pick-a-me?"

The challenge was one of a basket full of Easter traditions peculiar to Baltimore, rituals that included parades, butter shaped like lambs, and Easter Monday picnics in Druid Hill Park; customs that have faded with time.

The cry of "Who's got an egg?" would bring youngsters out of their homes, ready to do battle with hard-boiled eggs dyed in shades of blue and pink and yellow.

The game, which today endures around Easter tables in certain families, worked like this:

One kid wrapped a fist around his egg, leaving only the point exposed through a hole between his thumb and index finger. The challenger used the point of his egg to aggressively tap his foe's egg until one of the shells cracked. The eggs were then turned over and the game repeated with the butt end of the eggs.

The stronger egg would usually win at both ends, and the owner of the weaker egg would forfeit the ovum that had failed him. If there was a draw, the uncracked point would battle the uncracked butt. The loser surrendered his egg.

"Picking eggs was a big thing around the neighborhoods. I don't really know where it started," said Gene DeCarlo, Sr., 68, who keeps the tradition alive in Highlandtown with his grandchildren. "You've got to remember, in them days eggs weren't as plentiful as they are now. You won a hard-boiled egg from another kid — that was something good to eat."

Old-timers remember the sight of champions running the alleys with the pockets of their Easter Sunday trousers bulging with eggs.

" I think picking eggs was just something they did around Baltimore," said Dorothy Kraft, 68, who grew up on Decker Avenue. "I never heard of out-of-towners doing it."

For generations it was part of local Easter along with cakes that looked like chickens and lumps of butter shaped like lambs; pre-dawn street processions with Easter lilies; taking baskets of food to church to be blessed; boys chasing girls on Easter Monday — known to some as "dingus day" — to beat them on the legs with switches; sunrise services at Memorial Stadium; and the annual Easter parades along Charles Street and Pennsylvania Avenue.

"People would dress up in their Sunday best and parade up and down Pennsylvania Avenue and we stayed dressed up until late in the evening," said Walter Taylor, a longtime resident of West Lafayette Avenue who didn't want to give his age. "It just was so beautiful, so exciting. I always liked to wear white: a white suit with a white shirt, white socks and black and white shoes."

The parades included people with Easter lilies. "The lily is resurrection white, for purity," said Wadsworth Robinson, whose family has sold flowers from a shop on East Monument Street since 1935. "Carrying a cut lily reminds me of authority, like a papal staff. They look delicate, but they're very tough."

Pat Beczkowski remembers carrying a lily through Fells Point before the sun came up on Easter Sunday.

"We had to carry it from home to St. Stanislaus where we put them on the altar," she said. "It was tradition."

On Charles Street, said 85-year-old Rose Ellen Clarke, the Easter parade was "something wonderful" until too many automobiles began crowding the boulevard after World War II.

"This was back in the '20s and '30s, when it was in its highlight," she said. "People would walk in their finery coming from church; all the way up Charles Street people joined in. There was no planning, it just happened."

In the city's Polish neighborhoods, once Lent officially ended at noon on Holy Saturday, families brought baskets of food to church to have them blessed.

Yesterday, Father Joseph Grybowski, pastor of St. Casimir Roman Catholic Church on O'Donnell Street, blessed about 400 baskets.

One of them belonged to Catherine Smertycha, who keeps alive the Polish tradition of making lambs out of butter at her rowhouse on South Linwood Avenue.

Her basket, covered with a white cloth embroidered in the Ukraine with a Bible, chalice and flowers, included homemade kielbasa, horseradish, a braided, Polish bread called bobka, raisin bread, hard-boiled eggs dyed with onion skin, salt and pepper, and a lamb made from butter.

"My mother had metal molds that came from the old country and every year at Eastertime she made butter in the shape of a lamb," said Mrs. Smertycha. "It's the sign of new life."

The blessed food will be eaten today after morning Mass.

"And if it was blessed, you better be sure you didn't get no crumbs on the floor," Agnes Borkowski said.

April 11, 1993

In midst of urban chaos, a Buddha sits

THE BRICK BUDDHA OF BALTIMORE SITS STILL AND SERENE IN THE FACE OF mortals in transit.

Every day, some 100,000 people pour into the city on the Jones Falls Expressway and 5,000 more come by light rail. More than a few, surely, have glimpsed the tan Buddha behind the former Cannon Shoe factory on Mount Royal Avenue since May.

But until two months ago, only one — a young Vietnamese woman named Amy "Cuc" Huynh — took time to pay respects. Since her maiden pilgrimage, dozens have arrived each Sunday to picnic and pray at the feet of a project left behind by a Maryland Institute, College of Art graduate.

"I saw the ear of the Buddha one day, but nobody believed me," recalled Ms. Huynh, 25, who began using the JFX to commute from her Randallstown home to her Highlandtown dry-cleaning business. "Something told me it was over there, nobody believed me. Then I dreamed Buddha was there — nobody believe."

To prove it, Ms. Huynh pulled off the expressway one afternoon in a hard summer rain and drove in circles for a path to the Buddha. She parked and began tramping up and down Mount Royal Avenue for a way to get behind the buildings that back up to the JFX. Soaked with rain, she prayed: "Let me see it, and I will take care of it."

In the space between the AAA Maryland offices and the Maryland Institute's Fox Building — the former shoe factory — a set of steps appeared.

Ms. Huynh walked down the steps and around the corner to a trash-strewn, poison ivy-infested lot used by students for temporary installations of large sculptures. Bounded by the light rail tracks, the hideaway was frequented by dog walkers, beer drinkers and graffiti vandals.

The only thing Amy Huynh saw was her Buddha, sitting pretty.

"I called my Mom and said: 'I found the Buddha! I found the Buddha!' She said: 'Take it home! Take it home!' I said: 'Too big.'"

If Buddha won't come to Randallstown . . .

That weekend, a caravan of Ms. Huynh's friends gathered for a little yard work. Like Ms. Huynh, most were ethnic Chinese from Vietnam and believers in the Buddhist teaching that life is permeated with suffering driven by desire, suffering that ceases when desire ceases.

They picked up trash, weeded, poured concrete, laid tile, spread gravel, planted shrubs and were about to build a $900 roof until the school discouraged them. One elderly woman donned gloves to yank out poison ivy by the roots. Gifts were left: fresh flowers, coins, food.

An odd lot became a holy place.

About 40 worshippers visited Sunday, dressing the altar for a feast — bowls of apples, oranges and pears, big pots of vegetable curry, sweet rice and peanuts, fried noodles with carrots, and coconut cake.

A tape player launched sacred chants against the expressway's din, and people waited their turn to bow before the Buddha with clasped hands. They knelt to offer incense, showed toddlers how to pray, and graced the statue with beads on string and beads on sticks — fat black ones that look like skewered Greek olives. Oriental fortune tiles were dropped for hints of the future.

As commuters on a light rail marked "Glen Burnie," pointed through the windows, Amy Huynh explained why she alone comes every day to thank the Buddha.

"Not easy to see Buddha from highway," said Ms. Huynh, who fasts from meat in the presence of the Buddha and says her business has improved since finding it. "Everybody say I'm lucky, but I pray for him to take care of everybody."

Said her mother Hao Quach: "All Buddhas are the same, but this one is special because Amy is his messenger. God gave Amy the fate to see the Buddha."

As it was Noriko Ikaga's fate to build it.

A 1994 graduate of the Maryland Institute's ceramics department, Ms. Ikaga returned to Japan in September and could not be reached. But department chair Ron Lang remembers her deep spirituality as a rarity in his 16-year tenure.

Mr. Lang challenges his students to answer: "What do you believe? What do you want to say?" He reasons that if young people become passionate for a project, they will find ways to hurdle technical problems.

Ms. Ikaga confessed that she'd never been asked to express herself. Her first attempt produced hands in prayer.

"She mass-produced the hands and set them all over the floor with cut-out shadows of different colors," said Mr. Lang. "And then she started making beautiful hearts, idealized hearts, broken hearts and hearts under attack by tools. She'd show a delicate, lattice-work heart under attack by a saw. When I questioned her, she told a story about the devil and how he tries to trick his way into our hearts."

Unquestionably, this was not the work of the typical undergraduate.

"Very early on, Noriko expressed a deep spirituality," said Mr. Lang.

"Spirituality on top of creativity made her work refreshing. And she stuck to that."

For her senior project, Ms. Ikaga proposed a Buddha, an idea that perplexed Mr. Lang. An exact rendering of an existing object — be it a Buddha or a tree — does not reveal the individual who made it. Knowing Ms. Ikaga was sincere, he resisted asking her to do anything that might be construed as irreverent.

"She wanted to know how she could technically execute a large Buddha and make it believable. I asked her how she was going to make it hers," said Mr. Lang. "She thought about it, came back to me, and said she'd make it brick [in homage] to the architecture of Baltimore."

Metaphorically, the Buddha is brick. Actually, it is an iron armature covered with sun-dried clay, or adobe, with mortar lines chiseled in and striped with white paint. Striping surfaces to look like brick is an old Baltimore tradition, popularized on rowhouses between 1850 and 1880.

Examples can still be found in the Buddha's Bolton Hill neighborhood and parts of East Baltimore.

"Adobe became the workable solution to real bricks," said Mr. Lang. "But it's not permanent and in our climate, it's not going to last forever. It has a finite time to exist."

The idea of a finite Buddha is not acceptable to Amy Huynh and her loved ones, who thanked Noriko for bringing them a god and have already coated the statue with water sealant. Although it weighs about a ton, they are thinking of moving it if the weather takes too much of a toll.

Said a friend of Ms. Huynh's: "Amy didn't go out looking for a Buddha. It came to her."

October 15, 1994

Heavenly inspiration graces earthly garden

THE FRIENDS OF GOD HAIL VISITORS TO LITTLE ITALY FROM AN EXETER Street rock garden, a baker's dozen of Catholic saints in a sidewalk shrine built to bolster people's faith at the end of a troubled century.

"The energy of the saints comes to people in many different forms," says Larry Fenaroli, a chef who made the garden in front of his house. "If people believe that this energy is still with us, it might give them hope as they pass by. We have no one to look up to today. Everything seems so self-serving."

Although not a practicing Catholic, Mr. Fenaroli is a spiritual man with a strong nostalgia for the traditions that shaped his childhood. Growing up at 209 N. Front St. in the St. Vincent de Paul parish in the 1950s, he helped the Rev. John Sinnott Martin build a churchyard rock garden.

"Working with stone and plants makes me happy," he says. "This is a talent I haven't been able to express well in the city."

When Mr. Fenaroli started his project in May, making a wall of flat rocks from a creek that runs through his friend Ty Hodanish's farm in New Jersey. He merely intended something to complement the Formstone on his rowhouse.

But then his next-door neighbor thought it would be nice to have the Blessed Mother in with the flowers and gave him a white ceramic statue of the Virgin Mary. By the time the garden was finished in late June with shamrocks, lilies and passion fruit, everybody had gotten into the act.

"Someone said, 'Oh, you need this' and 'You need that,'" said Mary Sergi, who donated the statue of Mary, which is turned toward her house. "The next thing you know — there it is!"

Mr. Fenaroli focused on saints especially beloved by the Italian people, and from their homes came an altar's worth of foot-high statues.

Frances Caliri on Trinity Street donated St. Gabriel, St. Francis and Our Lady of Mount Carmel.

"I say prayers to all of them," said Mrs. Caliri, 74, who keeps a small altar at the top of her stairs.

Angie Guerriero, whose house faces the shrine, contributed a statue of St. Jude. Sts. Rita, Lucy and Rocco came from a gift shop at the Basilica of the Assumption on Cathedral Street. St. Gennaro landed in Baltimore's Little

Italy from New York's Little Italy. St. Joseph and St. Teresa were bought at Joseph's Gift and Religious Goods on Harford Road. St. Anthony came from the Rev. James Purvey, a friend of Mr. Fenaroli's assigned to St. Michael's Church in Overlea.

And St. Vincent Pallotti was a gift of the Rev. Flavian Bonifazi, a Pallotine priest with St. Leo's church. "The saints are the friends of God," Father Bonifazi says. "If you need a favor of somebody, you go to their friends."

The only representations of Jesus, for whom these saints lived and died, are a babe in the arms of Mary and on crucifixes held by a few of the female statues.

"In the tradition of the Catholic faith, they are our bridge to Him," said Father Bonifazi, who is going to print brief biographies for the statues.

Mr. Fenaroli's favorites are St. Joseph, the carpenter and foster father of Jesus ("Because I like to work with my hands," he says); St. Francis, because he is fond of animals; St. Rita, for whom his sister was named; and St. Jude, who gives strength to those in desperate straits.

An unfortunate but necessary cage rises up in front of the garden, protecting it from malice. "The fence takes away from it, but I know why he did it," Ms. Sergi says. "People would [destroy it] just to be mean."

When neighbor Arthur Gentile was helping Mr. Fenaroli put the fence up, Mr. Gentile's mother stopped by to give Mr. Fenaroli hell for not including St. Ann.

"I told her I didn't have room," says Mr. Fenaroli, who likes the way the painted plaster statues bring color to the street. "By the time she came by, we were filled up."

Just as pedestrians seem to be filled with a warm feeling when they stroll by the shrine after taking dinner in one of the neighborhood restaurants. From her house across the street, Angie Guerriero has seen tourists make the sign of the cross and stop to take pictures.

"You should believe in something," she says. "I think your day works out better when you start it with a prayer."

July 10, 1995

One family's faith in the '90s

IT FALLS TO 16-YEAR-OLD CORRINE LIVINGSTON TO CARRY HER FAMILY'S Catholicism into Christianity's third millennium. A senior at Mercy High School, she attends Mass when she can fit it in, which isn't too often. "With work and school and doing plays, I never have time," she says.

Her 39-year-old father, Michael, who left his parents' East Baltimore rowhouse at 13 to enter a seminary high school, makes Mass only about twice a month.

The spotty attendance distresses 69-year-old family matriarch Marie Livingston, whose life has been devoted to St. Wenceslaus, the old Bohemian church that struggles to survive across the street from her North Collington Street home.

"In my day, there weren't any excuses," says Mrs. Livingston. "Whether you could walk or not, you went." Mrs. Livingston, the only member of her family with a ticket to see Pope John Paul II at Camden Yards on Sunday, celebrates Mass three to four times a week.

Compared with the Depression-era Catholicism that defined Mrs. Livingston, it would appear that the years have diluted the fervor of her family's faith.

Mrs. Livingston carries a rosary wherever she goes, dipping often into her pocket to finger the beads and recite Hail Marys. Michael Livingston sometimes prays the rosary on his fingers during long drives. Corrine was taught the devotion, but rarely does it. Family rituals such as kneeling around the dining room table together to say the rosary during Lent have not survived.

On matters of doctrine, the generational differences are pronounced. Corinne is the most liberal, standing apart in her desire for a church that ordains women and belief that each woman has a right to choose on the issue of abortion. Unlike his mother, Michael supports birth control, favors abortion in cases of rape or incest and believes priests should be able to marry.

"In real life, I can't agree with everything I was taught," says Michael, a data processing supervisor for T. Rowe Price. But "I know what I have inside — faith in God and a strong background in doing what's right. I may say a prayer to myself going down the street, but it's not something I'm going to talk about in a bar."

In a time when the American Catholic Church has been fundamentally changed by the Second Vatican Council, the women's movement, a shortage of candidates for the convent and priesthood, and postwar prosperity that transformed working-class urban Catholics into middle-class suburban ones, the Livingstons have remained indelibly Catholic.

Michael and his wife, Diane — a Catholic who works for the Mission Helpers of the Sacred Heart nuns in Towson — invited a priest to bless their new home when they moved from Bradshaw to Havre de Grace about two years ago. Their son Benjamin, 12, goes to St. Stephen School in Bradshaw.

And the first thing Corrine did when her folks moved into the Bayview Estates development was hang a crucifix on her bedroom wall.

"I know that God's with me, that He'll help me through things," says Corrine, who learned the value of faith two years ago when an uncle died suddenly. "I pray before I go to sleep, I've prayed for help getting jobs or passing tests or when I felt sick. And when I've had a fight with friends or my family, I talk to God about it. Just because I don't make it to church all the time doesn't mean I'm not Catholic."

Her father credits Catholic schools for much of Corrine's character.

"I wanted to give my kids the foundation for starting off in life, and Catholic school teaches values; hopefully it teaches you respect," he says. "Even when I was making $4 an hour, we were going to get them there."

About the only time Michael and his brothers return to the streets of their childhood is to visit their mother, virtually the last of the old parishioners who still lives within walking distance of St. Wenceslaus. Through the years, Mrs. Livingston's family members have tried to get her to move out, but they have learned to save their breath.

"The only place I'm going is from here to the funeral parlor and then to St. Wenceslaus" for her Mass of Christian burial, she says.

Her family worries about her safety in a neighborhood that has deteriorated severely in the past 25 years. "She said she was outside when a shooting occurred and saw the bullets flying," says Corrine. "I'm like: 'Grandma, you're out of control.'"

Homes where friends and relatives were born and raised are blighted and boarded; keeping trash from accumulating is "hopeless"; and attendance at St. Wenceslaus' 700-seat sanctuary has declined in Mrs. Livingston's lifetime from a half-dozen packed Masses every Sunday to fewer than 200 people for three weekend services.

Buoyed by an influx of black parishioners who've brought African-American Catholic hymnals to the pews, St. Wenceslaus escaped closing this year when the Archdiocese of Baltimore "twinned" it with St. Ann's, another once-vibrant but long-suffering parish at Greenmount Avenue and 22nd Street.

"You know it won't ever be the way it was again around here, but it could be better," says Mrs. Livingston, now helping the parish plan a 125th anniversary celebration for 1997. "People are afraid to come here. I just pray that the ones who do will be safe."

The historically Bohemian St. Wenceslaus parish — named for the 10th-century Duke of Bohemia and the patron saint of Czechoslovakia — was founded in 1872 by Catholic immigrants seeking to worship apart from the Poles and Lithuanians settling southeast Baltimore.

The neighborhood the Bohemians staked out as their own blocks of rowhouses north of Johns Hopkins Hospital along Madison Avenue and Monument Street was once known as Swampoodle.

Mrs. Livingston — daughter of a Czech immigrant named Frank Michal and Barbara Novak, a first-generation American from Madeira Street — was baptized at St. Wenceslaus in 1926.

From her first breath, she entered a world where family, neighborhood and school fused in a kind of village Catholicism: Everyone she knew went to the same church, learned to read and write at the same school, memorized the same catechism and traced their lineage to the map in the Old World.

St. Wenceslaus was flanked by a Redemptorist rectory, a convent for the School Sisters of Notre Dame, a church school and an auditorium to celebrate baptisms and weddings. Here, Catholicism seeped into kids' bones whether the youngsters liked it or not.

To this day, Mrs. Livingston can rattle off the old Baltimore Catechism like it was her phone number. "We had to know who made us and why," says the 1944 graduate of Seton High School. "It was simple: 'God made me to know him, love Him and serve Him.'"

The old ways and the tight-knit neighborhood endured together until about the time Michael made his First Holy Communion, just before the changes of Vatican II in 1965 began filtering down to the neighborhood. Four years later, white flight that began in the 1950s was accelerated by riots after the assassination of the Rev. Martin Luther King, Jr.

"When I started school, you looked at the back of the priest during Mass. Then they turned it around and the nuns took off their habits," says Michael. "It was easier for me to accept the changes than my mother."

Corrine, who belongs to a Christian youth group and works the annual St. Stephen carnival, has gone to Catholic schools since kindergarten. Asked the old catechism question — "Who made you and why?" — she repeats the question, as if it's the strangest thing she's ever heard.

But after thinking about it a moment, the teenager says: "God made me so I could make a change in the world. I believe He made everybody and He made me. He wants me to put my mark in the world. I want to do that by designing sets in the theater."

At one time, Marie Livingston believed she was made to enter the convent. "When I was in high school, that's all the nuns preached to you," she says. "I always thought I would be a Daughter of Charity and wear a big boat hat. It just didn't work out."

Instead, after leaving Seton and working for a few years, she married Arden Livingston, a Protestant from Wilkes-Barre, Pa., who joined St.

Wenceslaus in an era when converts were discouraged from ushering at Mass or joining the Holy Name Society. Mr. Livingston outlived that time to become an ordained deacon.

When Mrs. Livingston joshes that her granddaughter might "become a nun," Corrine shakes her head, amused at the absurdity of the notion.

With three silver earrings in each ear, a pager in her pocket and a taste for rap music, Corrine has listened politely to school presentations on the value of religious life, but becoming a nun is definitely not on her agenda.

When it's time to fall in love and marry, however, she says she'd prefer a Catholic. "I want a husband who believes what I believe. Someone who believes in the salvation of God."

At Mercy High School — where the administration enforces hemline regulations and tuition is $4,500 a year — students take religion courses with titles such as "Bio Ethics" and "Life Choices for Christian Women." They learn scripture, church history and study papal encyclicals on abortion, capital punishment and the moral debt the world's rich owe the world's poor.

"Sometimes it can appear that our programs are not as demanding or stringent as in the past, but I think in terms of actual awareness, our young women have a much broader picture of Catholicism," says Elizabeth Lambertus, a former nun who chairs the religion department. "These young women are allowed to come to their own conclusions, but my position is to present the teachings of the church, whether or not they want to hear it."

Michael Livingston thought he heard the call to the priesthood while serving as a St. Wenceslaus altar boy. His older brother, Arden Jr., already was at St. Mary's, a Redemptorist seminary high school in North East, Pa., and Michael was going to go, too.

"I wasn't forced into it, but once I decided, Mom and Dad were so happy, I saw that gleam in their eye," he says. "A 13-year-old probably doesn't know what's involved, but 'Father Mike' sounded nice to me."

After graduating from the 12th grade, the lure of girls and cars and having fun began speaking more strongly to Michael than studying Latin and the Gospels. Arden already had quit the seminary, and his little brother wasn't looking forward to breaking more bad news at home.

"For one whole week after graduating, all I thought about was 'Do I really want to go through with it? Should I do it to make them happy?' I probably cried when I told Mom," he says. "She was hoping one of us would do it. Back then, everybody wanted a priest in the family."

Now, Mrs. Livingston prays that the Roman Catholic Church will sustain her family once she's gone and that her grandchildren will teach the faith to their children.

"It's something you don't have control over, but I hope they carry it," she says. "They've all been brought up to carry it, to do the right thing."

October 6, 1995

Spirit crosses religious divide

THIS IS THE STORY OF A JEWISH LIQUOR KING AND THE NUN WHO LOVED HIM.

More than eight years after Benny Rubin's death, Sister Mary Joannene of the School Sisters of Notre Dame attends synagogue several times a year recite Jewish prayers for his soul. It is something you don't see every day, just like their friendship.

Because of the devotion they had for one another — he a big-time booze merchant in the glory days of downtown Baltimore and she a Catholic nun with a lifetime of service at schools and orphanages — nearly $1 million is available today to send women to college.

"Benny was my father's very, very good friend," remembers the former Grace Merendino, whose dad sold whiskey to Mr. Rubin's store. "I think I was the daughter he never had."

After Mr. Rubin died of prostate cancer at age 84 in 1987, the Associated Jewish Community Federation of Baltimore received notice that a Jew who'd never made his bar mitzvah had left almost $800,000 to endow scholarships for bright, deserving women from all backgrounds.

Mr. Rubin's will stated that if the Associated wanted the money, Sister Joannene and her buoyant spirit had to be on the board that gave the cash away.

She was his best friend for more than a quarter-century, the one who sat with him under a tree at the Inner Harbor on sunny afternoons, who cleaned his house when he was sick and decorated it at Christmas, the gentle soul who held his hand and prayed as he died.

And he was the guy with the deep tan and white hair who loved the way the convent cook made short ribs, the sport who drove golf balls on the grounds of Notre Dame Preparatory while waiting for Sister Joannene so they could go out to dinner.

"Everybody thinks I had something to do with Benny leaving that money," says the 73-year-old nun, a teacher of world cultures assigned to Notre Dame Prep since 1969. "Benny was a millionaire in the liquor business, but I didn't know what he was going to do. All I know is that he was interested in children, and he saw me so many times correcting papers."

Her hunch is that "this whole thing is his great love of his mother. They were poor, and he was always working to take money home to Mama. I guess he didn't want other women to have to work as hard as his mother did."

Named for his mother, Mary, the Rubin Scholarship Fund is worth $936,500 and has helped nearly 200 girls and women continue their education. Recipients must maintain a B-plus average.

At board meetings of the scholarship fund. Sister Joannene has been known to tell a room full of Jews: "I fell in love with a Jewish man, and his name is Jesus, and I thank you all for him. "

Says the Associated's Marta Braverman: "Our contact with Benny comes through Sister. When she addresses the board, she speaks for Benny, telling us there was no one to help him when he needed it. When we were notified of the gift, people said: 'Benny who?'"

Here's who: the longtime and prosperous owner of People's Liquors at Howard and Fayette streets back when downtown was the pulse of Maryland's economy: a 12-hour-a-day, six-day-a-week working man who liked steak for breakfast, a glass of beer when he was parched and was known to make book before the end of Prohibition provided him a new venture.

Benny Rubin was a brusque, tough businessman from the old school, a sport who hid a compassionate heart under a barrel chest and a Great Depression character who could have come out of Damon Runyon's typewriter as easily as he emerged every morning from his mother's boarding house near Greene Street to take on the world.

"He was a greenhorn who knew he had to fight his way through," says Sister Joannene. "But he always talked about Miss Irma, his third-grade teacher who hugged him when he was catching on to English."

Said Preston Burger, a retired liquor salesman: "I liked Benny, but I didn't like Benny. He was a tough man to do business with, but he was smart. And he could handle himself with his dukes if he had to."

A man who rarely shared stories from his private life, Benny Rubin was born Boris Rub in Ukraine in 1903 and grew up riding horses and tending cattle. Safe in the United States when the Nazis were murdering entire cities of Jews, he legally changed his name to Benjamin Moses Rubin so there'd be no question as to his heritage.

The Rubins landed in America when he was a young boy, and years later he would describe the scar that ran along the side of his mother's body, a stripe earned, he said, by carrying him through barbed wire as they fled the town of Poltava.

In Baltimore, the Rubins settled near Greene Street, close to where University of Maryland Medical Center is today. There, Mrs. Rubin ran two boarding houses and raised three boys. Benny was the youngest in a family without a father.

"He worked in Lexington Market as a boy putting up the fruit and vegetable stands on the sidewalk, and he always got a raise because he didn't steal from the German man he worked for," says Sister Joannene. "Later on he delivered Western Union telegrams."

After graduating from Polytechnic Institute, surviving the Depression and hustling to put together a nest egg, Mr. Rubin opened People's Liquors in 1933 and ran it for the next 40 years. Margaret, his Polish Catholic wife, worked the cash register, and sales grew from undercutting the competition on price. The Rubins had no children.

"Before the days of shopping-center liquor stores, Benny was it — he was the liquor store to the department stores back when Howard Street was mecca," remembers Herb Kasoff, a young salesman for Quality Brands in the early 1960s. "Benny would fight you tooth and nail on the one hand, but if he thought you needed something, he'd help you."

Mr. Rubin's empathy for people in need was a big part of his relationship with Sister Joannene, a girl from the Blessed Sacrament parish in Govans who entered the convent at 16.

Benny was good friends with her father — an immigrant from Sicily named Frank Merendino who sold whiskey for Standard Distillers — and enjoyed keeping up with the young nun's career.

"I had heard of Benny for many years before I knew him, and he had seen many pictures of me before we met," says Sister Joannene. "When daddy died in 1958, Benny kind of took his place."

As Sister Joannene moved from assignment to assignment — from orphanages in Philadelphia to high schools in New York and New Jersey — Benny stayed close.

"He loved the nuns, and wherever I was stationed, he was very generous. He'd say, 'Are the penguins ready for a party?' and throw us crab and shrimp feasts," Sister Joannene says. "He couldn't understand how we didn't have kids of our own but could have so much love for others."

Being a sharp, successful guy, Benny liked to treat himself to new cars, and in the early 1960s, he sprang for a Thunderbird convertible. Among Sister Joannene's greatest memories — one of the images that defines Benny for her — is the time Benny drove the T-bird up to her orphanage in Philly to thrill the teen-age boys there with a ride.

"That's the kind of thing he did for me," she says.

In return, she showed him love and affection until his dying day and tried in vain to make chicken soup just like his mother did. By the summer of 1987, Benny's time was running out. By the 21st of September, it was up.

"That day I sat down beside his bed at 5 p.m. and held his hand until 10 when he died," she remembers. "I sat there reciting the second part of the Hail Mary: 'Holy Mary, mother of God, pray for us sinners, now and at the hour of our death, Amen.'

"Benny loved his mother so much, and I always talked to him about the Blessed Mother being a Jewish mother. His scholarship is a tribute to every Jewish mother."

December 26, 1995

Jesuit priest's staying power

THE REV. FRANK ERNST HAS BEEN A JESUIT PRIEST FOR NEARLY 40 YEARS, yet when asked about any dramatic spiritual events in his career he answers softly: "None that I can remember."

Looking back, the 69-year-old product of St. Brigid's parish in Canton thinks that perhaps the whole of his career — the day-in and day-out effort to fulfill a decision made as a teenager — is quiet spiritual drama in itself.

"There were times when I felt I was at a dead end. Sometimes I think: 'Should I have been a priest?' But it's irreversible at my age," says Ernst, who was ordained in 1957. "I've had periods where things were pretty rough with insecurity, depression and anxiety, but my struggle was always to stay. I wasn't going to join the parade of those leaving religious life.

"It was a sacrifice. You get lonelier as you get older; you see children that might have been yours and wonder about what you didn't have. The fact that I've struggled is to my credit. Giving up was non-negotiable."

In an age when the number of American priests is in sharp decline — only one will be ordained in the Archdiocese of Baltimore next year — the church is grateful that old-timers such as Frank Ernst decided to stick it out.

Last month, Ernst landed what may be his final assignment: associate pastor at St. Ignatius Loyola Church on Calvert Street in downtown Baltimore. Most weekdays find him celebrating noon Mass in the chapel. The Jesuit parish draws an eclectic crowd from around the metro area, and "Father Frank" hopes to become a part of their lives the way he was for so long at Our Lady of Victory on Wilkens Avenue.

At that church, where he served as associate pastor from 1976 to 1993, he still is thought of as a member of many families. Getting invited to dinner, attending weddings, being remembered on holidays and simply being remembered at all seems to have helped him as much as he helped the faithful.

"Just being alive was sometimes painful for me. You would think with that attitude I would have been a hermit, but I'm almost compulsively social," he says. "Because of my own difficulties, I'm quite compassionate and a good listener. I've known priests blessed with more gifts than me, and some of them have been so arrogant and self-confident it might have hurt" their ministry.

Francis Paul Ernst was born into a virtual Catholic ghetto on the northeast corner of Hudson Street and East Avenue just before the Great Depression.

His father, a mailman named Austin, had no interest in religion and his mother, Nellie, was devoted to the church. Among the boys his age at St. Brigid's school — across the street from his house — Ernst knows at least seven who went off to seminary.

There was "a deep atmosphere of faith in the neighborhood — you could almost touch it," he remembers. The catechism he learned from the School Sisters of Notre Dame in the 1930s and 1940s was, if not infallible, certainly indelible.

He decided to become a priest in his junior year at Loyola High School, soon after a car hit and killed his cousin, Jimmy Coyne, 16, in front of Patterson Theatre.

"We were born the same month of the same year, and his death got me to thinking that this world is passing," he remembers. If life on Earth is fleeting, he reasoned, why not dedicate it to the God who awaits us in the world to come?

Still, he wishes he'd at least known what it was like to date a girl before delighting his mother, who'd lost two sons in World War II, with his decision. He doesn't find similar regrets among the new generation of priests. Today's newly ordained are usually older than 30 and the priesthood is at least their second career.

"I think that's much healthier," says Ernst. "They're more mature and their decision is more mature. Some of the guys going in are not virgins. They know what they're giving up; we didn't. I've had to renew my decision to be a priest over the course of my life."

Despite the scholarship he achieved as a Jesuit — graduating from St. Isaac Jogue's in Pennsylvania and earning the equivalent of a master's degree in philosophy and theology from the order's now defunct college in Woodstock, Md. — it's the things Ernst absorbed as a shy boy that marked him.

Of the days when the parish priest wielded more authority than the cop on the corner, he says: "I always have good memories of that period even though we were taught things that were a bit silly, like your hand would burn in hell if you masturbated or that God is a traffic cop waiting to pounce on you as soon as you did something wrong. I must confess, that stuff is still a part of me and I'm not really happy about it.

"There was a lot of emphasis on sins of chastity, yet charity, social justice and racial justice — serious issues — were things we didn't hear much about," he says. "I was extremely happy with the changes [made by the] Second Vatican Council. I found it a great relief."

And over the years, from daily Mass in the old neighborhood to sabbaticals that have allowed him to study in Rome, his favorite Gospel story remains the Apostle Peter walking on the water.

"Peter begins to sink and cries out to Jesus, who takes him by the hand and pulls him up," he says. "When I say 'Lord save me,' I come up again. I like that."

August 28, 1996

Chapter 8

The Orthodox

In the shelter of a Jewish covenant

AN ANCIENT, GOD-CENTERED WAY OF LIFE IS THRIVING IN BALTIMORE beyond anyone's expectations. Or prayers.

As old as Moses and as fresh as the kosher pizza sold on Reisterstown Road, Orthodox Judaism is booming here.

"We talk about it every day," said Rabbi Herman Neuberger, president of Ner Israel Rabbinical College, the cornerstone of local Orthodoxy.

Of the 100,000 or so Jews in the metro area, about 20,000 are Orthodox: followers of the 613 laws and attendant rituals derived from God's covenant on Mount Sinai with the children of Israel.

The fruit of such fidelity is a community in which the ills plaguing the rest of American society are nearly absent.

"Crime as it exists in the general public does not exist with us," said Rabbi Moshe Heinemann, one of the most powerful figures in local Orthodoxy. "There may be some white-collar crime, but there are no murders among us. Drug abuse is so unusual, the news spreads like wildfire. Divorce is rising, but it's still much lower, maybe 2 percent. There is no illiteracy, and I haven't heard of an unwed pregnancy."

Jews have lived in Baltimore since Colonial days, long before the advent of Conservative and Reform movements, which relaxed many strictures still held sacrosanct by the Orthodox.

In 1845, Baltimore Jews built the first synagogue in Maryland, a still-functioning prayer house on Lloyd Street.

On tides of prosperity, persecution and assimilation, succeeding generations moved farther and farther from original neighborhoods near the harbor. The pickle-and-herring bustle of Lloyd and Lombard streets was abandoned for the great townhouses of Eutaw Place and Druid Hill Park, which in turn were left behind for the promise of suburbia in Park Circle, Park Heights, Liberty Heights and Randallstown.

Today, as Reform and Conservative Jews push deeper into Owings Mills and other areas beyond the Beltway, the Orthodox have dug in along the city's northwest corridor. The population is particularly dense between Greenspring Avenue and Reisterstown Road.

"This area is a ghetto where you can get all of your needs met," said Marilyn Fox, a New Yorker who moved to Baltimore after marrying a local man.

Passing motorists, may see only waves of black hats and beards in the weekly Sabbath parade, but Baltimore Orthodoxy is not homogenous.

The male-dominated faith is often criticized as demeaning to women, yet there is a growing feminist movement.

Dietary laws dictate what a devout Jew can and cannot eat, but more than a few Orthodox have become kosher vegetarians.

Across this spectrum are varying degrees of adherence to the essential obligations of the faith, some of which are daunting to even the most conscientious.

Passionate debate over nuance and interpretation is part of Orthodoxy. But local rabbis take pride in the extraordinary cooperation among Baltimore's Orthodox leaders.

"There is no strife," Rabbi Heinemann contends.

In Baltimore since 1967, the rabbi's stewardship at the Agudath Israel congregation and his authority over the city's kosher food industry have led local Orthodox to a more stringent observance.

Although this Orthodoxy is reasonably free of extremes on either end, there are simmering disputes between the left and the right. While they argue over whether recreation and education should include both sexes, moderates work for common ground between the liberals and sticklers.

"Centrist Judaism is a euphemism for a little bit to the left," said Rabbi Sheftel Neuberger, an administrator at the Ner Israel college and the son of its president. "The center of Baltimore Orthodoxy is closer to Agudath."

Most Orthodox wouldn't think of driving a car on the Sabbath, which would break the law against starting a fire by "igniting" the engine. Because of this, many Orthodox buy homes within walking distance of the synagogue.

Such practices have helped stabilize home ownership along upper Park Heights Avenue, which has at least eight Orthodox synagogues.

Another four or five dot side streets.

The Sabbath is not only a day for rest, but also for savoring family and judicious recreation.

Despite laws against any form of creation, such as writing, there are families who believe that banning a Sabbath game of Scrabble is going too far.

So rich in synagogues is Baltimore that any Orthodox Jew should be able to find comfortable sanctuary.

At last count, there were 27, including one for Iranian Jews who had fled persecution.

"We came here from Atlanta, which is a one-synagogue town," said Jay Taffel, a CSX Corp. economic analyst. "In Baltimore, the choices were overwhelming."

In 1967, there were about 700 Sabbath-observing families in the metro area, according to Rabbi Heinemann. Through a slow, steady growth that surged in the 1980s, the number tripled.

Today, about 35 to 50 new Orthodox families settle here every year. So many Jews are walking to synagogue for Sabbath services that there is talk of lobbying the city to widen the sidewalks along Park Heights Avenue.

"There was no plan to bring Orthodox people" to upper Park Heights, said Stuart Macklin, an Orthodox who volunteers with the Jewish community group called CHAI. "I don't remember any meeting we had 10 years ago to attract the Orthodox, but it happened."

It happened in Baltimore for a host of reasons — religious, economic and inextricable.

To the Orthodox, nothing is more important than educating their children to God's sacred covenant. Such families, often large ones, created a need for schools. The schools need teachers, who must have housing and synagogues and kosher markets.

To educate their children, Orthodox teachers and parents will make great sacrifices. Baltimore's standard of living — with housing and food prices about a third of those in New York or Los Angeles — makes that sacrifice easier to bear.

Young teachers and rabbis start their own families and the cycle continues to the point where, in Baltimore, the community is so self-sustaining there is an Orthodox used car lot and an Orthodox phone book in which to find it.

The taproot is the 62-year-old Ner Israel Rabbinical College, a world-renowned institution that has turned out three generations of Orthodox scholars, many of whom remain in Baltimore after graduation. Every local Orthodox institution has at least one major player educated at Ner Israel.

Baltimore Orthodoxy also has prospered through the unanticipated, global phenomenon of ba'al teshuva, a return from assimilation to observance.

Primarily a movement of young to middle-aged adults, ba'al teshuva is especially pronounced in Baltimore. Such newly returned Jews are found in every local congregation and one — Tiferes Yisroel on Park Heights Avenue — is largely made up of Jews who were reared in nonobservant homes.

"Those who have not found meaning in the secular world are very central to ba'al teshuva," said Rabbi Menachem Goldberger, who leads Tiferes Yisroel.

"Becoming an Orthodox Jew is not a magic potion for making life good," he said. "Life is difficult, and the world is often a brutal place. Orthodoxy offers the chance to find meaning in the struggle."

Along with migration from other cities and the return of lost souls, the number of local Orthodox is rising, boosted by birth rates dramatically higher than the rest of society.

In size, Orthodox families of the 1990s often resemble Roman Catholic families of the 1950s.

Unlike Catholics, the number of children at the dinner table is not the result of a religious ban on birth control. Instead, it's an attempt to fulfill the commandment to "be fruitful and multiply" while perpetuating Judaism in a time of high assimilation and low Jewish birthrates overall.

"Anywhere between four and six kids is average and there are plenty with 10, 11 and 12," said Sheftel Neuberger.

Whether the Orthodox Jew in Baltimore is an aged Bible scholar or a ba'al teshuva whose first step toward his ancient ancestors is giving up cheeseburgers because of the law against mixing meat and dairy, there is room inside the eruv for all.

A rabbinically sanctioned loophole in Judaic law, an eruv permits an observant Jew certain exceptions to the rule against carrying any object outside the home on the Sabbath. It does so by extending a household's boundary. It is an unbroken "fence" invisible to the untrained eye, an enclosure made up of such things as telephone wire, highway walls, cemetery fences and hedges that meet prescribed codes of density.

Where no suitable objects exist, string is deliberately hung to complete the fence.

As Sabbath draws near, "Is the eruv up?" rings through Orthodox neighborhoods. If there is doubt, such as when snow or ice play havoc with string and tree limbs, the anxious Jew can call the eruv hot line for an update.

Baltimore has a generous eruv — 28 miles around Northwest Baltimore and the suburbs just beyond it. Since 1981, its size and uncontested legitimacy have been a great draw for Orthodox Jews from other cities and sweet comfort to those already here.

"It's not that we're trying to finagle; we're recognizing our limitations," said Rabbi Shalom Salfer, Baltimore's chief eruv inspector. "We're not in charge of ourselves and our homes, the Almighty is. If people could carry on the Sabbath, they'd [eventually] carry on business. The eruv is a reminder."

Inside this reminder are schools, restaurants, bookstores, day care, prayer houses, and ritual purification baths for men, women, and cooking utensils.

Baltimore also has an Orthodox court to settle disputes within the community, organizations that offer free loans to the needy and kosher meals to shut-ins, and apartments for out-of-towners with relatives in local hospitals.

All of which have come together in Baltimore to create a quality of observant life that some Orthodox rank higher than New York.

"This is better than New York," said Rabbi Chaim Landau of the Ner Tamid Congregation on Pimlico Road.

"Baltimore offers everything New York has in a much safer environment and an economic standard that is easier to attain," he said. "The number [of Jews] isn't in the millions, which is overwhelming, and the Orthodox community is contained geographically. Orthodox Jews are coming here from major cities where crime is epidemic. It's not that there's no crime in Baltimore, but Baltimore is safer."

And better than L.A.

Michael Langbaum, a 35-year-old neonatologist reared Orthodox in Los

Angeles, moved his family to Baltimore in 1991 to take a job with Johns Hopkins. The idea was to stay for a year and go home.

Now, home is Baltimore, and he's trying to persuade his parents to move here.

"It's nice to get back to a warm, hometown atmosphere that Los Angeles was when I was a kid," said Dr. Langbaum, who looked at houses in Baltimore County before deciding his family would be more content in the heart of the Orthodox community. "My kids are growing up more like I did, able to ride their bikes down the block with their friends. My kids never played in the front yard in Los Angeles."

March 5, 1995

Courtship by the book

OF ALL THE MYSTERIOUS STATEMENTS IN THE TALMUD, ONE OF THE BEST KNOWN says that finding a true partner in life is as difficult as parting the Red Sea.

In the world of Orthodox Judaism, where family is second to God alone, people are always working to part the seas so men and women can get married, fulfill the commandment to multiply and ensure the faith for another generation.

As the father of a recent bride put it: "Matchmaking is the favorite indoor sport of Jews."

Whether they are professionals using computers, a yeshiva rabbi intimate with all the qualities and quirks of his students, or Aunt Malkie who just happens to know a nice boy from a good family, somebody is always trying to fix people up.

Certain Hasidic families in the United States still choose mates for their sons and daughters as they did in 18th-century Poland.

Before Orthodox Jews get to the wedding canopy, they must navigate a dating process governed by religious laws and customs that most of society would find unthinkable, beginning with informal but detailed checks of family, character and health.

(One young man just starting to date has kept a recent surgery secret so as not to hurt his chances of finding a wife.)

The way the Orthodox see it, the average American does more homework deciding to buy a car than choosing a spouse. The Orthodox divorce rate, estimated at about 5 percent, suggests they do their homework well.

Dating prohibitions include touching, which is said to hamper the work of picking a mate since physical contact intoxicates the senses. Time spent completely alone is forbidden, since it might set the stage for touching, and outings just for fun are frowned upon.

Such boundaries lead to a lot of evenings sipping soda in the lobbies of big hotels while trying to fathom another person's dreams and visions.

Other safe places include museums, the zoo and a place that's become something of an inside joke: the airport.

"I've been on an airport date once or twice, hasn't everybody?" Chuckie

Epstein, a 25-year-old Orthodox pilot, says with a laugh. "It's a cliche now, but the airport is a good place for a first date. It's not heavily populated at night, it's quiet, there's a lot of room to walk around, it's indoors, which helps in the winter, and it's safe."

Movies are usually out of the question until a couple is engaged, and even then, many Orthodox Jews do not partake of pop culture. Because laws of modesty largely keep the genders separate from about grade school until dating begins, early dates are often awkward experiments.

"It can be pretty tough," said an Orthodox man, who did not want to be named for fear that his views might hurt his standing in the Jewish community. "I can count on one hand the crushes I've had. If a boy or girl has a reputation for flirting too much, it might be harder for them to get married."

On one of his first dates, this young man was mortified to discover that the bench he'd picked in New York's Battery Park for conversation was in a gay area.

The rules are often stretched (some daters hold hands, others kiss) and can be broken in ways anyone who has been on a date can understand. One young woman breached the law that demands sensitivity to the feelings of others when she kept looking at her watch as her date attempted to explain his goals in life.

Shadowing everything is the idea that this dating has tachlis, or purpose. That purpose is to find your bashert, or "meant to be."

Dating usually begins at 19 or 20 for a woman, about 21 for a man. Some young people let their parents know when they're ready, others need to be prodded by their parents to get in the game.

Our rabbinical student, let's call him Yaakov, describes a typical case: "For starters, everyone's a nice girl. The shadkhan [matchmaker] tells you when it's OK to call, and the guy gets very nervous trying to create a conversation with someone he's never met.

"You say you'll pick her up at a certain time and get spitzed up in a suit and hat. A lot of guys hate wearing the hat on a date, but it shows respect. Mom and Dad answer the door, and she's hiding in her room so you have a few minutes to meet the parents, who ask stuff they already know: 'Where do you go to yeshiva?' 'What does your father do for a living?'

"And then the girl walks in, you say hello and turn right back to talk to the parents again. You're thinking: 'This could be my wife.' She's thinking: 'This could be my husband.' And the parents are thinking: 'This could be my son-in-law.'

"It's hard even if it goes well," he says. "If it doesn't go so well, it's horrible."

The rabbis tell the young men the same thing mothers advise young women: Trust the system, everything will work out.

As it did for Rivkah Goldfinger, 21, and Dovid Stein, 24, married May 19 after knowing each other for eight months in an almost storybook example of Orthodox courtship, complete with the kind of surprises that pop up while you're busy following rules.

"Usually people spend a couple of weeks looking into each other's backgrounds before agreeing to a date, but this time I got the phone call without even knowing his name," remembers Goldfinger, who grew up in Northwest Baltimore.

They were brought together after Stein's rabbi moved to Baltimore from Australia. The rabbi's wife knew a friend of Goldfinger's mother, and that's all it took for wheels to start turning.

After being told about Stein, Goldfinger requested more information. That got garbled into a message that she was willing to go out, which soon put her in an awkward conversation.

"I had a sense that I didn't want to go out with him; he sounded too much like the standard yeshiva guy. I decided he wasn't unusual enough," she recalls. "But I couldn't say no. He'd been told I wanted to go out."

What Goldfinger regards as the "standard yeshiva guy" — someone pursuing a worldly career simply because their parents are afraid they'll starve with an education in Talmud alone — is acceptable to many Orthodox women.

Margie Pensak, one of about six traditional matchmakers in Baltimore, has nearly 750 clients, about 90 percent of them Orthodox.

Working for a small registration fee to cover her expenses (mostly long-distance phone calls), Pensak says she often feels like a "waitress taking orders." Wish lists include everything from age and weight to tastes in music, to willingness to live in Israel and unwillingness to watch television.

Some people who have used matchmakers are put off by being reduced to a paragraph of statistics "like the back of a baseball card — I'm deeper than that," says one Baltimore man. Others are content to find "the generic Orthodox Jew — kosher home, observe the Sabbath, Torah study and raising kids to go to yeshiva," says Pensak.

Generic just wasn't going to do for Goldfinger, who comes from a very observant yet whimsical and open-minded Hasidic family — a woman whose independent thinking is symbolized by her choice of Catholic-run Loyola College for a biology degree.

She knew her bashert had to be Hasidic — someone given to wearing satin caftans and round fur hats, who favored oil to light the Sabbath candles over wax — but beyond that she "couldn't put into words" her notion of a soul mate. From the 20 or so dates she had before meeting Stein, she knew what she didn't want.

There was the art museum date, with a guy who "walked by all the pictures I wanted to see."

There was the 45-minute "sit-in" around the dining room table with a devoutly Hasidic man while her parents entertained his parents in the next room.

"He couldn't believe I knew the Talmud and was shocked that an Orthodox girl had taken a class in evolution," she says. "I wasn't about to tell him I was going to be a doctor."

And then she found herself having dinner with Stein without having seen him. But four months and nine dates later, after long evenings talking in hotel lobbies, they were engaged.

"The right one is preordained. My job was to meet a number of girls before I met the right one, " says Stein, an Australian studying in New York. "Some girls were too loud, some girls were too quiet. I went out with good-looking girls and not such good-looking girls. They were all nice girls, fine Orthodox girls. But you want someone with the same ideas as you. Rivkah had the right combination of all of them."

Stein plans to become a pulpit rabbi while Goldfinger is about to embark on medical school, an arduous beginning for any marriage. "It will be hard but rewarding in the long run," says Goldfinger. "I love the idea of being a rabbi's wife, and he thinks being a doctor is one of the greatest jobs a person can have."

Ted Friedman also thinks being a doctor is great and has been looking for someone to share a doctor's life for about five years. The music on his home telephone answering machine has Bruce Springsteen singing: "I just want someone to talk to and a little of that human touch. "

The 37-year-old endocrinologist from Los Angeles, who became observant as a teen-ager, has had well over a hundred dating adventures, ranging from a Chinese convert he encountered on the Internet to a mountain climber he met in Alaska with a Jewish hiking club.

He'd exhausted at least one matchmaker in Los Angeles before meeting Pensak at a religious retreat for singles.

A few weeks ago, Pensak set Friedman up with seven dates over two days, all in New York. None panned out.

"In general, people seem good at first but they hide things or mislead you," says Friedman, who is looking for a woman between ages 25 and 33 to start a family.

Many of the very observant women he's been out with weren't educated enough for him, and many of the professional women were not religious enough.

As the old Jewish saying goes, the right girl at the wrong time is the wrong girl.

For now, it's back to Pensak the matchmaker, who has 12 marriages to her credit since 1988. When a match ends in a marriage, it is traditional for the bride and groom to buy the shadkhan a gift. Friedman hopes he'll be sending something Pensak's way soon.

"The right person will come when the time is right," he says. "It's going to happen when it's going to happen."

May 26, 1996

Taking time to pray at the old ball game

BORSCHT BELT THEOLOGIANS LIKE TO POINT OUT THAT THE WORLD BEGAN with baseball. It says so in the Bible, with the very first line of Genesis.

"In the big inning..."

For observant Jews who enjoy taking in a ballgame at Camden Yards, the big inning is the bottom of the 5th, when a little room behind Section 32 begins filling up for evening prayers.

"It's not really a synagogue area," says Jerry Shavrick of the tight spot behind the Kosher Food stand, a narrow cubby hole of concrete and cinder block without a mezuzah, where youngsters wear yarmulkes under their Oriole caps and trade baseball gloves for prayers books. "But people know it's the place to come. The word is spread."

Mr. Shavrick is executive director for Project Ezra, a Jewish safety and health group that runs the kosher stand as a break-even public service. Because nothing is more healthy for a religious Jew than keeping the laws of God, gathering to pray evolved naturally from the food concession.

"You can't miss one day without it, no matter where you are," said Rabbi Boruch Braun, an instructor at the Torah Institute on Northern Parkway who brought a group of 15 kids to a game this month. "It's our life. We weave it into everything we do."

Compared to the continuity of daily Jewish prayer — some 3,500 years and running — Cal Ripken's streak is barely a blink in the cosmos.

" It's a highly unusual thing to find a maariv service in the secular world," said Harry Horn, a rabbi from Teaneck, N.J., who attended a recent game between the Orioles and Cleveland Indians. "New York has a much larger Jewish community than Baltimore and we don't have something like this at Yankee Stadium."

Known in Hebrew as "maariv," evening prayers are generally said between the time the stars come out and midnight and are one of three worship services observed daily by Jews around the world: morning, noon and night. Obligatory for those who have made bar mitzvah — males over the age of 13 — the prayers include a combination of chants and silent devotion that last about 12 minutes.

It begins: "He, the Merciful One, is forgiving and does not destroy. Frequently He withdraws His anger, not arousing His entire rage. [God] save! May the King answer us on the day we call…"

While the prayers can be said in solitude, believers attest that praise and petitions are more effective, indeed are better received by God, when chanted in a group. A minimum of 10 males over bar mitzvah age are required for a Jewish quorum, known as a minyan. At Camden Yards, the kosher stand has only once failed to gather a minyan and that was on a rainy night.

"I see something like this and it makes me feel good, a place I can come and pray with fellow Jews," said Irvin Zeidel, also from New Jersey. "I work with an outreach group who try to bring Judaism to people who are not observant and this kind of thing makes it more convenient for everyone. At the ballpark, you'll see a yarmulke here and there, but to see them all together praying in a small room is something special."

During the service, ventilating fans spun and refrigerators hummed as more than 40 of the faithful bowed at the waist and bent at the knees while chanting.

Out in the stands, folks may be praying for a late-inning rally, but in this makeshift synagogue, Jews remind themselves that God commanded Moses to tell the Israelites to wear fringes on the corners of their garments "throughout their generations" and "not explore after your heart and after your eyes after which you stray."

Orthodox Judaism is driven by 613 different laws interpreted with varying degrees of stringency, commandments that have created a culture so insular at times that some have never been to a movie theater. While rabbis generally place athletics on a higher plane than motion pictures, certain sticklers take a dim view of professional sports.

"The Jewish religion doesn't have too much respect for [professional] sports in general. It is useless, it doesn't promote anything," said Rabbi Moshe Heinemann, head of the Agudath Israel congregation on Park Heights Avenue and a powerful authority in Baltimore Orthodoxy. "Improving one's health [through exercise], that's a religious thing, a sacred duty. But to go and watch someone else play is a different story. It's not forbidden, but it's not considered very worthwhile."

With all due respect, 16-year-old Nachliel Friedman, a rabbinical student at Ner Israel in Owings Mills and a fan of the American pastime, takes a different view.

"Some people think it takes away from spirituality to come to the ballpark, there are those who want to pray at a higher level. But my attitude is you can pray and have fun too. Does God want us to have fun? Yes, to a certain extent."

Out in the stands, a roar goes up after the service has ended and the boys scatter for their seats.

" You try to keep the game out of your head while you're praying." said 12-year-old Shabsai Shuchatowitz. "But it's hard sometimes."

August 30, 1995

The hat of manhood

WHEN THE BLACK HAT OF ORTHODOXY FIRST SETTLES UPON THE HEAD OF AN adolescent Jew, the boy beneath the brim begins giving way to manhood.

"The mothers say they can't see their little boy anymore," says a rabbi who supplies hats to Baltimore's Orthodox community. "They want the smallest brim because they don't want the child to disappear beneath the hat."

Though a symbol of strict adherence to Jewish law, the wearing of a black hat is custom and not law. In the United States, it was almost exclusively the domain of rabbis and yeshiva students until about 40 years ago.

And it is no small statement of fashion, even among a people taught to value modesty and humility.

Young men looking to cut a dashing figure favor hats of smooth felt with wide brims. In Baltimore in the early 1980s, a 1-inch brim was the norm and 2 was considered far out. Today, 2-inch brims are standard bar mitzvah fare and 3 inches — the stuff of cowboys to many old-timers — is the cutting edge.

At weddings, the father of the groom may indulge in a fine suede for photographs. And boys, who get their first hats at the bar mitzvah age of 13, are known to brag and gossip about the size, style and price of their kovim the way secular youths compare athletic shoes.

Together with a full beard (also customary but not required), the black hat is the easiest way to recognize an Orthodox Jew on the street.

But it takes a while for a young man to grow a beard, and for a bar mitzvah boy, getting a grown-up hat while assuming the obligations of adulthood is a rite of male passage. Such rites are rare elsewhere in society.

"I felt like I was on the team," says Binyomin Schwartz, a 13-year-old eighth-grader at the Talmudic Academy on Old Court Road. "When everyone in your society is like that and you're not there yet, you wish for that day."

It is a time that the young Jewish male tells fellow Jews he is not only ready to don the hat, but also a certain seriousness: that from now on, when he prays he will dress as if in the presence of a king.

The custom, mentioned in commentaries on Jewish law going back hundreds of years, also is used as a reminder to resist the temptations of assimilation, telling the world in no uncertain terms: I am a Jew.

Just before he became bar mitzvah in December, Binyomin was taken by his parents to buy a size 7 Stetson, a prized possession he stores in its box when he's not wearing it.

"It marks the end of one era and the beginning of another," says his mother, Priva. "It gets you in the heart."

His father, Yaakov, a teacher at the Talmudic Academy, also wears a Stetson (size 7), but, although he grew up Orthodox, he did not adopt the black hat custom until he came to Baltimore's Ner Israel Rabbinical College from Columbus, Ohio.

"My parents always joke that some people are the black sheep of the family, and I'm the black hat of the family," he says.

It was his desire to be like his Ner Israel teachers, such as the fabled Rabbi Yaakov Ruderman, that led Rabbi Schwartz to don a black hat not long after he arrived there at age 19.

"I will revere Rabbi Ruderman all of my life, and when I picture him in my mind I see the beard and the hat, and I seek to emulate what he stood for, his depth in learning and moral greatness," says Rabbi Schwartz. "In secular culture, people root for the Orioles, admire Cal Ripken and wear the team's hat and T-shirts. It's a way to connect."

At the Hattery, a clothing store run out of a rabbi's basement in Northwest Baltimore, the connection can be made for as little as $55 for a Pinizza to $169 for a top-of-the-line Borsalino. In the middle are Stetsons and Huckels.

The rabbi who runs the store, where most Orthodox Jews go to get their hats in Baltimore, does not want his name used because, although he is a licensed merchant and pays sales taxes, his basement is not zoned for retail use.

Since a more stringent Orthodoxy hit Baltimore a generation ago — an Orthodoxy in which most young men want to imitate the rabbis they honor — the Hattery can hardly give away its surplus of blue, brown and gray hats.

The rabbi sells 50 dozen or so hats a year, and his customers demand black.

"The rite of passage when you made your bar mitzvah used to be the fountain pen; now it's the black hat," says the rabbi, who sells hats to supplement his income from teaching fifth grade.

"I tell parents to buy the $55 hat the first time out. It's going to get stuck in a locker, he'll ride his bike with it, it'll get crushed. I feel that all first hats will disintegrate."

Some Orthodox families in Baltimore — kosher, observant and as respectful of the Sabbath as anyone — have found themselves on the fence over the black hat.

Howard and Judy Elbaum of Mount Washington have become increasingly strict in their practice of Judaism as their children have moved through Jewish grade school and high school. A few years ago, their son Ari, now 15 and enthralled with the knowledge that his ancestors in Poland were rabbis, started talking about getting a black hat.

Mom and Dad have not said Ari can't have one, but neither are they quite ready to rush out and buy one. In this country, at least, it has not been the family custom. They would like their son to wait a bit longer before deciding.

Yet, Ari appears eager to wear one.

"A black hat is a beautiful thing. It's a sign of respect when you're standing and praying in front of [God], a symbol of going up the spiritual ladder," says the 10th-grader at the Hebrew Academy of Washington. "My goal is not to base my life on whether or not I wear a black hat; my goal is to be the best Jew I can. I have a lot of learning to do."

And it would not surprise anyone in his family if, before long, he is doing it in a black hat.

January 18, 1996

Orthodox means of travel

SO MANY THINGS ARE CRUCIAL TO THE INTENSELY ORDERED LIFE OF AN Orthodox Jew: a synagogue within walking distance of home, a trustworthy rabbi, and schools to teach the galaxy of nuance inherent in Judaism's 613 separate commandments.

The outside world rarely gets to see the striped shawls and tiny boxes filled with sacred Scripture worn by religious Jews at daily prayer. But the next time you're cruising the streets of Northwest Baltimore, be alert for an obvious sign of the Orthodox way of life — the faded and rusting full-sized American station wagon.

"When I'm driving down the Jones Falls Expressway and I see a big old wagon, I automatically assume it's an Orthodox family," says Hillel Tendell, a local attorney. "And when you come out of [services] and see two identical wagons side by side, you ask the next guy, 'Which one is yours?'

"Go to the corner of Clover and Highgate, and you'll see both sides thick with station wagons," says Tendell. "This is the way we live."

The hulking wagons and boxy passenger vans that seat up to 15 people reflect the size of the Orthodox family. Even when a couple has only four or five children, they are invariably part of a car pool ferrying children to and from Jewish schools.

"Generally speaking, a person isn't allowed to cease having children for reasons of convenience," says Rabbi Yitzchok Adler, a father of 10 who recently bought a 1989, 12-seat Chevy van with 80,000 miles on it for $6,800. "We need big vehicles, and we need inexpensive vehicles."

The preponderance of these autos are 7-year-old Chevrolet Caprice wagons or Oldsmobile Custom Cruisers — lumbering, four-wheel boats that tend to be gray or blue and sell for about $6,000 if they're in good shape.

American automakers are no longer manufacturing full-sized wagons — they've been overtaken by minivans and sport utility vehicles — but so many wagons remain among Baltimore's 2,100 Orthodox families that children waiting to be picked up from school often check who's behind the wheel so they don't go home with the wrong people.

And most of those wagons come from Sher's Auto Sales and Maven

Motors, Orthodox used car lots three blocks apart on Reisterstown Road.

"Meir Sher is the main source; he's known far and wide," says Tendell.

Like all used car salesmen, Sher likes to close a deal with a handshake — except when the customer is a woman, because Jewish laws of modesty caution him against touching any female other than his wife.

Sher's wife is Chaya, a verbal dynamo who does most of the selling — sometimes getting more than $11,000 for a one-owner late-model wagon with low mileage — after Meir buys the vehicles at auction and wholesale. While the most-observant Jew struggles to fulfill all of the faith's dictates, particular pains are taken to sell used cars by the good book.

"Jewish law doesn't accept the concept of buyer beware," says the 49-year-old Sher, a rabbi who used to study the Torah until midnight and then stay up for hours rebuilding a carburetor. "If there's a dent that's been fixed, I have to tell you. And if an unknown defect is found where the person would not have bought it had they known, then the deal is no good either."

A Sher deal is built on Chaya's passion for verifying a vehicle's actual miles. The only way to do this is by tracking down the original owner. Chaya claims success about 80 percent of the time.

"I had a one-owner Buick Roadmaster wagon with 52,000 miles on it. It had gone through our 100-point Sher check, and we had it sold to a woman in New Jersey," says Chaya, 48, who between deals has arranged marriages for customers. "When we finally reached the original owner, she was livid — she had sold the car with 112,000 miles on it. So there goes the myth that if you take a used car to a mechanic you trust, they'll know if the miles are true or not. We couldn't tell by looking."

For a dozen years, the Shers have provided religious Jews from Miami to Manhattan with the right ride, the past five years from a scruffy lot at 5420 Reisterstown Road, south of the heart of Baltimore's Orthodox community.

On a metal bookshelf in the office is a complete set of the Talmud, the voluminous body of Jewish teaching. Meir doesn't get to lose himself in its pages as often as he'd like, but many a customer has sat down to study while waiting for a car to be fixed.

And while the Book of Deuteronomy exhorts Jews to write the laws of God "upon the doorposts of your house," Sher's is the only place Neal Golbin has seen with Scripture alongside roll-up garage doors.

Golbin, a nonpracticing Jew hired by the Shers to drum up sales among gentiles, has been in the car business for more than 10 years. He was a partner in a dealership in Harford County for a while and has never seen anyone do business like the Shers.

"They're selling cars sight unseen over the phone to people out of town. It's unheard of," says Golbin. "They have a list of people who want a certain type of vehicle, and when Meir's at auction, if he sees what they want, he gets it."

Golbin, who used to send station wagons to the Shers when he had his own business, has worked for the family about six months. He connected with Meir at an auction one day when his life was on a downswing.

While no more observant of Jewish law than he was when he joined the Shers, Golbin's spirituality has grown on the job.

"These people have a daily conscious contact with God, and that's something I need," he says. "Commercialism has become our culture's substitute for that."

Academics who have studied the effect of religious ethics on business have found that integrity invariably helps sales.

"The fundamental premise of a market economy is trust, and trust presumes underlying honesty," says Shirley Roels, an economics and business professor at Calvin College in Grand Rapids, Mich. "Trust is what has carried capitalism in this country, and people will go out of their way to buy it."

Meir Sher has been known to talk customers out of buying a car when he believed there was nothing wrong with their old one.

He says: "You don't always get rewarded for good deeds in this world. Being as fair and honest as I can be, I might lose deals, but that person is going to tell his friends about me."

August 18, 1996

Chapter 9

Characters

'Telescope Man' hustles stars from street corners

CALL THIS GUY THE TELESCOPE MAN.

For some loose change, the chance to make small talk about big dreams and the sheer and simple thrill of it, Herman Heyn will give you a peek at the heavens.

In this land of sidewalk opportunities there glows a galaxy of ways to persuade pedestrians to drop money in a hat.

Some guys whine Bob Dylan songs, strumming a battered sixstring and croaking their hearts out about the many things that "God said to Abraham…"

Some guys juggle cabbages, some paint their faces and pretend they can't talk and others shove fire down their throats.

But Herman Heyn — 57, part-time math teacher, affable astronomer for the common man, and chaser of many an eccentric hustle — has been averaging $28.48 a night by setting up an 8-inch Meade telescope on Baltimore Street corners, pointing it at the sky, and giving passers-by the chance to see a crater on the moon.

Or Jupiter with a six-day moon beneath it; maybe an anonymous shooting star as it passes through town; the Pleiades and red-giant Betelgeuse; the Orion Nebula; or the Domino Sugar sign if that's the universe you happen to be in the mood for.

"You don't live for the spectacular — that's great when you can get it — you live for day-to-day observing," says Mr. Heyn, a man who surrendered after a grade school science teacher drew the Big Dipper on the blackboard.

And there the dipper hung that night when little Herman stared out his bedroom window.

"My role," says the Telescope Man, "is helping other people see what's out there. Stuff they would never see on their own.

"One guy in Fells Point told me, 'If I die tomorrow I'll die content that I at least got to see one of Jupiter's moons before I went.'"

And while you can't put a price tag on giving someone a thrill they've never known, there is that hat lying beneath the telescope tripod and it doesn't take a Copernicus to figure out what it's for.

Mr. Heyn says he doesn't ask for it, but the money has been there each time the Telescope Man and his $1,200 peephole have ventured out of his Waverly row house since last November.

Part scientist, part businessman, part Barnum of the Big Bang, Mr. Heyn has kept a faithful log of his astral gigs as they have been acted out in Charles Village and Fells Point, enthusiastic attempts to "have another source of income and teach people about the stars."

The good:

- Jan. 30, 1988. Fells Point, Saturday, 9 p.m. til 12:30 a.m. 12-day moon. One person commented that it did not show the whole moon... but all lookers were pleased. First half of evening had a layer of thick clouds that made image a bit flat. Second half was clearer, sharp. Moon was in Gemini and very high, so scope was pointing almost straight up. Collection: $72.21 ($47 in bills and $24.21 in coins.)

The not-so-good:

- Feb. 6, 1988. Saturday. Fells Point. Arrived at 7 p.m. Looked at Jupiter, Venus and the Great Nebula in Orion. Looked amazingly good. Reported temperature was 18 degrees with wind at 18 mph. Just too cold. Few people and very few contributions. Total $2.80. Packed up at 8 p.m. Too cold, probably, for people to reach into their pockets for money. Pleiades looked nice through the view finder. Orion's Belt fitted into finder!

The all-too-typical:

- Local weather so messed up you can't glimpse much of anything.

"Maryland weather isn't bad, it's perverse," says Mr. Heyn, who, in constant pursuit of financial solvency, has given astronomy slide shows for Baltimore public school children, Penitentiary inmates and friends at private parties celebrating such phenomena as the passing of the Comet Kohoutek.

At dusk last night, with Mr. Heyn and his telescope established on the corner of St. Paul and 31st streets, the atmosphere was "great, it's not cold, not windy, and the sky is crystal clear."

Ellen L. Edwards, a 39-year-old nurse on her way to purchase a Lotto ticket, ambled up to the scope and peered through the lens pointed at the sky high above the Homewood campus of Johns Hopkins University.

"I can see Jupiter and four moons!" she said, setting her sights on the spheres that go by the names of Ganymede, Io, Europa and Callisto. "And a lot of blue clouds or something with stripes across it. What a thrill! I love to look at the sky."

Mr. Heyn hopes many will do so tonight when Venus and Jupiter approach each other for a near cheek-to cheek meeting — at least that's how it looks from Earth — expected to result in their brightest, most visible pairing in years.

So bright, in fact, that Mr. Heyn could have naked-eyed them as a kid before owning his first lens, a 3-inch diameter Mogey his Dad bought him just after World War II, an instrument powerful enough "to see the rings of Saturn."

A boy and his scope. It was a love affair that dominated young Herman's emotions until he turned 18.

"In high school, what social life was for other people, for me was staying home on a Saturday night reading an astronomy book," said Mr. Heyn, who lives among the clutter of the universe in the shadow of Memorial Stadium. "Mom was always pushing me to go to parties and get dates, but I just wanted to read. When I look in the sky I still see the constellations the way I learned them in those early books."

After graduating from City College, however, he sold his telescope for $180 to finance a trip to California with friends. For the next 18 years, his passion waned.

And then, sitting at the breakfast table one mid-November morning in 1966, Herman Heyn saw a buried newspaper item that made his pulse race. That very night promised the return of the famed "Leonid Meteor Shower," a flying flash of entertainment visible within "the sickle" of the constellation Leo that hits a spectacular peak about every 33 years.

"I had missed it as a child because I was only 3 in 1933 and I remembered being a kid thinking, 'Gee, I hope I'll be alive when it comes back,'" said Mr. Heyn. "But I had totally forgotten about it."

That night, he waited in the dark in the backyard of his Bosworth Avenue home with a 35-mm camera propped up against a tree with its shutter open. It was Baltimore. Cloudy and heavy. The view was reportedly great out in Utah, but Mr. Heyn spent several hours without seeing much of anything.

His camera, however, did pick up some star trails, and the experience was enough to set the Telescope Man off again. Combining astronomy with photography, Mr. Heyn's renewed vigor moved him to haul his family up and down the coast — sometimes off the coast— for eclipse vacations. His growing expertise landed a few of his photographs in astronomy books and an Italian encyclopedia.

Today, Mr. Heyn designs and markets T-shirts — he's got a magnificent one of Halley's Comet and Mark Twain, whose life began and ended with appearance of comet — teaches math and high school equivalency courses for the city of Baltimore; rents a room to a Johns Hopkins University graduate student; works at the Waverly Farmer's Market in the summer; loves folk music and folk dancing; and provides a window to the Milky Way for anyone with enough time to put their eye up to a lens.

He calls himself "Baltimore's Streetcorner Astronomer", and now is struggling with city bureaucrats for a formal permit to peddle the stars wherever he pleases — particularly at Harborplace, with summertime around the corner.

It's all an acknowledged hustle — "Heaven if you're a hustler and hell if you're not," reads the sign above his desk — but for Herman Heyn, the Telescope Man, it sure beats the daily race of rats that ran him ragged so long.

"I hand-to-mouth it," he says, a smile spreading across his gentle, bearded face. "But I feel great."

March 6, 1988

Prisoners of war

LELIO TOMASINA HAD NEVER SEEN SUCH ORANGES.

Mammoths!

The oranges of America, as big as a baby's head!

It was late 1942, Lelio's first days in this strange land of gigantic bounty called the United States.

His gateway to the New World was not Ellis Island, but the belly of a prisoner-of-war ship.

And he knew very little, almost nothing, of life here when the Americans herded him and hundreds of his surrendered countrymen into a mess hall at Camp Buckner near Raleigh, N.C.

The prisoners whispered among themselves: "No wonder America is so big, look at the big oranges they have!"

The Italian soldiers were just a few weeks removed from the battlefields of Sicily and North Africa, where they ate what they could find and bugs crawled on their bodies as they tried in vain to hold off British tanks with pistols and rifles.

Compared to such hell, the sight of oranges worthy of Eden left the Italians awe-struck.

"At first we were afraid to touch them," he said. "Geez, they were so beautiful and big!"

When the prisoners bit into the magnificent fruit the smiles on their faces turned sour.

Lelio Tomasina and his comrades had eaten their first grapefruit.

It was a small surprise in a constellation of change that transformed the young soldier and some 50,000 of his surrendered companions once the United States took custody of their fates.

The Italian prisoners were distributed among Army camps across America, and eventually, Lelio would be shipped to Maryland's Fort Meade, where more than 600 POWs were held between 1942 and the end of 1944.

When Italy surrendered in September 1943 — leaving Germany and Japan to fight alone against the rest of the world — the armistice required the immediate release of Allied prisoners in Italian hands, but made no provision for Italian prisoners held by the Allies.

Most of the captives signed "cooperation" papers, which transformed them from prisoners to "co-belligerents." By consenting to help the American war effort in non-combat duties, mostly dull kitchen and construction work, the POWs at Fort Meade received liberties they never dreamed possible.

Says Lelio, who held rank in the Italian artillery somewhere between a corporal and sergeant: "We were prisoners in a way, but not exactly prisoners."

Not exactly.

Not the way his father was a prisoner during World War I and traded his watch to German captors for a handful of potato skins.

Compared to their time as hapless, hungry, bug-infested soldiers in Sicily and North Africa, the stateside sojourn of Lelio and his comrades was a marvel of feasts with Baltimore's Italian community; warm beds, hot showers and new uniforms; and moonlit dances with local girls.

"We were treated better than we were as soldiers in the Italian army, as if we were family," said Lelio, who still carries a picture in his wallet of himself at Fort Meade with Sue Gentile, the Baltimore girl he eventually married and remained with 24 years until her death in 1972. "I never got mad one day about my prisoner days."

His first week in America — where he kissed the ground after arriving by ship in Norfolk, Va., on his 22nd birthday — was like a movie, Lelio said.

It was so unbelievably magnificent, he said, that he was sure the Americans were just being nice before they shot everybody.

"After I kissed the ground they began counting us off, 20 at a time and they put us on a first-class train," Lelio said. "It had red velvet and crystal chandeliers and we're thinking: 'What are they going to do to us?' A black porter in formal dress came up to us with a silver tray of doughnuts and coffee. I had never seen a doughnut in my life."

He was thinking of his father giving up his watch for potato peels and remembers chuckling to himself at the sight of American soldiers guarding the prisoners at both ends of the passenger car.

Lelio thought to himself: "Who is going to try to escape from this?"

At Fort Buckner, they were given a physical, soap and shaving gear, new shoes, and clean clothes with POW stamped in red on the back of their work shirts.

And then nearly 400 of them sat down to eat dinner, the dinner of the great oranges.

"About this supper I could write a book," says Lelio, laughing.

After the grapefruit was served, the Americans served them a huge pot of spaghetti. Despite the bounty, the prisoners were so unsure of their next meal that they divided the pasta among themselves, noodle by noodle.

"It took us a long time just to count out the noodles 20 at a time to make sure everybody had the same amount," he said.

After the spaghetti came a cart of hot dogs. A pair of hot dogs were put on each prisoner's plate and everyone was free to go back for more.

With gastronomic pride, Lelio Tomasina — now a U.S. citizen, now retired from 32 years with Bethlehem Steel at Sparrows Point — remembered his first encounter with the all-American hot dog.

"Do you know how many hot dogs I ate? I'll never forget it," he said. "I ate 22 hot dogs that day. I was 154 pounds when we landed in Norfolk and three months later I was 190 pounds. After we ate everybody was sitting around rubbing their belly, saying: 'Boy, America is nice.'"

To the Italian soldiers locked up at Fort Meade, Guy Sardella was a war hero.

A hero who brought together lonely prisoners and the city of Baltimore with the sound of his voice.

"Everything happened because of Sardella," said Lelio Tomasina. "We are all here today because of him."

Now 80 years old and living in Cockeysville, Guy Sardella was the voice of Maryland's Italian community for nearly 40 years as the host of a weekly radio show.

Born across from the Flag House on Albemarle Street and raised in Italy, he taught Italian at the Peabody Institute; knew everyone of even passing importance among local Italians; was named Baltimore's Italian-American of the year in 1960; and twice has been knighted by the Italian government.

In 1944, when he discovered that the Fort Meade barracks were crowded with hundreds of the fallen sons of Italy, he decided to use his influence to make their stay more pleasant.

He organized a soccer team among the prisoners and combed Baltimore for a team willing to kick a ball with the enemy; he helped put together a band from the musicians among the POWs and took them to local variety shows; made introductions with local families; invited prisoners into his home; brought Baltimore Mayor Thomas D'Alesandro, Jr., to Fort Meade to give a speech to the prisoners in their native tongue; celebrated Mass with the prisoners at the outdoor chapel they had erected.

He acted as an around-the-clock diplomat between the prisoners and a public wary of such intimacies with the enemy.

He fielded angry letters from local men who complained that their wives were spending every Sunday afternoon socializing with POWs at Fort Meade.

"Everybody in town was talking about the prisoners," he said. "I was there almost every day. What a memorable summer that was."

The memories that were the summer of '44 began with a simple announcement over WCBM radio that Italian prisoners of war who had agreed to cooperate with the Allies had been rewarded with the privilege of receiving guests.

"I said: 'Ladies and gentlemen, you would feel good if you went to visit,'" said Guy. "After the second announcement there was a string of cars going down to Fort Meade filled with people and food for immense picnics. The prisoners built an outdoor stage and put together a little orchestra and after awhile people were going down there by the hundreds on Sunday afternoons to meet prisoners from their old home towns in Italy."

The good times ended late that summer when half of the prisoners were returned to the Italian government. By the fall of 1944, all of the prisoners were gone from Fort Meade.

"When I arrived on the last day, the Italian officers saluted and ordered their soldiers to start cooking," said Guy. "It was so touching to see all of them, the way they made a speech thanking me for all I did for them, for alleviating their prison life. The first six or seven years after they left I would get piles of Christmas cards and then it started to dwindle off. I still get a few."

And he still has boxes of gifts given to him by the prisoners before they were shipped back home, presents of gratitude that included a big oil painting of prisoners attending Mass next to a tree in an open field.

"That was the best part of my life," said Guy. "We were treated like kings there, but what I didn't do for them. What I treasure most is a big plaque they gave me with the words: 'We will never forget what you did for us…'"

It was raining hard and the prisoner orchestra began playing "Stormy Weather."

A big storm.

Thunder cracked and lightning streaked the windows of the Fort Meade field house as Bruno Brotto walked across the dance floor to ask a pretty girl for a dance.

"I'll never forget it," remembers the former Gabriella Fabi, daughter of a Little Italy barber. "It was 1944. I was 20 years old."

Gabriella and her girlfriends were part of a flock of hundreds who answered the call of Guy Sardella. She later was one of about 30 Baltimore women who followed their POW sweethearts to altars in Italy.

They started off riding down on buses from Broadway on Sundays, and soon began driving cars down during the middle of the week, carrying along baskets of roast chicken and platters of gnocchi.

In a July 1944 Sunday *Sun* article illustrated with photographs by A. Aubrey Bodine, reporter Flora Murray wrote:

" … the girls, conscious as most are these days of the scarcity of dancing partners, are happy to attend the dances and interested to meet people from their parents' or grandparents' native land."

Said Gabriella, now 68: "My parents told me to go to the dances and look for my cousins. I didn't find any cousins but I found Bruno."

"I liked her," said Bruno, "because she was speaking Italian pretty good. We understood each other."

Said Gabriella, "I fell in love with him. You couldn't ask for a nicer guy. All of the girls found someone, we all fell in love."

It was another stormy night when Bruno and Gabriella parted in October

1944, as he was sent with other prisoners back to Italy.

"We promised that we would write and we did, for two years," she said. "I felt that I was committed to him."

Back home in Padua, Italian girls teased Bruno about his American sweetheart.

"The girls in Italy would laugh at you when you said you had a girlfriend back in America," he said. "They would say: 'She's not going to come and visit you.'"

But Gabriella did, and she brought her mother.

"It had been 20 years since my mother was back home," she said. "In September of 1946 we went over on a Liberty ship. It took 14 days."

Sue Gentile, Lelio Tomasina's love, sailed for Italy, too. In time, many of the American girlfriends followed their soldier sweethearts across the Atlantic and made good on their promises to marry.

On Dec. 9, 1946, Gabriella and Bruno were married.

"I stayed over there for a year and I didn't want to come back. I didn't have the personal comforts I was used to here, but I got used to it," Gabriella said. "I was young and it was a great adventure. There was no car; Bruno had a bicycle and I would sit sideways on it and that's how we traveled around. It was great fun. But everything in Italy was bombed out from the war so we decided to come back."

Many of the former POWs and their new wives later immigrated back to the United States, and after almost 50 years, Gabriella and Bruno are one of about a half-dozen of the POW couples still living in the Baltimore area. Bruno still works part time at his Eastern Avenue barbershop.

Said Gabriella, gazing lovingly at Bruno not long ago over a plate of pasta: "If you gave me the chance to go back to those times, I wouldn't change anything."

February 21, 1993

Bawlmer — don't you love it, hon?

CHECK OUT DEM PLATES, HON!

When Dave Desmarais looks in his rearview mirror, he often sees people in the car behind him pointing at his beat-up Subaru.

Motorists following Mr. Desmarais get all worked up when they see his celebration of a way of life emblazoned on vanity license plates.

The tags on the '82 Subaru scream: BAWLMER.

Bawlmer: the colloquial slurring of the jewel on the Patapsco.

Bawlmer: the unself-conscious universe where people affectionately call friends and strangers "hon"; where rowhouse dwellers paint their window screens so people can't look in on hot summer nights and see them sitting in front of a fan in their underwear; where the Baltimore Colts Marching Band plays on and on nearly a decade after its team left town.

As the city's population dwindles with each burial of another old-timer from the working class and each moving van that hauls yet another family over the city line, Bawlmer shrinks toward an existence solely in memory, folklore and Dave Desmarais' license plates.

"It's a way of letting people know that I love the city," says Mr. Desmarais, a 35-year-old resident of Arabia Avenue in Northeast Baltimore. "I don't pretend to be the epitome of the Baltimore 'hon' person, but I'm not poking fun either. When Motor Vehicles [Administration] said you could put seven characters on a tag instead of six, I rushed down to claim the plate.

"Of course, a lot of people don't get it."

Dave Desmarais didn't get it for years.

With a French-Canadian father from New England and a Pennsylvanian mother, Mr. Desmarais moved to Baltimore at age 4 and grew up in Northwood. While young Dave had everything a kid might need, the boy was so culturally impoverished that by age 18 he had yet to eat a steamed crab or vacation in Ocean City.

This is a guy who introduces himself as "Dave, from Baltimore" when he's out-of-town?

"I've got this BAWLMER tag," he says, "but I don't have the deep, deep roots."

It wasn't until he left Calvert Hall High School in 1976 to study at

Randolph-Macon College in Ashland, Va., that the idea of Baltimore as a place unique upon the Earth began to enchant Mr. Desmarais.

"I knew I was a true Baltimorean when I found myself defending the city against people who didn't know anything about it," he says. "I began to get this emotional sense: 'Hey, I'm from Baltimore,' and decided to educate myself so I could defend it with some knowledge."

To that end, he wrote a college paper on the city's Inner Harbor and dollar-house renaissance and, after graduating in 1980, he returned to the burg he had so viscerally defended — home to Baltimore to explore in person what he mostly knew from books.

"I walked and drove everywhere. The harbor is the pretty face that people fall in love with, but I fell in love with the personality beyond the harbor," Mr. Desmarais says. "I went through all of the western part of the city, all of the forests in Leakin Park and Dickeyville. I walked the old Ma and Pa [Maryland & Pennsylvania] railroad line from North Avenue through Wyman Park and over to Cold Spring Lane through Roland Park, talking to people along the way and taking notes."

After immersing himself in the historic Baltimore of Mount Vernon and Bolton Hill, Mr. Desmarais began wandering the city's "industrial wilds," nosing his way along Erdman Avenue, North Point Boulevard — areas he has yet to exhaust — and stretches of Canton waterfront not yet transformed into marinas and condominiums.

"A lot of these places have been cut up by highways," he says. "I like to investigate the parts in between, the remnants."

Dave Desmarais' adventures take place between trips to pick up and drop off clothes for Park Charles Cleaners, his downtown business. If recently you found yourself behind him in traffic and hankered to see just where BAWLMER leads, you might have been delivered to the fabled Sip & Bite diner on Boston Street, a crab house in Dundalk or Mr. Desmarais' latest discovery: Morrell Park and the communities along Washington Boulevard.

Mr. Desmarais first glimpsed the area from the sterile elevation of Interstate 95, a modern highway of convenience that allows people to travel quickly without having to stop or meet anyone.

"I like to get off the highway just to look around," he says. "I saw a neighborhood that I knew nothing about just sitting there. I don't have any great revelations about Morrell Park to share except that it has some nice homes and some run-down areas. But it's exciting to stumble across a piece of the city I didn't know before."

And when Mr. Desmarais is entertaining out-of-town guests, exploration gives way to tried-and-true touchstones such as the ruby magnificence of the Domino Sugar sign in Locust Point.

"I like to tell them it's a neon sign the size of a football field," he says. "No one ever believes it."

As Mr. Desmarais roams the streets and alleys of Crabtown — thrilled now and then to find himself idling next to the car with DUNDALK vanity plates — does he detect a wane in the city's idiosyncratic pulse?

"I think the 'hon' way of life is disappearing," he says. "The hons are leaving the city and moving out to White Marsh and Perry Hall. The hon stereotype [derived from white ethnics] is the Bawlmer stereotype. The people in Roland Park don't talk that way, and they've been entrenched forever. Blacks don't talk that way, and they've been here as long as anybody."

The "hon" part, says Mr. Desmarais, is the fun part.

Having worked with a local preservation group, his community association and the Downtown Partnership merchants association, he knows that the erosion of Bawlmer is nothing compared to the erosion of Baltimore.

"It takes a certain kind of person to live in the city by choice these days. I live and work in the city as a matter of principle," he says. "But the school system is dying and people get murdered every day — I don't cower from crime, but the deterioration of the neighborhoods and the flight of the middle class, that's the real tragedy.

"Young people like me buy their first homes in the city and then leave when their kids get ready to go to school," says Mr. Desmarais, who is single and certain, for now, that he would remain in town if he has school-age children.

"We've got to reverse the population decline. We've got to pay attention to the neighborhoods, the schools and the libraries."

August 29, 1993

160

Scavenging for art

THE TREASURE DAVID KLEIN SEEKS RESEMBLES HIS BELOVED BALTIMORE: old and worn, perhaps discarded too hastily; yet resilient, with enough life and character left to warrant salvation.

David Klein rescues wood, weathered wood dappled with paint.

He scavenges in alleys and Dumpsters and abandoned buildings; discerns the gems — like pale blue shelving from a long-gone confectionary on South Eden Street — and takes it home to make furniture.

"I dig taking something that was once and making it happen again," he says.

From the place where Mr. Klein's imagination meets a pile of trash come cabinets and beds, tables, hutches and benches; sturdy pieces of art that sell for $6,000 to $12,000 and make their way into galleries from New York to L.A., the *New York Times Magazine* and homes in Guilford.

Yet the adventure is as much about Baltimore — where he has lived for all of his 52 years — as it is about wood. "My wife wants to know what I do all day," he says. "I tell her: 'Run around having fun.'"

The fun started in the 1940s in a Lithuanian neighborhood on Hollins Street, where he sold shopping bags at the old open-air market for a nickel apiece and got a good whipping for shooting BBs at the windows of his alma mater, St. Peter the Apostle grade school.

"I came from a neighborhood, and when you're born into a neighborhood, you have a feel for the city," he says. "I have a bizarre affinity for anything old. Baltimore's definitely the old and thank God for what little of it we have left."

A recent journey through what is left began at Mr. Klein's Hampden studio and wended through Charles Village and Pigtown on a southbound route to narrow waterfront streets named Cooksie and Cuba.

Along the way, he passed and passed up great piles of wood and furniture. He can tell if it came from a basement or a roof, if it was window trim or door jamb and, most importantly, whether it's worth getting out of the truck for.

What he prizes is wainscoting, porch ceilings, floor boards and wide, straight planks with paint peeling to reveal another color: yellow, pink, gray, blue, white or green.

"I go with color as I find it," he says. "Green must be an easy color for people to live with [because] most of the wood I have has some kind of green on it."

Better yet are surprises — like the Canton rowhouse's wall of wainscoting that helped persuade Mr. Klein to leave straight carpentry for art. "We were tearing out this kitchen and I found some beautiful wood behind cheesy $2 paneling," he says. "I took it home and used it for the back of a cabinet."

Some places, like the garage at the corner of McHenry and South Carey streets, remind him of past bonanzas. "I can't go to the lumber yard for this stuff," he says. "My stuff has to be found."

His savvy for where to look comes from the friends and hobbies and jobs he's had since graduating from Edmondson High School: photographer of South Broadway vagrants in the mid-1960s; owner of downtown hippie "head shops" in the late 1960s; old-school theatrical agent in the '70s with his father, Irv Klein; seller of matchbook ads and builder of bars, making a buck where a buck could be made.

"I beat around for 20 years, never knew what I was doing," he says. "Whatever came along, I'd go with it until I got bored."

Until he discovered — after playing around with planks from a century-old barn in Harford County — that wood and the things you can do with it had never bored him.

"I realized, after doing it for 20 years, that I was a woodworker," he says.

While between jobs in 1987, he stumbled across a copy of *American Craft* in a Belair Road junk shop. Inside were photos of furniture "that rocked me through every nerve in my body."

It was the work of Stephen Whittlesey, a Cape Cod artist who uses barn wood and planks from lobster boats and bunk houses. But the initial thrill led Mr. Klein into a blue funk — at the moment he realized what he really wanted to do with his life, he saw that someone else was already famous for it.

When his depression passed, Mr. Klein picked up a crowbar and went looking for wood.

He wanders through neighborhoods that thrived in his youth but are now decimated by poverty and crime. Two guys with grocery carts at the city's old public school headquarters on 25th Street, a fire-damaged building being torn down for a supermarket, offer Mr. Klein a hand, but he just waves them on before disappearing into the burned hulk.

He emerges a few minutes later, ecstatic. "Oh, baby!" he cries. "This place is a mother lode — it's a treasure trove! There's enough wood in here for the rest of my life. Why should it be buried forever when I can preserve it? It's up to me to pull out the beauty."

May 3, 1995

Canton's 'crazy ladies'

THE CHITTER CHATTERS SAVE THEIR RETIREMENT NICKELS FOR BUS TRIPS TO Wildwood, N.J., but they don't get in the water. As 77-year-old Dolores Rogers puts it: "Nobody's seeing my body but the undertaker."

The group gets together once a week to gossip (but not in an ugly way), and every so often, between bingo and a nice ham and cheese sandwich with a deviled egg on the side, they'll lock a lifelong friend in the bathroom just for the hoot of seeing the door handle jiggle in vain.

"Crazy ladies," says a woman who has watched this crew in action for years. "They're all going back to the nut house tonight."

Wild women, these Chitter Chatters.

For the past 30 years, in the long Baltimore tradition of neighborhood pleasure clubs, a group of women in Canton has been getting together every Tuesday night in a century-old saloon at the corner of Decker and Fait avenues.

"Just to have something to do," says Dolly Fuchs, who founded the club with Bessie Sibiski in 1965 and is known for her crude gags, like the blow-up doll she often hangs out of the window on bus trips to moon passing motorists.

"Chitter-chattering," explains Mrs. Sibiski.

Dues are $2 a week, an extra 25 cents each goes into a "sick fund" to buy flowers or a fruit basket when someone is on the mend, a 50-50 raffle keeps petty cash flush, and getting in is as easy as having a current member vouch for you.

At its peak in the 1970s, the club had 23 members, but is now down to 10. They can't remember turning anyone down, and the record shows that once you become a Chitter Chatter, you'll most likely die before you quit.

"When we had the bigger group, there were a lot more widows," said Mrs. Fuchs, who has been president of the club for 19 years, even after moving to Parkville with her husband when their children were growing up.

The only member who doesn't live within walking distance of the bar, Mrs. Fuchs says of East Baltimore: "Highlandtown is most in my heart. I never got real close to my neighbors out here. My closest friends are still in Highlandtown."

How have they lasted so long?

"No men in the club to give us aggravation," says Janet Biedronski, who at 53 is one of the youngest members.

163

This week, they got together to celebrate the 80th birthday of their oldest member, a charter Chitter named Frances Rohlfing, who packed hominy into tin cans at a neighborhood factory until it shut down when she was 79.

"I'm hanging in there," says Mrs. Rohlfing, who received "a working apron" and bubble bath from the club as birthday presents.

Crowded around a row of small red saloon tables pushed together, the ladies rave about how moist Renee Bollack's mandarin orange cake is — "Ain't that good cake?" — and remind each other that they're not as young as they used to be.

"We used to close the bar at 2 o'clock, now we're home in bed by 10," says Mrs. Rogers. "In the old days we'd have a few drinks and do the chicken dance around the pole in the middle of the bar."

The club meets in a side cubbyhole off the main barroom, and the whole place is not much bigger than the parlor of a Patterson Park rowhouse. A buffet lines the wall at the once-a-month "social," and on the other weeks, a tumbler of bingo numbers stands at the end of the row of tables.

"It's their life, what they look forward to. Once they get in the club, the only way they get out is die," says Gary Sibiski, the oldest of the Sibiski children at 52. "We've talked about getting a pool table, but it ain't going in there. It's got to be that lineup of little tables."

An offshoot of the neighborhood's old Mother Seton Club, the Chatters began in November 1965 when Mrs. Sibiski and Mrs. Fuchs began knocking on doors to see if any women wanted to get together on a regular basis.

Then, as now, the headquarters was Hen's, the unmarked bar at Decker and Fait where Bess and Henry Sibiski raised five kids on the second floor. Legend has it that Wild Bill Hickok drank there when his Wild West Show pitched a tent on a vacant lot, back in the days before the east side of Canton was part of the city.

Hen's still looks as if Wild Bill would be comfortable throwing back a shot of liquor there, with a beautiful wooden bar adorned with a pair of steer horns 6 feet wide, a round kitchen table under the window, simple stools and a tin ceiling.

In the old days, you could take home a half-gallon of beer in your own bucket for 60 cents. Now, a can of Budweiser goes for $1.40.

"The man who told me the Wild Bill story said he stood on our steps and watched the Baltimore fire in 1904," says Mr. Sibiski. "I don't know if the tin ceiling was here when they built the place, but it was up when I bought the bar in 1957. I think it's been washed twice since then."

About the same time the Chitter Chatters got rolling, a bunch of guys who liked to quench their thirst at Hen's started the Potomac Pleasure Club.

"Some of them said our club would never last because women couldn't stay together," remembers Dolly Fuchs. "Well, we're still here after 30 years and they folded after two."

"They wanted to merge with us," says Mrs. Rohlfing. "But we wouldn't have it."

February 2, 1996

'El Greco'

SOMETIMES HE IS EL GRECO AND SOMETIMES HE'S THE ELECTRO MECHANIC, but always he remains Theodoris Roditis.

When elbow-deep in the guts of a half-century-old Singer sewing machine, Mr. Roditis is the Electro Mechanic. When composing electronic symphonies on keyboards buried inside his Fells Point repair shop, he answers to El Greco.

His credo?

"I can fix," said the 64-year-old native of Rhodes, Greece, eyes smiling, his accent almost undecipherably thick.

Not only can he fix almost anything, Mr. Roditis will patch your sewing machine for a song and throw in a tape of his soothing compositions to calm you while you run a zig-zag stitch.

That's what happened to Dolly Jacobs and Linda Weiderhold, sisters from the Eastside who savored the full El Greco/Electro Mechanic experience last month.

"When I walked in his store, I almost dropped over," said Mrs. Jacobs. "There's only a pathway through all that stuff, but he knows where everything is."

Mr. Roditis had already fixed a sewing machine for her for $45 (about an hour's worth of labor at other service centers) and the family decided to revisit his shop after taking in a crab cake dinner at the Sip & Bite restaurant.

Mrs. Jacobs wanted to pick up a used typewriter, hundreds of which Mr. Roditis repairs and exports to Pakistan, along with old bicycles. Mrs. Weiderhold had hauled in a broken sewing machine of her own, and they wanted their mother to meet the eccentric Teddy Kennedy look-alike who had been so nice to them.

"He gave me extra needles and bobbins, and he put a plate on it for me to do zig-zags," said Mrs. Weiderhold, who had her Capitol machine fixed for $55. "And then we went home and listened to his tape."

The family is making copies of Teo's tape — dreamy, synthesized keyboard music with an almost New Age feel to it, a sound he describes as "my personality" to pass around to relatives.

"This is my religion, you know that," he said of music, which he began studying in grade school on the trumpet. He also plays the violin. "I don't work for money, just love, to work for my music. I don't make a million, just enough for living."

For the past seven years after spending five in Philadelphia, where he has an ex-wife and two grown sons, nearly all of Mr. Roditis' life has taken place behind the glass storefront at 1742 Eastern Ave.

The narrow first-floor shop, which doubles as his home, is stuffed with parts from old cash registers, broken adding machines, amplifiers and cassette decks.

A wooden pole is thick with eyeglasses, light issues from weird sci-fi lamps with stalactite-shaped shades that look as if they have fallen from the ceiling of Luray Caverns, and a revolving display case is crowded with unused tubes of watercolor paints.

No spot is free of clutter: buttonhole makers, staplers, accordions, a Seal-A-Meal machine, violins, books, baby dolls, snare drums and tape dispensers.

But mostly there are sewing machines, lime-green Singers from the 1950s and jet black ones with gold-leaf trim from the 1920s.

The sewing machines are for sale. The dolls are not.

Dolls, he maintains, carry the spirit of people, and such a thing should not be sold.

"Buy a sewing machine," he says. "But no buy my dolls."

In the sewing industry, mechanics are traditionally known as adjusters.

The ability to fix a variety of machines from the treadle models Isaac Merrit Singer pioneered in the 1850s, to post-World War II electrics built inside cabinets, to the latest computerized stitchers, is a rare skill.

"There are very, very few good mechanics that can cover a wide range of machines. Most adjusters have retired, and they haven't been replaced," said Jim Slaten, who runs a Singer dealership and sewing machine museum in Oakland, Calif. "It's a handed-down kind of thing."

Mr. Roditis, who is better on old models than on newer ones, said he learned his trade working for a Singer outlet in Athens, Greece, for 25 years.

In Baltimore, he has worked for J. Dashew & Co., a distributor of machinery to the garment industry for nearly 100 years, and Acme Pad Co., founded in 1938 to make shoulder pads for men's and women's clothing.

"He worked in our repair shop," remembered Alvin Gorn, a Dashew vice president, adding that anyone who talked to Mr. Roditis for more than five minutes knew that he was passionate about music. "He had a certain grandiosity about him. I can't tell you why he struck me that way, but you felt it," he said.

Since being laid off by Acme in 1992, Mr. Roditis has worked only for himself, making ends meet with shipments of typewriters and bicycles to

Pakistan on Third World vessels that call on Baltimore every three or four months.

Why Pakistan?

"Poor people, no buy new," he explained. "A lot of English schools in Pakistan."

As his own boss, he locks the front door to his shop anytime he likes to indulge in his music, sitting deep in the center of his great pile of stuff at his true workbench, a stack of keyboards littered with blank composition paper, inspiration coming from such diverse sources as modern Greek poetry and personal ads in the *East Baltimore Guide*.

If the words are powerful enough. he said, putting his hand to his heart, they stir him to "touch my keys."

In addition to the money he earns repairing sewing machines, he makes $10 to $15 for every typewriter he sends overseas and about $5 for each bicycle. But in 12 years of writing music in the United States, which takes up so much of his time that he claims not to have many friends, he hasn't made a dime from his compositions.

"Today I am a poor composer," he said. "But maybe not tomorrow."

March 22, 1996

Chapter 10

Readings

On dark city nights, stories provide the illumination

Downtown on West Baltimore Street, as the hands of the Bromo Seltzer tower clock move toward a cold midnight, men in black leather and thick gold chains duck into Crazy John's for greasy sausage and video games.

Street scavengers go over the day's haul of aluminum cans, slump their matted heads on each other and rummage through plastic bags. A few feet away, inside the Eldorado Lounge, men drinking liquor watch women without clothes dance on top of the bar.

Five tall stories above the city that reads, in the vast and peeling carcass of an old garment factory sweatshop, young minds gather to entertain themselves with literature.

"He had sworn to quit the neighborhood of man and hide himself in deserts, but she had not," declares a bearded young man with the crescent of a silver moon hanging from his ear, reading aloud by candlelight to a silent group of listeners. "And she, who in all probability was to become a thinking and reasoning animal, might refuse to comply with a compact made before her creation.

"They might hate each other," he continues, seated at a table made from a derelict wooden door balanced on empty tar buckets. "The creature who already lived loathed his own deformity, and might he not conceive a greater abhorrence for it when it came before his eyes in the female form? She also might turn in disgust from him to the superior beauty of man; she might quit him, and he be again alone, exasperated by the fresh provocation of being deserted by one of his own species."

Another Friday night. Another chapter of Mary Shelley's "Frankenstein."

The weekly readings — organized by poet Raphael Dagold, 23, and sculptor Marc Braun, 25 — began on New Year's Eve, and word of the readings has spread through friends of friends and homemade posters tacked up around town inviting anyone with interest to present themselves at midnight at 322 W. Baltimore St. "It's a great story to read out loud," says Mr. Dagold, who photocopies his poetry and gives it away.

"We were trying to find something that would tie together every week," says Mr. Braun, whose sculpture includes pieces of iron fashioned into a huge wrench with a score of antique wrenches welded inside. "You know, like, 'stay tuned.'"

Attendance varies, from a half dozen to 15. The listeners are usually known to each other, people from stray orbits circling the Maryland Institute of Art.

When the readings started, they doubled as pot-luck dinners. But, says Mr. Braun, money comes to artists when it comes. While they don't have food anymore, the story endures.

In 4,500 square feet of darkness illuminated by candles — just enough light to make out the shadows of old beauty parlor chairs and cats scratching pale green paint from walls of hammered tin — the audience drinks cheap beer, coffee out of ceramic bowls, and wine from juice glasses. Several listen with eyes closed.

Mr. Dagold, who was smitten with the story of the lonely, loveless monster while an English major at Swarthmore College, lays his unabridged Marvel Comics edition on the table and continues.

He becomes the book's narrator, Dr. Victor Frankenstein, creator of the monster. Here, in Chapter 20, the good doctor has gone back on a promise to build a mate for the fiend and is haunted by the price the world will pay for his decision.

"The night passed away and the sun rose from the ocean; my feelings became calmer, if it may be called calmness when the violence of rage sinks into the depths of despair," reads Mr. Dagold. "I left the house, the horrid scene of last night's contention, and walked on the beach of the sea, which I almost regarded as an insuperable barrier between me and my fellow creatures... If I returned it was to be sacrificed or to see those whom I most loved die under the grasp of a demon whom I had myself created."

By the end of the chapter, a villager has been found murdered, and Dr. Frankenstein is being brought before a magistrate to answer for the death.

"Whoa!" shouts Mr. Braun. "So the monster is framing him again!"

"It looks like it," says Mr. Dagold, closing the book as a discussion begins.

Is the monster a symbol for the dehumanization of man in the industrial age?

Who is more depraved, the monster or the madman who made him?

And isn't the original fiend a far cry from TV's Herman Munster?

Not everyone hangs around to fish for answers. Richard Bolan, 41, and Brien P. Williams, 32, head for the door when the chapter has closed.

Mr. Bolan, who has attended three of the readings and brought Mr. Williams for the first time, says it isn't the story that is important to him.

"I just flow with the words," he says. "I meditate to the voice and the candles."

Mr. Williams feels differently.

"I was following the narrative, probably more closely than if I'd been reading it myself," he says. "Instead of being aware of the structure and the underlying meaning, I was just following the story. It was refreshing."

They walk down 95 steps that make up the five flights of stairs to the street, where the drama on the sidewalk hasn't changed much in two hours.

Tough teenagers zip between Japanese sports cars parked curbside and the all-night fluorescence of Crazy John's, the men in the doorways remain unconscious, and the Eldorado's doors are being locked.

Upstairs, Mr. Dagold begins to read a poem left for him by Mr. Bolan as the city that reads waits for dawn.

April 21, 1989

'Guide' captures a flavor
that suits east side tastes

WHERE CAN YOU FIND BETTY BOOP, MIMI DIPIETRO AND A MAN WITH HIS hands tied behind his back running naked down Conkling Street?

In the pages of the *East Baltimore Guide*, of course.

Such combinations of characters — along with senior citizen news, rhetoric from local politicians, advice on skin problems, crime reports, birthday wishes and hundreds of cramped column inches of advertisement — have made the *Guide* an east side icon as enduring as the pagoda in Patterson Park.

Men sentenced to prison have been known to subscribe by mail just to keep up with the old neighborhood.

"They call it the Bible out here," says publisher H. Milton Lasson, a balding, spry man of 70 who smokes cigars, tends to wear a hat over his white hair and has owned the paper since 1939. "It's the bible of East Baltimore."

It is an east side bible, ironically owned by a man who has resided all his life in Northwest Baltimore — a prosperous give-away tabloid that earns Mr. Lasson more money than he cares to acknowledge.

Since it began as the *Shoppers Guide* in 1927, the paper has been bringing news from down the alley and around the corner to the row houses of Little Italy, Highlandtown, Fells Point, Canton and most areas in between.

Each Thursday morning, 30,000 copies of the *Guide* are delivered to nearly every residential and business door in Southeast Baltimore by the same people who give out supermarket circulars.

And even though the *East Baltimore Guide's* free, if a resident doesn't get his copy — or if it's sopping wet — *Guide* management hears about it the same day.

"One hundred percent market penetration in the East Baltimore area where we distribute," says Jack Rumel, who spent 27 years selling advertising for the *News-American* and joined the *Guide* about a year after the *News* folded. "That's President Street on the west, the harbor on the south, East Point on the east, and Monument Street to the north."

Sometime between 8 and 8:30 every Thursday morning, people begin gathering outside the *Guide* offices on Conkling Street near Fleet Street to get the latest poop when the doors open.

Readers — young ones who dart in, but mostly older ones like John who take things a bit slower — come in throughout the day, say hello to 23-year-old classified ad manager Debbie Richardson, who sits up front behind a desk, and grab a few copies to take to churches and neighborhoods around town.

Every job Mrs. Richardson has ever held, including her current one, came through *Guide* classifieds.

"I got all my jobs out of the *Guide*," she says. "Up Goldenberg's warehouse on Conkling Street when I was 19, then I worked at Dr. Cerveny's — he's a dentist right down the street, I got him outta the *Guide* — then I worked at USF&G, got that job outta the *Guide*, and then I got this job outta the *Guide*."

Classified ads cost $3.20 a line, with a total of 35 letters or spaces per line. The price goes up 50 cents every June 1.

"We accept almost everything," said Mrs. Richardson, pausing while taking an ad over the telephone.

Particularly popular items are photographs and captions announcing birthday and anniversary wishes, excellent report cards, engagements, memorial tributes, first communions, novenas and military achievements.

An example: "Happy First Birthday — Timothy John Wickman will celebrate his first birthday on June 30. He will have a party on June 24 at his grandparents' house in Dundalk ... Happy birthday Timothy, We love you bunches!"

Around this and other features, such as the "Did you know?" trivia cartoon, recipes, and editor John Cain's "Raisin' Cain" column, is news.

Some of the stories are the *Guide's*. Many others are rewritten from the local dailies.

Mr. Lasson, who took over the *Guide* with his late brother, Nelson Lasson, 50 years ago when the family bought out the Boone Press Co. at 129 West Barre St., has sole responsibility for the eclectic stories that run into each other on page one.

The short, one-column stories sometimes number up to a dozen and span the world of news from the Steven Spielberg-Amy Irving divorce to manhunts for homicide suspects from South Exeter Street.

"If you just had one or two long stories on the front page, it would be very blah," said Mr. Lasson, who clings tightly to a cultivated low profile. "I personally think that the *Guide* front page is very attractive."

There are no editorials, but since Mr. Cain became editor in April 1988 the *Guide* has pursued news about development along the Canton waterfront far more intently than it did before he arrived.

A 49-year-old Canton native who returned to Baltimore several years ago after working as an actor in New York, Mr. Cain says that his very active membership in the Waterfront Coalition, an alliance of east side neighborhood groups seeking to control waterfront growth, does not compromise his objectivity.

"I wanted the job to put real community news in the paper," he said.

"I told Mr. Lasson I would benefit the paper because I'm on the inside of the development fight. There might be a slant one way or the other, but if I'm going to harangue, I do it in my column."

A recent harangue came to the defense of Virginia Baker, the longtime head of the Mayor's Office of Adventures in Fun, whose job was recently threatened by city budget cuts.

"You know, hon," wrote Mr. Cain, "these characters in City Hall get dumber by the day."

Councilman John A. Schaefer apparently isn't one of them.

Although each of the First District councilmen receives frequent notice in the paper, Mr. Schaefer has long been known as a close friend of Mr. Lasson and gets nothing but positive publicity in the *Guide*.

In contrast, political observers believe the *Guide's* repeated publication of letters critical of former Councilman Donald G. Hammen led to Mr. Hammen's defeat in the last city elections.

Recently the *Guide* gave John Schaefer credit for single-handedly passing the five-cent reduction in city property taxes in a front page story headlined, "Councilman John Schaefer Engineers 5-Cent Property Tax Reduction Thru City Council." In fact, he was just one of several council members who supported the cut.

To which Mr. Lasson responds: "The people in East Baltimore don't know [the outside] councilmen. They know John Schaefer and he's the head of the budget committee."

Such inconsistencies don't appear to bother the publisher, and the readers and advertisers keep coming.

"Even I wonder what makes the paper tick," said Mr. Lasson. "Sometimes I am amazed at the demand."

July 9, 1989

A long-lost jewel of Union Square
may glow again as a beacon hope

RUSSELL BAKER REMEMBERS THE LIBRARY OF HIS BALTIMORE CHILDHOOD AS "a wonderful, mysterious place with cathedral beams in the ceiling — I tried to read my way through the whole place one summer."

It was the late 1930s, and the future writer's dreamland stood at the corner of Hollins and Calhoun streets. Old branch No. 2 of the Enoch Pratt Free Library, just down the block from H. L. Mencken's house, was one of the four original libraries bequeathed by Mr. Pratt to the city in 1886.

"I remember those great ceilings and the sense of richness on the shelves," said Mr. Baker, a *New York Times* columnist and former *Sun* reporter whose book "Growing Up" won a Pulitzer Prize in 1983. "The library did a wonderful job of putting their own hard bindings on books, lovely colors: dark blues and greens and deep reds. The shelves were a medieval tapestry of color."

In his own youth, apprentice curmudgeon Henry Mencken was likewise enchanted by the world within the library's Romanesque arches, high-peaked slate roof, terra cotta panels and floral chimney decorations.

In a chapter of his memoirs titled "Larval Stage of a Bookworm," Mr. Mencken wrote: "I had a card before I was nine and began an almost daily harrying of the virgins at the delivery desk."

Yet, if you visited 1401 Hollins St. today you would find a sad, boarded-up building weary from its 108 years; a dark haunt strewn with surplus furniture and junk: odd hand tools, old air conditioners, a roll of chicken wire, kitchen sinks, television sets and rusty frying pans. Replaced in 1964 by a bigger branch library at the corner of Hollins and Payson streets, old No. 2 housed Urban Services workers for about 20 years before languishing as a Pratt storage shed.

Now, 30 years after its shelves were emptied of books, the structure described by preservationists as the most important building in the Union Square neighborhood, could return to its original purpose with the help of a $125,000 state grant.

Along with the Union Square Improvement Association and the nonprofit Neighborhood Design Center, the Pratt hopes to resurrect the building as a library with a single purpose: community redevelopment.

And though at least another $175,000 is needed, the principals expect renovations to begin with roof repairs in the fall.

"Libraries have never done anything like this before; they've never seen neighborhood groups as their client base," said James C. Welbourne, assistant director of the Pratt. "Union Square is trying to take back its neighbor-, hood and they're asking institutions like the library not to leave."

By itself, the Pratt is unwilling and incapable of spending the estimated $300,000 necessary to repair a building that is no longer a part of its neighborhood-branch system.

Still, the Pratt has been reluctant to abandon the fabled edifice and has kept up with minimal maintenance, spending $13,000 in the last year for a boiler and furnace repairs. So, when Union Square leaders and members of Neighborhood Design Center pitched a plan to bring No. 2 back to life with volunteer labor and outside funding, the Pratt listened.

Under the plan, the Pratt would retain ownership of the building and fill it with urban development literature, including classics on fund raising, and an electronic database of community programs from across the country.

The Neighbor Line database eventually will be accessible from other Pratt branches and city agencies.

"Around that core collection we'll add titles that particularly relate to Baltimore as well as documents from the city planning department," Mr. Welbourne said. "And there will probably be some aspect of Mencken as well."

The Neighborhood Design Center, which aids communities statewide and helped plan the redevelopment of the old Green Spring Dairy property on 41st Street, will staff the space, use it for offices and play host to redevelopment workshops.

Louise Hintze, who works out of the building as a free-lance social worker, will stay put to continue her work. And Union Square will get needed public meeting space for children and adults, while erasing some of the blight in its midst.

The design center, said executive director Ellen Casale, will bring in neighborhood groups to brainstorm with builders and architects on problems ranging from making use of old industrial sites to shoring up bad alleys.

"This building is a peach — it's a little shabby, but structurally sound," said Phil Hildebrandt of the Union Square Improvement Association.

Said Ferrier Stillman, president-elect of the design center's board: "One of the reasons we chose this as our new home, instead of, say, revitalizing a bus station, is because libraries connote the importance of education — a library is something everyone can be part of."

May 7, 1994

177

'It was like a time capsule'

THE WELL-INTENTIONED ARE ALWAYS DONATING SACKS OF BOOKS TO THE
Baltimore Hebrew University on Park Heights Avenue. It usually happens
once relatives have cleaned up after a loved one has died. The books are
often of little value.

One morning this August, a small, elderly man with a Yiddish accent
appeared in the school library and asked for some help carrying in books.
There were about a dozen heavy packages, each carefully wrapped in brown
paper and tied with cord.

After he'd unloaded everything — some 40 books and numerous pam-
phlets, telegrams, posters and artworks — the man asked that no one find out
from whom they'd come. The university knows, but won't identify him
except to say he was an Eastern European Jew who escaped the Holocaust.

"He treated it like it was something holy. I don't think he knew what to do
with them after all these years," said Steven Fine, acting director of the university's Meyerhoff Library. "For us, it was like a time capsule had popped
into our hands."

The packages were carted into the staff room, the twine was cut and it was
discovered, said Fine, "that we'd been given books from the concluding
years of the Holocaust — Jewish books that bore the stamp of the Nazis the
way Jews themselves did."

The man had delivered an odd trove of works from the 18th, 19th, and
20th centuries written in Hebrew, Yiddish, Latin, Aramaic, Hungarian,
Polish, French and German. It included books looted from Jewish libraries
in Europe and slated for an institute in the "New Germany" for the study of
a vanished race.

That race, of course, is the Jews, who because of the codified faith that has
sustained them for three millenniums have come to be known as the People
of the Book.

Inside the brown wrapping, Fine and the chief librarian, Elaine Mael,
found books wrapped again in American newspapers from 1952, as if read-
ied for a new home. That home was not found until now.

Others, like a commentary on the five books of Moses by the 19th-century

German rabbi Samson Raphael Hirsch, had been sent out for new bindings and were still sheathed in the bindery's tissue paper.

"No one had touched them since they came back from the bindery," said Fine.

"It was eerie," added Mael. "I couldn't stop talking about it for days."

Several title pages in a four-volume, early 18th-century Amsterdam edition of the "Mishna Torah" by the fabled Jewish philosopher Maimonides are marred by the official Third Reich stamp of an eagle atop a swastika.

Of particular interest are posters of old tombstones from Jewish Spain and of special irony are volumes of the Gemara, the monumental records and minutes of Jewish legal debates conducted by the faith's ancient sages. The set given to Baltimore Hebrew was printed by the American government in Germany after the Nazi surrender.

The chief rabbi of the U.S. occupied zone dedicated that work to the American army:

"This special edition published in the very land where, but a short time ago, everything Jewish and of Jewish inspiration was anathema, will remain a symbol of the indestructibility of the Torah."

Another book carries the seal of the Volozhin Yeshiva, once the leading Lithuanian institution for study of Jewish laws and custom. Others are stamped "Offenbach," the American military post where a huge depot of stolen books and other cultural material stolen from the Jews was assembled for return to their rightful owners at war's end.

By that time, many of the institutions from which they were stolen — an estimated 957 libraries, 375 archives, 531 research institutes and 402 museums, according to Holocaust scholar Philip Friedman — had been destroyed. Most of the private owners had been murdered.

The ownerless property was distributed to Judaic libraries and institutions, the majority of them in Israel and the United States, by Jewish Cultural Reconstruction Inc. of New York.

Fine said that Baltimore Hebrew University already owns other Offenbach booty, relatively marginal volumes dispersed after the big collections had been parceled out by Reconstruction Inc.

And while the most precious item in the recent gift is the 1708 Maimonides commentary, now valued at somewhere around $2,000, money is not the true measure of the donation, according to Fine.

"None of what we received is earth-shattering," said Fine. "But a lot of this was saved by acts of heroism, by Jews forced to work as Nazi librarians. Sometimes they got burned and their works didn't. This is their legacy — here we are some two generations removed from the Holocaust and things are still turning up on our doorstep."

October 9, 1996

Chapter 11

Local Heroes

East Baltimore 'hoodle' patrol keeps the streets clean

UNDESIRABLES BEWARE: REGINA'S RAIDERS STAND VIGILANT AGAINST ALL manner of "hoodles" intent on bringing down the quality of life in a small patch of East Baltimore near Patterson Park.

Regina Myers and her elderly band of a dozen or so community commandos have battled prostitutes, drugs and the people who sell and use them, absentee landlords and bars they find offensive.

"If we think we're right," said Mrs. Myers, 67, "we'll take on anybody."

"We got a nice place to live here," said Stanley W. Zielinski, 79, speaking of the area bounded by Washington Street on the west, Montford Avenue on the east, Gough Street to the north and Fleet Street to the south.

"But the only thing is, we got too many hoodles," said Mr. Zielinski, using the East-side vernacular for hooligans.

The group, now 10 years old, calls itself the "Concerned Citizens." It meets once a month in the Holy Rosary church hall on Chester Street.

"When anybody wants anything, we're always there," Mrs. Myers said. "We always try to solve things ourselves because — it's a heck of a thing — lawyers are so expensive."

The group's latest victory came earlier this month when it successfully petitioned the city against granting zoning that would have allowed the liscensing of a tattoo parlor at 2233 Eastern Ave.

Jeff Fogel, a veteran local tattoo artist who did not want to be interviewed, had plans to establish a tattoo parlor between Mike Weber's shoemaker shop and Joe Thomas' taxidermy business. That spot was last used to house the Hog's Breath Inn, which lost its license in 1984 after the Concerned Citizens teamed up with police to document liquor board violations.

According to Gil Rubin, director of zoning, the city Health Department had no objection — in fact, a health official testified that Mr. Fogel had operated a sanitary and trouble-free tattoo parlor on Howard Street for many years. The Fire Department had no objection and the city traffic department had no objection.

But the Concerned Citizens, along with area businesses and at least one church, wanted no part of it.

A carpet store, they said, would be OK; an ice cream parlor, wonderful; even another video store — but no tattoo parlor.

Fearing the spread of hepatitis and AIDS because of the needles and reluctant to face the kind of people they believed would come to Eastern Avenue in search of tattoos, the group gathered 123 signatures and took their fight to City Hall.

"I asked 15 people I know with tattoos, men and women, why they did it," said Mr. Thomas. "And they all said they were intoxicated when they got them."

"They have places on [The Block] for that kind of stuff. We're trying to raise families over here," said Gus Orfanidis, who runs a pizza shop at the end of the block. "In this neighborhood I want my kids to be able to go out there on the sidewalk and talk to people and make friends. I want a community here.

"I have nothing against tattoos, but let them go somewhere else. If I want a tattoo, I know where I can find them."

Mike Weber, 67, is proud of what he and his friends have accomplished, but he's a reluctant Raider.

"I'd rather be fishing," he said. "But we've had a lot of trouble here with prostitutes, both boys and girls, and we got that taken care of, and then we had the Hog's Breath that brought a lot of prostitutes and trouble.

"We try to keep the neighborhood as drug-free and prostitute-free as possible. I told [Mr. Fogel] we had nothing against him at all. He couldn't understand why the people didn't want tattoos here. We told him we weren't used to it."

The biggest item on the group's community wish list is a foot patrolman. They've been asking the Southeastern District commander for one for years, and they haven't given up.

December 19, 1989

Baltimore's maven of mischief

VIRGINIA S. BAKER STANDS AT THE CROSSROADS OF MONUMENT STREET AND Belnord Avenue and looks back through the long scope of the 20th century for the magical place of her youth.

"This," she says, "is where I learned all my tricks."

Her tricks were mastered during a 1930s East Baltimore childhood spent running the streets around her family's confectionery store. Back then everyone for blocks knew the kid who ruled the sidewalks on roller skates as Queenie.

It was a world of horseplay and monkeyshines that forged Miss Baker into Baltimore's undisputed, all-time champion of fun and games — a playground pioneer with 53 years at full throttle in the city's Department of Recreation and Parks. She is perhaps the only civil servant in America in charge of an office called Adventures in Fun.

Along the way, she has lasted through the administrations of nine Baltimore mayors, through the evolution of fun from spinning tops to virtual-reality video. She has worn out more pairs of tennis shoes than most people will ever own, while delivering entertainment and exercise to three generations of Baltimoreans.

The kids who were on the playground her first day on the job in 1940 are now the grandparents of the kids who come to her for soccer balls, board games and art supplies at the city's Clarence Du Burns Soccer Arena in Canton.

When Baltimore public-school students got their report cards in June, a note was slipped in with the grades — a memo telling families who to call for free activities to fill the idle hours of summer.

The phone number school officials gave out rings on Virginia Baker's desk.

Fun, as Miss Baker knows it, is simple: chicken-clucking, peanut-shucking and hog-calling contests; frog hops; turtle derbys; puppet shows and magic acts; an Aug. 2 swap day at the Broadway Market Square in Fells Point, where kids can trade old toys but not their brothers and sisters; and, in the same place, the annual Aug. 16 celebration of Elvis Presley.

All of it is for kids.

You see, the children of Baltimore have always been Virginia Baker's kids — the ones who screeched on swings, skinned their knees, and whooped and hollered and carried on outside the way they never could at home. Just the way little Queenie carried on back in an age when toys were simple and most of the games kids played came out of their heads.

In the age of Nintendo, it's hard to conjure a time when simple things were considered fun.

Yet, when Virginia Baker lines kids of the '90s up for beanbag tosses or sack races, they have a ball.

"A kid," she says, "is still a kid."

The foundation for a half-century of teaching kids how to get a healthy kick out of life was laid at the corner of East Monument Street and North Belnord Avenue — a sidewalk laboratory for a life's work of play.

And it was mixed up with enough mischief to give Huck Finn a run for his money through the narrow alleys of a long-ago Baltimore, a city fading away in old photo albums but vibrant in the memory of the 71-year-old woman who helped pioneer playground recreation in this town.

"We played every game you can imagine out here," she says during a visit back to the corner, looking around the place she called home from infancy until her father died in 1954.

"God, we had fun here!"

Queenie rode scooters.

Shot marbles.

Played tag.

Spun tops.

Made yo-yos sing and puppets dance.

She made kites out of newspapers and sticks.

"I used to fly a kite right here," she says, looking south on Belnord Avenue. "And I made the kite myself. I was 8 years old."

And she roller-skated from home to the Northeast Market near Johns Hopkins Hospital and back again.

She got black eyes from roughhousing, and the local butcher put beef on them to keep the swelling down.

Miss Baker is asked:

"Were you a bruiser?"

"Yeah," she says.

"Did you get into some scrapes?"

"Oh, yeah."

When Queenie disobeyed, fibbed, or otherwise landed her backside in hot water — which was not infrequent — her beloved skates were taken away as punishment.

Like the time she refused to tattle on the kid who threw a doughnut at the head of a diminutive neighborhood man with the unfortunate name of Mr. Bigger.

She says: "We used to hide behind corners and shout: 'Grow a little bigger!'"

Getting her skates back meant much to Queenie, who today remembers she wore out many wheels rolling around her neighborhood.

Schumann's is where Queenie used to buy her replacement skate wheels. "Cost me 7 cents a wheel," she says. "That's the trouble with kids today, they throw the skates away when the wheels wear out. You can go to a hardware store that sells the wheels."

Schumann's Hardware at Monument Street and Kenwood Avenue, a block from the confectionery store, is still in business today. But Miss Baker doesn't know that Schumann's doesn't sell skate wheels anymore. And Schumann's doesn't know of any hardware store that does. "You've got to be kidding," said a man who answered the phone there.

As a kid, Miss Baker collected matchbook covers and wagered hundreds of them at a time in card games of pitch, poker and pinochle down at Sprock's Garage on Lakewood Avenue.

"I'd be sitting on those white marble steps in the morning when the street-cleaning man would be coming through our area," she says. "I'd say, 'You want coffee?' And give him coffee and one of those good Czechoslovakian pastries. We became good friends. I told him about my match-cover collection and every day he'd bring me about 200 match covers he found cleaning the streets."

In 1940, a year after graduating from Eastern High School, Virginia Baker joined the Department of Recreation and Parks and was assigned to a Durham Street "tot lot" in Fells Point. There she began a playground ministry of making city life less harsh for thousands of Baltimore youngsters.

From Durham Street she made the rounds of playgrounds citywide; became the director of recreation in Patterson Park, where a center now is named in her honor; launched miniature boat regattas at wading pools all over town; and held Twister contests in War Memorial Plaza when the wacky tie-yourself-up-in-knots game swept the nation in the '60s.

Her knack for getting publicity swept her into City Hall in 1972 to head the Mayor's Office of Special Projects for her old buddy William Donald Schaefer.

Miss Baker's energy and gut-instinct for boosting the city made her a favorite of Mr. Schaefer back in the early renaissance days when he was mayor and "Baltimore is Best" was stenciled on every park bench in town.

In 1987, Kurt Schmoke moved her office from City Hall to the Broadway Recreation Pier. There, Miss Baker found volunteers to rebuild a battered roof-top playground; brought back the fabled "rocky boat" ride beloved by kids in the 1940s; and inspired the neighborhood to replace 410 lights that spell "CITY PIER BROADWAY" on the side of the building that faces the harbor.

When crews for Barry Levinson's television series, "Homicide: Life on the Street," made its headquarters at the Rec Pier, Miss Baker and her staff of three were moved to the Burns soccer arena, where she works to this day.

Looking back on her career, she says: "I've made a lot of kids happy. That's what I get paid for."

Virginia Baker's old neighborhood was just about new when she was born there in 1921. It was a community of Czechs and Poles and Germans and Bohemians when her parents opened their store at the corner of Belnord and Monument.

Her father, Frank Pecinka, changed his name to Baker when he came to America from Czechoslovakia. Her mother, Hattie, was a Baltimorean of Czechoslovakian descent.

Today, Virginia Baker's former stomping grounds between the Catholic parishes of St. Wenceslaus on Ashland Avenue and St. Elizabeth's on Baltimore Street are showing their age: The neighborhood looks poorer, the streets rougher, the residents more weary. The white marble steps at the Belnord Avenue entrance to the old Baker candy store, steps that now lead to the kitchen of a combination carryout/liquor store, sum up the look.

"Oh, golly gee, they didn't have those bumps in them when I was little," says Miss Baker. "They were beautiful. I used to use a pumice stone on them to keep them clean."

Tiles are missing from the front steps; signs advertising pizza and cold beer are taped to the front of the building; and black steel grating covers all of the windows except the ones that have been bricked up.

"It used to have pretty green and black glass in the front," says Miss Baker. "I had to wash those windows and I made sure at Halloween that nobody put soap on them."

Inside, the current owners serve customers from behind walls of thick, bullet-proof plastic. Immigrants from Korea, they don't speak English very well and are too busy making a living to pay much attention when Miss Baker shows them a picture of her father behind the counter in a white pharmacy jacket, boxes of El Producto cigars and candy behind him.

"Daddy mixed the syrup for the sodas and milkshakes and Mama cooked the chocolate for the sundaes," she says. "Boy, did this neighborhood smell good!"

Now, she laments: "Look, our beautiful windows, all cemented up now. I squirted this pavement about three times a day, and if a bad kid went by who gave me a hard time, they'd get the hose. I scrubbed these steps all the time. I played jacks and ball on the steps, waiting for the mailman. I was collecting stamps and corresponding with people all over the country. That hobby made me a good geography student."

The windows used to have painted screens in them and it was Queenie's job to take new screens up to the Oktavec family on Monument Street to have pictures drawn from Czechoslovakian postcards daubed on them.

A gaggle of neighborhood kids who wouldn't know Virginia Baker from Barbara Bush gather to gaze up at this grandmotherly-looking woman inspecting the neighborhood sub shop like it was some kind of big deal.

In a voice so provincial that Washington disc jockeys regularly put her on the radio just to let Washingtonians believe that all of Baltimore thinks and talks like Virginia Baker, she bellows:

"Hi, kids, I was born here!"

The children laugh and run away.

Miss Baker watches them squeal down the sidewalk and remembers: "My father would say to my mother: 'Oh, that Queenie, she's running the whole block!'"

She wants to come back and run it again, real soon.

She wants to make her old neighborhood jump again with a "Belnord Avenue Fun Day," a day to bring back all the days from 53 years in recreation.

A day that hasn't even been planned yet, but percolates off the top of Virginia Baker's busy head like all of her ideas.

The fun will be delivered to Belnord Avenue on wheels.

"I invented the fun wagon," says Miss Baker of the small trailer with a basketball hoop on the back, a mobile rec center packed with hula hoops and roller skates, board games, bats and balls.

"We'll rope off Belnord Avenue right here where I was born. Take some brooms along and teach the kids to sweep up and pick up glass to play safe."

A special day to relive a childhood when every day was fun day for a girl named Queenie.

July 25, 1993

For sale: A palace on Patterson Park

THEY COULD HAVE MOVED ANYWHERE THEY WANTED WHEN THE TIME CAME to leave the big old house that faces Patterson Park.

Guilford.

Severna Park.

A luxury condominium at the Inner Harbor.

Anywhere.

But Ed and Eleanor Rybczynski moved two doors away.

They say they decided more with their hearts than their heads — choosing to keep their view of the Patterson Park pagoda that Mr. Rybczynski fought to save in the early 1960s; to remain in walking distance of Holy Rosary Church where they were married in 1954 and all 10 of their children were baptized; to stay put in the old waterfront neighborhood where their Polish-American roots go back to the turn of the century.

With retirement near and all but one of their children gone, the Rybczynskis stood at a crossroads faced by thousands of middle-class families in the last three decades, a time when Baltimore's population fell from 939,024 to 736,014 as faltering neighborhoods were abandoned for the new promise of the suburbs.

For the second time in 30 years, the Rybczynskis committed to life in the city.

"This is where I grew up," said Eleanor Rybczynski, 62. "I sing in the church choir and teach Sunday school. I help with their big Polish dinners. This is my neighborhood. I guess it's emotional."

"We looked around in other neighborhoods," said Mr. Rybczynski, a 63-year-old eastside attorney. "But never seriously."

The last time Ed and Eleanor Rybczynski went house hunting they had six kids, another on the way, and space had long run out at their South Potomac Street rowhouse. Back then, in the summer of 1963, Mr. Rybczynski's lawyer friends were telling him to get out of the city.

"They were amazed that we had made a decision to stay," he said. "They believed the only place to raise children was the suburbs."

Instead, he paid $10,000 for a 19th century urban mansion at 332 S. Patterson Park Ave. with high ceilings, stained glass, marble fireplaces and Georgia pine floors. Before moving in, he spent another $11,000 to repair the 15-room house. It would be the Rybczynski home for half of their lives.

While it wasn't easy — drug traffic, break-ins, prostitution and litter have increased steadily and their youngest child was once mugged in the park — the memories from 332 are the most vibrant in the Rybczynski family album.

The big front room with the 13-foot ceiling and windows that open on the park — the room where all 10 kids took piano lessons and learned to polka — has swayed to so many parties that people the Rybczynskis don't recognize often tell them of great times they once had there.

"People we don't even know say they've spent happy moments at our house," Mr. Rybczynski said.

On New Year's Eve, the party would begin around the Christmas tree in the front room before spilling through the house as midnight approached. Eventually, the celebration wound up on second- and third-floor porches behind the house for a grand view of fireworks — a vista of ships, tugboats, cranes and barges spanning the harbor from the Key Bridge to the Domino Sugars sign.

"At dusk we'd see people sitting in the park admiring our house, looking in the windows when the lights came on," said Tom Rybczynski, 35, a real estate agent with the tough job of trying to unload his childhood memories for $215,000.

Expecting to miss the house more than his siblings, Tom has been trying to burn images of the good times into his memory as he gives tours of the house to potential buyers.

"I was 5 when we moved in," he said. "The third floor was vacant then, and we used to go treasure hunting up there. It was always sunny, and we'd look in all the cracks and crevices and imagine finding treasure. One of the rooms had a porthole that looked north. My brother Paul told me the house was really a ship that had run aground in Canton and they dragged it up the hill to make it a house. I believed that story until I was 7."

Children visiting the chaotic, charmed universe crowded with toys and tykes "called our home the White House because it was so big," Tom said. "They'd marvel at the ceilings — one friend said it was like looking up at the sky."

After three decades that witnessed gallons of spilled milk, a grove of Christmas trees from the scraggly to the magnificent, daily homework times 10 and nightly prayers times 12, Ed and Eleanor called an unprecedented family gathering last year.

It was time to go.

"We discussed the idea that one of us children ought to buy it, but none of us could afford to keep it or fill it," said Tom Rybczynski, noting that while he and many of his siblings now have families of their own, none has proved as prolific as Ed and Eleanor's.

Still empty, the old house has been on the market since April.

"Everyone says the house is too large for personal use." says Mr. Rybczynski, who said it costs between $300 and $500 a month to heat the house.

"Someone mentioned turning it into a bed and breakfast. I'd discourage institutional use, such as a home for recovering addicts. I'd keep it before I let that happen," he said.

Against the advice of well-intentioned friends, and despite their own doubts, the Rybczynskis decided to live out their golden years at 328 S. Patterson Park Ave.

The longtime home of Marie Jerzak, a nice lady known around the neighborhood as "Miss Marie," the narrow, two-story house had only seven rooms and was in ruins.

Mr. Rybczynski bought it for $38,000 with no intention of moving in.

"Miss Marie had passed away, and I bought it from her estate for protection," he said. "I got word that a bad slumlord was about to buy it, the kind that doesn't care who they rent to. I was going to fix it up and rent it out and the wife said: 'We ought to move in.'"

Ed Rybczynski resisted the idea. Flagrant prostitution, "innumerable burglaries," and a resilient narcotics trade long ago convinced him that the quality of life around his beloved Patterson Park had not only slipped but was in a slide.

But Eleanor persevered, persuading Ed that it was worth their while to invest an extra $50,000 to renovate the rundown rowhouse with rosebushes in the front yard. They had the house repaired from roof to basement and knocked out a first floor wall to insure that all 34 of them could sit down together for dinner.

"I'm comfortable here," said Mrs. Rybczynski. "I feel safe here."

A recent count on streets bordering the park showed 31 houses for sale out of 443, or about 7 percent.

Maj. Harry Koffenberger, commander of the city's Southeastern District, notes "much more intense 'for sale' signs in the last two years," blaming the flux on "a multiplicity of problems — all the frustrations that come with living in an urban area." Residents like Mary Sloan Roby argue that "people move and houses remain on the real estate market for a variety of reasons... For every negative in East Baltimore, there are many positives."

Although few can afford to buy rundown buildings simply to protect the neighborhood from further decline, a network of community groups called the Patterson Park Neighborhoods Initiative has organized to attract new homeowners. With the help of local savings and loans, the Initiative is promoting mortgages of $50,000 and help with closing costs for as little as $1,000 down.

"Thirty years ago we made a decision to stay in the city and enjoy the benefits here," said Mr. Rybczynski. "I honestly believed there was going to be a renaissance, and I was correct in certain neighborhoods. I also anticipated that we would have very good gun control by now — that guns would be at least reasonably controlled — and I was wrong. I'm disappointed in our leadership. I think there's been a failure of leadership at all levels of government."

However grieved and disappointed at the fall of their ideal, Patterson Park remains the heart of everything dear to Ed and Eleanor Rybczynski.

Because of that faith, the entire family was able to gather for

Thanksgiving dinner last year with a view of the Patterson Park pagoda, just as they had for the last 30 years.

And they will do it again this year, two doors away from the good old days with a little less elbow room at the table.

"It's crowded," said Ed.

"But we get everyone in," said Eleanor.

November 22, 1993

A sweet mission of mercy

CAN DOUGHNUTS SAVE THE POOR SOULS OF BALTIMORE?

Johnny X thinks they might. Upon that belief, he has given away thousands of them.

"Our government should feed the American people first — the poor unfortunate souls who sit on them broke down steps and call it home. Don't starve 'em!" declares John Stackowitz, whose middle name is Xavier, from which the X is taken.

"And that don't stand for 'x-cess' baggage!"

But it could stand for extra sweet and extremely sticky, like the 35 dozen doughnuts bouncing around in the back of Johnny's 1987 Chevrolet wagon while he made a recent morning run, the fragrance of honey dips, chocolate glazed and Boston cremes churning in the sun as he careened toward Arbutus.

"I get everything for free," says Johnny, 75, wheeling through a wide intersection en route to South West Emergency Services on Maple Avenue. "And I run all over the damn place giving it away."

In an egg crate alongside the doughnuts are his philanthropic files: a receipt from the American Rescue Workers mission on West Baltimore Street for 30 dozen doughnuts; an invoice for six cases of milk and juice, eight gallons of lemonade and a box of bread delivered to South West Emergency Services; and a note of gratitude from the sugar-and-jelly smitten police of the Southwestern District, who enjoyed free doughnuts one snowy morning last winter courtesy of you-know-who.

Who is this Mister Doughnut of mercy?

He's the kind of character who says "Jiminy Christmas" when he's surprised and ends phone calls with: "Double-0 Seven, signing off."

A guy who gives out business cards identifying himself as "Johnny X: The Poor Man's DJ" but only provides music — everything from polkas to Tony Bennett — at a weekly shuffleboard league.

A self-styled ladies' man whose first wife, Mary, ran off years ago with some guy she met in boxer Red Burman's saloon; whose second wife, Alice, died in 1990 ("I hope and pray I can find one just like her"); and whose current sweetheart is also named Alice.

But above all, John Xavier Stackowitz is a proud veteran of World War II, a Good Conduct Medal winner who served with the Army in Panama, helping to protect the canal.

Part of a soon-to-be-gone generation that came of age when the United States triumphed over the world — and tends to think the country has gone downhill ever since — Johnny rarely goes out without his "World War II Veteran" cap pinned with the American flag.

The hat leaves his head only when he eats, sleeps, pays a bill in person, is greeting a woman or asks a favor of a stranger. "Out of respect," says Johnny, who, in July, will take over as commander of the Veterans of Foreign Wars Post No. 3217. "Respect is something lost in this country."

Johnny's face is a kindly pink mug, his thin hair as white as snow and his eyes droopy and a pale, watery blue. He sports a tattoo on each forearm — a kewpie doll on the right and, on the left, the words: "Mother and Father — True Love" and his older brother Frank's name above the words: "Killed in Action, Feb. 8, 1945."

Born on Gough Street in East Baltimore, Johnny is the son of Polish immigrants who spent their summers living in shacks outside of Aberdeen so they could make a few extra nickels shucking corn. He's dabbled in television repair, worked in garages and, for a while in the 1950s, tended bar at Frank Malinowski's gin mill at Gough and Ann streets. Today, he survives on Social Security and a pension from his days standing stowaway watch on foreign ships docked in Baltimore.

"I didn't miss nothing," he boasts.

Johnny's day starts before 7 a.m. when he leaves his Baltimore Highlands apartment to pick up the goodies — juice, milk, bread, yogurt and sometimes eggs along with the doughnuts — from good-hearted bakers and supermarket managers.

His doughnut gig began last Christmas when a VFW friend sent Johnny to see Steve Fogler, owner of Fogler's Bakery on Patapsco Avenue in Brooklyn.

For years, Mr. Fogler had an employee deliver unsold leftovers to missions and shelters. The man was killed in a traffic accident, and the practice lapsed until Johnny X showed up to fill the void. Ever since, he has hauled away 10 to 40 dozen doughnuts a day, six days a week.

"John's just a guy that likes to look out for other people," said Mr. Fogler, 38. "He's somebody looking for somebody to thank him."

And they can't thank him enough at South West Emergency Services.

"This is one of them places you go when you don't have anything," says Johnny, his personality way out in front of a grocery cart loaded with 35 dozen doughnuts, as he enters the center at Arbutus United Methodist Church.

"Help yourself!" he cries, smiling and flirting. "I've got plenty!"

From the back, volunteer Lois Smedley watches Johnny work the room with amusement and respect. "We didn't have stuff like this to give away before John started coming around," she says. "Families need the staples — if John didn't bring bread, we wouldn't have bread to give away — but if we can send doughnuts home to treat the kids, that's a good thing too."

In his khaki work pants, mustard yellow shirt, suspenders and black work shoes, Johnny blushes like a schoolboy before heading to his next stop.

"I like to keep moving," he says, pulling his Chevy off the parking lot. "If you spend too much time in that recliner, it shortens your life."

May 25, 1994

'Pope' still fighting for Reservoir Hill

THE POPE OF WHITELOCK STREET IS PRACTICING DUKE ELLINGTON TUNES ON A baby grand piano in the front window of his Reservoir Hill rowhouse. Atop the piano is a statue of St. Francis of Assisi. Beyond the statue lies a desolate stretch of Baltimore known as the 900 block of Whitelock St., the desert in which Catholic priest Thomas F. Composto has tried to do good since 1968.

A former Jesuit, expelled by his order for reasons neither he nor the Jesuits will explain, Mr. Composto keeps his chops sharp to pick up extra cash at senior citizen sing-alongs. Other money comes from counseling work and teaching courses on ethics and death. A few years ago, he was a maitre d' in Glen Burnie.

All to sustain himself for his life's work as staff and soul of St. Francis Neighborhood Center, a Catholic mission born amid the despair of Whitelock Street during the social activism of the 1960s.

Trying to do good on Whitelock Street for nearly half his life — almost 27 years of patience and labor that earned him the title of pope — has not been especially kind to Tommy Composto.

The city had so little faith in Whitelock Street that all that was left to do after two decades of indecision and decay was to knock it down and start over.

"Whatever we tried to do, it just didn't seem to ever work on Whitelock Street," said City Council President Mary Pat Clarke.

The city housing department is accepting bids from developers for a combination of private housing and businesses. What the agency won't take is carryout restaurants, drug testing or rehabilitation centers, any place selling liquor, or halfway houses.

"I just hope they don't take as long to build the block up as they did to tear it down," said Ronald Thompson, who has lived in the neighborhood since 1958.

Residents such as Mr. Thompson, who remember the glory days of Zurosky's meat market, G-Cleft Records, Montgomery's Barber Shop and Jerry Cohen's variety store, are eager to see business return, but finding merchants willing to take a chance on Whitelock Street may prove difficult.

Built in the first years of the 20th century, the 900 block of Whitelock St. percolated for decades as the Main Street of Reservoir Hill, a sprawling community of stately townhouses and about 8,500 residents between the Jones Falls Expressway and Druid Hill Park.

Where the Herling Brothers once delivered kosher meat to your door by bicycle, drug touts now direct a steady stream of customers from all over the city to supplies of cocaine and heroin.

"There aren't a lot of developers beating down the door to put up commercial buildings on Whitelock Street," said David Elam, a recently departed housing official.

The south side of the block came down in August, leaving rubble and bulldozers beyond the end of Tommy Composto's piano.

The north side is expected to tumble next month. When it does, St. Francis Center at 936 Whitelock St. will go down with it, along with the next-door dental office it spawned to serve the working class and poor.

When St. Francis and its rough basement chapel go, Tom Composto will say goodbye to the only real home he has known since leaving his mother and father to enter the seminary.

"St. Francis has paid attention to the ordinary, everyday people," he said. "All the people who've helped over the years have added to it, but it's hard to find people who don't quit after awhile."

You could call him stubborn.

Hard-headed would not be too harsh.

"Or you could call me dedicated," he said. "I'm combative because I've been hurt personally by higher-ups in public service or church service who wouldn't do what they dedicated themselves to doing. Most of them just want to climb. So many people have used this neighborhood as their social laboratory, and then they leave."

Although Mr. Composto is losing his home, a deal with the city gave him another one around the corner, at 2405 Linden Ave., for $500. It is something of a wreck, but he intends to fix it up and install a new chapel with $71,500 a judge awarded as compensation from the city for the taking of 934 and 936 Whitelock St.

His decision to stay is a renewal of his original commitment to Whitelock Street, even if some days that commitment doesn't go much beyond smiling and saying hello to a child who must navigate around gangs of drug dealers on the way to school.

"We've tried to be a voice for the marginal people of this neighborhood, to let them know that somebody gave a damn about them and cared enough to stay," he said.

The day Tom Composto first pulled up to Whitelock Street — back in the days when Reservoir Hill was the darling of young Catholics enamored of social justice — a large, skeptical resident stuck his face into the seminarian's car window.

He demanded: "Are you a priest?"

Pointing to the St. Francis Center, the man asked: "You going in there?"

And then: "You going to go away as soon as we get to know you?"

Mr. Composto remembers answering: "It's not my style to hit and run."

He was 29 then, less than a year from his ordination in his native New York. He's 56 now, with a Don Quixote belt buckle and hair gone to silver.

Although the Jesuits expelled him in 1990 and he has no authority in the Archdiocese of Baltimore to work as a priest, the sacrament of Holy Orders asserts once a priest, always a priest, so he remains "Father Tom" to himself and the neighborhood. The third vow of the Jesuits, after poverty and chastity, is obedience.

It is a virtue that does not lay easy on the temper and savvy of the Brooklyn-born Mr. Composto, an excitable man who doesn't flinch when drug dealers curse him out and isn't above using similar language in his chapel when something upsets him.

"I'm living in some turmoil right now," he said. "Every time I go outside, there's a new set of drug dealers on the street. They look at me and say: '[Expletive] you.'"

When Baltimore tried to take his house and the one next door for a total of $45,000 — the way they took the rest of the 900 block of Whitelock St. with urban renewal legislation passed in 1972 — Mr. Composto called his old friend Harold Glaser, a well-known local attorney who made his mark defending drug lords.

Trying the case pro bono, Mr. Glaser wound up winning Mr. Composto an additional $26,500 in a lawsuit that made the priest the last resident on the block.

"I think he's the Lone Ranger by personality," said the Rev. Robert Kearns, the pastor of St. Peter Claver parish. "Ecclesiastically, he's in no man's land because he has no [church] credentials and he's working in a tough, tough, tough area. I don't care who you are, you better be paying attention when you go to Whitelock Street."

His Jesuit superiors arrived at the St. Francis Neighborhood Center in 1990 to demand that Mr. Composto return to the order's New York province. He said his work was in Reservoir Hill and refused.

His superiors gave their regrets and said their goodbyes, and the Society of Jesus took its leave of Whitelock Street and Tom Composto.

Not much goes on at the St. Francis Neighborhood Center these days.

It has been that way for several years.

"I've got a 4,000-book library that used to be available to the community, back when I trusted them to come in my house. You can't trust a drug user," said Mr. Composto, who closed a summer Bible school two years ago, he said, because parents were afraid to send their children to Whitelock Street.

Mr. Composto celebrates Mass for a handful of people at 11 a.m. every Sunday; Alcoholics Anonymous and Narcotics Anonymous groups meet in the chapel a few times a week; and every now and then a funeral is held.

At John Taylor's dental office next door — where about 10,000 people have had their teeth fixed since 1972 at prices far below commercial rates —

clients continue to show up on Wednesday afternoons.

Although Dr. Taylor's mobile service to invalids and shut-ins will continue, the Whitelock office will close in deference to the looming wrecking ball.

"When you've got drugs, you don't need any other factors to kill a neighborhood," said a man who grew up on Whitelock Street and comes back only to have his teeth fixed. "Everything else tumbles down behind drugs."

An old friend of Mr. Composto's — an attorney involved in charity work who asked not to be identified — admires the mission's longevity but questions its effectiveness.

"Why hasn't the center flourished more than it has? It takes a feisty guy to live in that neighborhood, but I think Tom creates as many enemies as he has friends," the friend said. "Why do certain do-gooders attract volunteers and dollars and others don't? He hasn't made much progress compared to what other martyrs have done in the city."

It wasn't always this way.

"I knew Tommy best when he was part of the beautiful chaos of that house," said Joseph Healy, who arrived as a Jesuit seminarian in 1967 and put in about three years at the center before leaving his order to marry a woman he had met in the neighborhood.

"We tried to live the way the neighbors were living, but we weren't kidding ourselves; our mentality wasn't poor. Once you realize you can walk away from it any time you want, you're not sharing poverty."

Now director of international programs for Loyola College, Mr. Healy continues to use St. Francis for dental work and remembers the project as a party with its heart in the right place.

"We were open until midnight, and every night we always had a dozen people for dinner. It was happening, it was fun, and we were young. What did we know? We were having a ball and hopefully helping someone."

Having a ball ranged from helping families get heat for the winter to putting on clerical collars to testify on behalf of youths in trouble with police.

Leased for about $100 a month, the St. Francis Neighborhood Center opened in 1965 as an extension of St. Peter Claver on Fremont Avenue. The idea of former Jesuit and anti-war activist Philip Berrigan, it was an attempt to introduce "storefront Catholicism" to a neighborhood with no parish of its own. As Mr. Berrigan got deeper and deeper into the anti-Vietnam War movement, other seminarians took over.

"I didn't think any of us had a plan to stay there the rest of our lives," said Mr. Healy. "We were playing it by ear."

Brendan Walsh became the center's first full-time resident in 1967.

"Every Saturday, the nuns came in and did some sort of teaching and lunch program with children," said Mr. Walsh, who, with his wife, Willa Bickham, has operated the Viva House soup kitchen on Mount Street for the past quarter-century. "It was simple hospitality. As the war heated up, we used the place as an anti-draft board."

Asked how Viva House is able to attract dozens of volunteers who helped serve 37,000 free meals last year in a ghetto nearly as desperate as Whitelock Street, Mr. Walsh said, "Good work and goodwill go hand-in-hand."

Perhaps the brightest moment of the St. Francis project was the Ralph Young School for Boys, a free, private junior high for inner-city youths staffed by Jesuits and neighborhood volunteers. It lasted about five years until federal Model Cities money evaporated.

"We never followed up to find out what happened to the kids we educated," said Joe Healy. "How did they end up? I don't know."

Ask Tom Composto to name one youngster who fought his or her way out of the neighborhood and you get the same answer.

As bad as things might have been in the 1960s, they are worse now.

According to the police homicide unit, there have been at least 10 homicides on or around the block in as many years, including the still unsolved 1988 slaying of 11-year-old Latonya Wallace.

The Police Department's escape and apprehension squad is frequently looking for fugitives there. Last year, a man robbed a liquor store with a device he claimed was a bomb, and the drug dealing is entrenched and blatant.

"Looking back to 30 years ago, it seems inevitable now that if anyplace was going to become a crack haven, it would be Whitelock Street," said Ed Sommerfeldt, a Coppin State College math professor who, with Mr. Composto, was part of the last wave of Jesuit seminarians who descended on the neighborhood in the late 1960s. "You could argue that Tommy doesn't seem to have made much of a difference. But you could also argue that things could have been a lot worse without him."

Mr. Composto said the reality of Whitelock Street may constitute a record of "diminishing returns," yet he continues to see his mere presence as his greatest achievement.

"I give what I can give by living here," he said. "I'm less naive than I used to be, so I get more discouraged. I see all these people hurting and I get mad that I can't pass a miracle.

"The dealers call me the [expletive] preacher up the street, but I'm the one they come to when they need to talk," he said. "I tell them, 'You got talent, you got brains — you must have brains or you'd be dead by now. But you've got no friends, and at the end of the day, you can't even say you've done a good job.'

"I tell them, 'Whitelock Street is the [worst place in] Baltimore, and you're going to be here for the rest of your [expletive] life, as long as that lasts.'"

The same could be said of Thomas F. Composto.

December 4, 1994

The tree man of SoWeBo

GARY LETTERON IS A GOOD SOUL WHO SLAVES TO SEED THE CITY WITH TREES.
Where some guys trick out their Camaros with flaming paint jobs,
Letteron cruises Southwest Baltimore in a pickup truck with autumn leaves
drawn on its fenders, its bed heavy with zelkova, beech and ash.

His battle cry?

"Plant 'em green side up!"

The best-known street arborist in Baltimore, Letteron is a green Robin
Hood who rescues trees growing in the path of suburban bulldozers and
replants them in the weary city; the self-appointed horticulturist of SoWeBo
who supplies neighborhood kids with hot dogs and shovels in a frantic campaign to shade sidewalks and turn vacant lots into parks.

For a guy with the fragile heart of a poet, Letteron's audacity is legendary:
take something ugly, show people how to have fun making it better and then
dare anyone to say he had no right to do it.

"I started it because it needed to be done and it felt good," says Letteron
in the lush Eden of the 500-tree Hollins Street Nursery, planted on one abandoned lot and another donated by the bar next door, Scallio's Tavern. "And
then people patted me on the back for it, and that felt good too."

In the late 1970s, you might have encountered Letteron at Franklin
Street's fabled Marble Bar, where he played keyboards for Edie "the Egg
Lady" Massey, Fells Point's late queen of kitsch who appeared in the early
films of John Waters.

It was just the kind of action he was looking for when he left his parents'
home in Anneslie for downtown in 1978.

Today, you're likely to meet the 42-year-old West Lombard Street resident
the way Frank Rogers did, over beer and trees.

"I met him at a mulching party," says Rogers, who volunteers with the
Tree Tribe, an offshoot of the Parks and People nonprofit that gave Letteron
a job after marveling at what he had done on his own for years.

"I wanted a tree in front of my house for a while," says Rogers, who lives
near Letteron on Pratt Street. "One day Gary shows up with some sledge-
hammers and a couple of guys and they dig out a cement pit for some trees.

I got a liberty elm and my neighbor got a white ash. The city says it costs $300 to dig a pit in the sidewalk and they can't afford it, but there's really nothing to it.

"Gary's stepped into this gray area and made it his own. You can bang your head against the bureaucracy all day long, but plant a tree and it's an immediate improvement."

The city's tree specialist, Marion Bedingfield, is as frustrated by the municipal budget as anyone. He dreams of having a Gary Letteron in every neighborhood.

"A lot of the stuff that Gary does we can't officially condone, but he wants his part of the city green," says Bedingfield, who has known Letteron for 10 years. "When we tell him we don't do sidewalk cuts, he calls back a day later and says we didn't look hard enough, that there's one there. Then you find out he went out and rented a jackhammer at his own expense.

"Once he wanted to plant on a vacant lot on Stockton Street and we told him we couldn't give permission because it belonged to someone in Virginia," says Bedingfield. "Somehow, it got planted anyway. It was literally a dumping pit, half-paved, full of refrigerators and garbage. Now it's a park. If I know Gary, most of the money is coming out of his own pocket. He's a cool guy."

Subsidizing his mission with money made from spin-art stands at neighborhood festivals and whatever he can scrape together in the SoWeBo tradition of throwing a party at any time for any cause, Letteron sees his work as a civic duty.

"The nursery was built on a vacant lot of an allegedly deceased man named Minor Jones," he says. "We just fenced it off and said to heck with it. Anything too small to be economically developed becomes a blight, a dump site. It's the right and responsibility of every community to take vacant lots. A utopian dream in Baltimore, free land to everyone!"

Terry Smith was so weary of the drugs and trash and street robberies in Southwest Baltimore that he was ready to unload a house he'd already paid off just to get out. Then he met Letteron and some of his signature flowers and trees, and decided to tough it out a little longer.

"He does everything on a handshake and it gets done," says Smith, a 20-year resident of West Ostend Street. "It's like 1969 with him — instead of peace marching, he's tree marching. It's his dream to see squirrels flying through a canopy of trees over the city."

Just south of the 2800 block of Wilkens Ave. near Gwynns Falls, grass and trees from Letteron's hand grow behind an old garage. After planting the lot, Letteron put up a stern sign he found in his wanderings: WARNING! NO DUMPING IN THIS AREA. FIRE DEPARTMENT. BALTIMORE COUNTY.

"He's a good-hearted idiot who keeps believing in humankind in an area where that belief is misplaced," says Danny Fowler, who replaced the front door to Letteron's house this week after it was kicked in by daylight thieves who stole his favorite bicycle and a power saw. "He's nice and he tries to do nice things. Unfortunately, the rules in this society see kindness as weakness."

His kindness, sweat and ability to get others to help him are responsible for more than 100 new trees in the past year, and a half-dozen Hollins area parks — including a small peach orchard — sprouting from formerly trashed lots.

One of the best lots sports a sunken carved totem pole on Stockton Street between Lombard and Pratt.

"A fine example of the idyllic sites we have to work with," says Letteron. "One of our trees arrived sans leaves, but we planted it anyway. We've seen worse."

The city, the state Department of Natural Resources and the National Tree Trust almost always give Letteron what he wants because they know the trees will be planted and cared for. And when new neighbors such as Hilton Braithwaite show up at Letteron's door asking for a tree for their yard, he can make them happy by saying yes.

"I just moved into a house on Stricker Street and everybody's talking about Gary," says Braithwaite, a Howard University professor. "He's the man."

Right now, the tree man of Hollins Market has another idea at the back of his mind.

"I'd like to put a toad abode here in the nursery to raise tree frogs," he says. "I haven't done any of the research yet, but it would be nice to hear frogs croaking in the night."

June 7, 1996

Chapter 12

Doing
Business

He keeps bicycles oiled, legends alive

CHARLES F. LOGUE IS THE KEEPER OF LEGENDS PASSED DOWN TO HIM FROM "the old man from Swampoodle with the wheels in his head."

The old man was his father, the late Bernard J. Logue, Sr., one of Baltimore's pioneer bicycle enthusiasts who reportedly bought contraptions built for three, four, and five riders from Orville and Wilbur Wright in 1902.

Swampoodle, now nearly forgotten, was a Bohemian "hollow" — a neighborhood just north of Johns Hopkins Hospital that centered on a pair of tiny, parallel side streets named Barnes and Abbott.

It was in Swampoodle — where the Logue family lived for three generations — that the second family bicycle shop was established in 1912, at 931 North Broadway.

The Broadway location, a symbol of the bicycle's growing popularity and the Logues' corresponding prosperity, branched from the family's first bike business, a shop Bernard established at the corner of Lafayette and Division streets in 1896.

As for a bicycle man having "wheels in his head," it's no different from a reporter's heart pumping newspaper ink. It simply means that Bernard J. Logue, Sr. — who left his father's coal yard to promote Baltimore bicycle riding when the fad first hit the nation — lived for his work.

Those spoked wheels still turn inside the small, perky head of Charlie Logue, who, just shy of 70 years, says he can still — if so moved — climb atop a "high-wheel," the kind popular in the Gay Nineties, and take a spin.

Some of those historic bicycles, once marketed as Kangaroos and Grasshoppers, now reside in the last of the Logue family businesses, Charlie Logue's bicycle-and-parts cluttered "Sport Shop" at 2527 East Monument street, near Milton avenue.

"I don't have to be doing this," he said, seated in a grimy kindergarten chair at the front window of his shop, "but I can't keep still."

Stealing away from the window now and again for a sip of beer, he says after a short swig, "I love bicycle work. I love working with my hands."

On a recent day, Mr. Logue, who makes repairs six days a week with Sundays off, talked about the bicycle business, his fingers moving between a small oil can, the barely lit nub of a cigar, and a sprocket remover that's passed as many years as its owner.

"I'm from the old school," said Mr. Logue, who works in the window instead of a bench in the back; his way of keeping a mistrustful eye on "a dirty, noisy" neighborhood he says is going to the devil.

"Somebody comes in with a bent wheel, I'll put a new rim and spokes on their hub. You go somewhere else and they'll say you need a new wheel."

The bulk of Mr. Logue's business is 10-speed work from adults — "mostly bent wheels due to potholes and rough riding" — and BMX bike repairs for young boys. He says the bike business is on a roll now, booming since about 1970 and fully recovered from some lean times 30 years ago when he repaired fishing rods and reels to make ends meet.

General repairs at the Sport Shop run between $20 and $60, with rates decided job-by-job. Mr. Logue will take a look at just about anything, but if it doesn't need fixing, or you can do it yourself, he'll tell you so.

He'll also say you must pay in advance and pick your bike or rod and reel up before his 4 p.m. closing time. If you need a used bike, Charlie Logue has hundreds of orphaned two-wheelers to choose from, many that came in for repairs and were never picked up.

From a stack of old photographs in a box atop a shelf tumbling with bike parts, Mr. Logue pulls a picture of a sign proclaiming one of the family's shops "Baltimore's Best" well before a certain local mayor was born.

"My father was an incredible man," said Mr. Logue, pointing to his dad in the picture. "Three-year education's all he had. My uncle had the schooling, but he couldn't do nothing with these shops. My father was the greatest promoter of bicycles in the city of Baltimore."

Before he died in 1965, Mr. Logue's father explained the sporting way to disembark a high-wheeled Grasshopper (which Charlie rode in East Baltimore's "I Am an American Day" parade up until 1970.)

Bernard Logue maintained that the proper way a rider dismounted a high-wheeler was by resting his feet on the handlebars while the bike was moving and then pulling back on the handbrakes with his fingers before "leaping off like a paratrooper."

Charlie Logue put the photo back and sat down, legs crossed, eyes darting out to traffic on Monument street. He's the last Logue bike-man, he says, the father of two daughters who had sons who aren't interested in fixing bikes for a living.

The bicycle repair season, which coincides with the riding season, is on the wane now, except for a temporary jolt by Christmas sales that put a few dollars in Charlie Logue's pocket for new bike assemblies.

Mr. Logue says the riding season will stay more or less dormant until the warmer winds of April roll through the alleys and narrow streets between Baltimore's row houses; breezy winds that whisper to kids and kids at heart that it's time to hop up and coast.

And perhaps pay a visit to Charlie Logue for a new rim, a tightening up of the brakes, and a little grease on the sprocket.

December 11, 1984

Benny's store vends 'odds and ends and a lot of lip'

IF BENNY'S STORE WAS THE STANDARD FOR AMERICAN GROCERIES INSTEAD of the 7-Eleven, those quick trips out for milk, bread and a cup of coffee would never be the same.

For starters, you couldn't get a cup of coffee. Even though the landlord for Ben Niroda's neighborhood store in Federal Hill is Pfefferkorn's, a wholesale coffee distributor, Mr. Niroda doesn't sell any.

He says he doesn't have the room, but a fresh pot in the store would eliminate a good excuse to close up shop for a few minutes and take a walk down to the Cross Street Market and shoot the breeze.

What does he have room for?

Boxes of ladies' stockings that fasten to a garter belt, stacked together with nibs for fountain pens, rouge powder puffs, 15-cent lipsticks, loose-packed McCormick tea, lead for lead pencils, rubber baby pants (four pairs, 98 cents), no-frills cuff links that shine like blank coins, and pink plastic hair curlers as big around as a half-dollar.

"All that stuff — gone," he says. "People stopped buying 'em. Them days is gone for good."

Few of Mr. Niroda's "antiques" are on display, and none are really for sale.

But that's no reason to get rid of them. They haven't gone bad, like the half-dozen bottles of Elmer's Glue that sat so long the glue hardened and turned brown.

What is for sale in the unmarked, whitewashed, cramped cinder block store at the corner of Riverside Avenue and Grindall Street is a lot of soda, a lot of candy and junk food, a lot of detergent, a lot of dog food, a little lunch meat, a mountain of canned goods, and credit if he knows you well enough.

"Odds and ends," says the 52-year-old, "and a lot of lip."

Remember now, if every American convenience store operated on Benny's Business Principles, all the clerks would know your business.

"Well, Steve, how'd you make out with Mary? She going to the movies with you tonight?" asks Mr. Niroda as a kid about 16 walks in to buy a soda, a fraction of the 25-plus cases of pop he moves a week.

208

Steve, dressed in tennis shoes, blue jeans, a T-shirt and a sweat-jacket, thinks this is a silly question.

"Ben," he says, "when do I usually have a $20 bill and when am I wearing cologne?"

An old man named Will Schier ambles in, a customer who's been buying from Mr. Niroda since he opened the store in 1957, and remembers the grocer when he was just a kid helping out a lady named Annie Wolfe in her Grindall Street grocery.

"He's the best one around here," said Mr. Schier, willing to overlook a $2.02-a-gallon milk tariff in favor of the grocer's company. "He has what you want and he treats you nice."

Mr. Schier buys two Pepsis, a loaf of bread, a can of soup and a half-pound of spiced ham. Mr. Niroda rings up $4.78, and his customer pulls a little notebook from the pocket of his old blue sweater. The storekeeper marks the debt on Mr. Schier's tattered book, and talks about the old-timers that are gone.

"Only 13 left from years ago," he says. "We counted 'em the other day, 13 just from Riverside Avenue, about five left on Grindall Street."

Over his 15-hour workday, in between the teen-agers (sodas and cigarettes), old folks from the old neighborhood (sodas and frozen dinners), the young professionals who have turned Mr. Niroda's stomping grounds into a tourist postcard (sodas and dog food), and the gangs of Southern High School students who can be found in the store a good two to three hours after the first bell has rung (sodas and potato chips), there is the almost constant squeal of young children racing in and out the front door.

Kids are Mr. Niroda's boon and his bane. He loves 'em — "I got a soft heart" — but they get on his nerves.

Two little blondies scoot in, one's about 4, the other not far from it.

"What are you getting — bubble gum?" asks Mr. Niroda, leaning over the counter to look at the girls, his eyes intent, bright; a smile around his straight white teeth, thick chestnut and gray hair fluffing around his ears, his cheeks flushed.

"A pack of rainbow gum," says one little girl, her nose to the cracked glass of the candy cabinet. She points. "Look Benny, not that, that, the long one."

The grocer fishes out the candy, takes in some small change, and the girls leave. He blinks. They're back.

"There's boys out there talking nasty," they cry.

"What? Bad words again?" says Mr. Niroda with the feigned concern of a parent. "Stay away from him. All right, outside now, you're making too much noise."

In days gone by, he says, when couples had children instead of dogs, over half his inventory catered to children. Baseball cards and sponge rubber balls were hot items.

"The neighborhood changed, they don't have the type of kids that would buy 'em now. I used to get the first series [of baseball cards] in the neighborhood, every spring, some kids would come in and buy 15 packs at a time.

"I used to sell crayons and coloring books; they began falling off about '79, when people moved in who didn't have kids. You don't know how to [order] no more, it's changed so much. It's even hard to judge what they're going to eat today."

You could listen to him talk forever, and some people do, hanging around on milk crates in the store, counting up how many neighbors are left from the old days while Mr. Niroda deals with the riff and the raff.

In between the mischief-makers, rough-housers, and just plain folks, a local politician or two drops by. Mr. Niroda counts state Sen. George Della among his personal friends, and has known Joe DiBlasi since the South Baltimore councilman was a little boy.

When news hit that Mayor Schaefer had called Mr. DiBlasi a "dumb bastard" because of differences over the stadium issue, Mr. Niroda said he advised his friend:

"Ain't that something, Joe? I would've poked him right in the nose. Joe says, 'Aw, he don't mean it, Ben.'

"I said, 'Joe, people don't say nothing they don't mean.'"

So much of what makes Mr. Niroda the genuine Baltimore article is his speech, a somewhat hoarse, phlegm-heavy "Bawlmer" accent rolling with the rhetorical questions "Ain't it?" "Know what I mean?" and the multi-purpose "Yeah," used both as question and answer. The eloquence conveys simple truths.

A scruffy street punk drops in to buy a soda. He looks about 14. It's 11 a.m., a school day.

"What'd they do, leave school out?" asks Mr. Niroda, knowing better.

"I think they got half a day today," the punk says, doing his best to avoid eye contact with the older man.

"No," says the grocer, as if he's memorized the public school calendar. "They got a full one today and a full one tomorrow. You don't want to learn, that's all."

November 15, 1985

210

Baltimore shop known worldwide
for magic touch in shoe repair

A WOMAN DOWN IN AMARILLO, TEXAS, WITH A NARROW FOOT AND THE NAME Harriet Strimple had a pair of aqua, doeskin high heels that she simply adored.

"They fit so well," said Mrs. Strimple of the shoes she bought more that 20 years ago. "But the heel was out of style."

What to do?

Wrap the shoes in brown paper and mail them off to Baltimore to have the heels fixed, of course.

Because, according to the advertisements for Century Shoe Repair at 207 Park Ave.: "The most expensive shoes you own is the pair that you can't wear."

A business as old as its name with a cash register that doesn't go any higher than $9.99, Century was founded above the old Wyman Shoe Store on Lexington Street by Sam and Izzy Myerberg, brothers new to America from Poland.

The Park Avenue site is the last building still in use from a business that once had a dozen stores around town, a shoe repair garage where battered wingtips and wobbly Cuban heels ride between floors in a wooden box on pulleys.

They start out on the second floor where just about every day Isabel Bradley uses a putty knife to open packages from places such as India, St. Louis, West Germany, Minnesota, the Virgin Islands and Hopewell Junction, N.Y., as shoes arrive from little towns, big cities and the middle of nowhere.

The work is solicited by black-and-white advertisements from another age, art deco ads that have appeared over the years in *Vogue*, *Redbook*, *House & Garden* and *Glamour* and that run regularly today in *House Beautiful*.

The orders come with little notes. Mrs. Bradley, one of the handful of people with strange and varied talents who have made Century Shoe Repair known around the globe, uses them to satisfy her hobby in handwriting analysis.

Just as Century's master cobbler Charles Jones says, he can tell someone's personality by the way the shoes are worn out (if the backs are pushed down, the owner is probably too lazy to untie them), Mrs. Bradley says she can fathom what customers are like by the notes they write.

"I've made friends all over the world," she said, admitting a particular fondness for customers who, like her, own Scottie dogs. "I've never met them, but I know them."

Shoes made like fishermen's net arrive with rips to be stitched, shoes come in for paint jobs, and shoes come in to be stretched wider and pulled longer.

They come with notes like this one from M'Lise Bulloch of New York City:

"For two months I tried to find someone to cover some shoes in the same floral print as my dress, but could not. I finally handpainted the shoes to match, but I would rather have them professionally covered. Please send me your brochure. I know that I will use your services."

Those services are arcane and extensive: reglazing reptile leather shoes; zipper repair; hats cleaned; heel and sole work of any kind; shoes dyed or covered with fabric; attaching instep straps to "give your pumps a new look"; pointed toes made round, or round toes made into a point; shoes stretched wider or longer or made narrow; golf shoes to be made out of dress shoes; broken shanks replaced to correct "wobbly" heels; pumps cut down; shoes made toeless; pumps made into sandals; and all manner of handbag and luggage repair.

The work costs as little as $9.95 for dyeing and as much as $34.95 for new heels in alligator, lizard or reptile leather.

The shop even fixes old baseball gloves, but few are sent in for repair.

"If Century can't do it, it can't be done," said Beatrice Nathanson, daughter of founder Sam Myerberg and the widow of Sol Nathanson, who started the mail-order business.

One of Mrs. Nathanson's early jobs for the company was posing for its brochures — from the knees down.

Having outlived most of her relatives, Mrs. Nathanson is the current president of Century, assisted by her vice president and daughter, Judy Elbaum, a former nurse who is presiding over a renovation of the old store and hopes to replace the exquisite tackiness of its faded gold and black Eiffel Tower print wallpaper.

In all, Century has a dozen employees, from Walt Davenport, tearing down shoes in the basement, to Jackie Bond, repainting them on the fourth floor, where she shares space with hundreds of old shoes.

Between the top and bottom they make a stop on the third floor, where the nimble hands of 51-year-old Charles Jones have at them with a small hammer and an ancient Singer sewing machine.

"I made my first pair of shoes when I was 10," said Mr. Jones, a veteran of three decades at Century who learned the craft from his grandfather, master boot-maker Henry Bowen, at the old Bowen Shoe Shop, 515 Presstman St. "People like old shoe comfort, and we give them a new shoe look."

Mr. Jones, who used to sing doo-wop in town with the Vel-Tones, recalled one lady for whom he had changed the style on an old pair of black pumps three times since 1965.

"First I cut the toe out for her, then a few years later she had the vamp cut," he said, pumping the pedal on a Singer stitcher that overlooks Park Avenue below. "Now she wants double straps put on them."

Mr. Jones said he had taken on an apprentice from time to time but lately had not seen much talent come out of vocational schools. He worries that his craft may soon be lost to a market of disposable shoes.

"The trouble with shoe repair today," he said, "is you're dealing with so much artificial material."

Of all of Century's employees, the most familiar is 90-year-old Will Gross, dean of Baltimore's shoeshine artists.

A man of few words who tends to be in better moods after he has had his lunch, "Uncle Will" was born in 1900, a few years before the Myerberg brothers started their business.

He began working for Century in 1943 as a one-time fill-in for a friend.

Forty-seven years later, he still shows up every morning to unlock the doors and get business rolling.

"I did all right in my life," he said. "I went to work for Sammy and Izzy on 138 W. Fayette St. as a shoeshine. A friend of mine was working the polls on Election Day, and he asked me if I'd go down [to] Century in his place. A couple of days later my friend said the old man was looking for me. I went down and saw Izzy, and he gave me a job."

It's a job that has taught "Uncle Will," Charles Jones, Judy Elbaum and the rest of the crew at Century Shoe a lot about the peculiar demographics of footwear.

"You get your odd shoes from California, and your fashionable shoes from New York and Florida," said Mrs. Bradley. "From the Midwest we get the sturdier types and from Texas we get a lot of boots.

"And," she said, "we don't get too many shoes at all from the Deep South."

October 8, 1990

The last of the corner butchers

An old grocer's scale, the kind with a metal bucket suspended on a chain, hangs from white wooden shelves packed with canned goods. Put a cucumber or a couple of tomatoes in the bucket, and a red metal arrow races around the face until it hovers over an approximate weight. It is a half-century old if it's a day.

On top of the meat counter sits a state-of-the-art electronic scale. Lay three pork chops on it and cool blue numbers provide an exact digital read-out.

Living out their golden years between these milestones of grocery technology are the Wagners: Donald and Winnie, running a corner store that's been in the family since 1921, an unmarked neighborhood market just off the corner of Fort Avenue and Hull Street in the heart of Locust Point.

Two or three days a week, 67-year-old "Wags" Wagner runs to the B. Green warehouse on Washington Boulevard to stock up on inventory, shelling out about $500 for candy and detergent, Tastykakes, canned beans, pickles and mayonnaise (only Hellmann's because he says "it's the best").

When asked to estimate the profit made on $500 worth of wholesale groceries, the couple is stumped.

"God knows. We've never figured it out," says Mrs. Wagner, 63, granddaughter of William Frederick Gabrio, who started the store. "People don't do business like this anymore."

Donald Wagner is one of the last, if not the very last, corner grocer in Baltimore who still butchers beef and pork to order.

About once a week, he gets half a steer, a loin of pork and a couple of boxes of boned meat from the Henry Heil meatpackers in Hampden. As customers come in, Mr. Wagner hauls the meat out of his wooden walk-in cool box and breaks it down the way they like it.

Business is first come, first served, with some patrons requesting meat for a single meal and others, like Henry's Bar on Fort Avenue, ordering enough beef cubes to make stew for the whole saloon.

"Let's see," says Mr. Wagner to a middle-aged woman named Rose Hoffman, a customer since childhood. "That's a Yoo-Hoo, three pork chops and a bag of chips?"

"That's it," she says.

But she doesn't hand over cash. Instead, Mrs. Hoffman's name and her debt go on a sheet of butcher's paper held by a clip with other running tabs. Children sign for their parents.

Mr. Wagner jokingly calls the debt sheet his version of running "an ATM card" service for his customers.

Except that banks and supermarkets — corporations that spend a lot of advertising money telling the public how friendly they are — aren't in the habit of doing business on trust. And they don't close up shop to run errands for old people or patronize the competition because someone in the neighborhood is bedridden and needs something specific.

The Wagners do.

They are gentle people; kind souls with an evident love for one another, for children and for customers they count as friends.

When a gang of kids comes in and clamors around Mrs. Wagner for ice cream, she smiles down at them and takes their faces in her hands. As Mr. Wagner collects tiny handfuls of change, Mrs. Wagner goes back to the family's part of the house and brings out paper towels so the ice cream doesn't run over the youngsters' hands.

Max Staffa has been coming in since he was 7. Now he's 80.

"I remember your grandfather," he says to Mrs. Wagner. "Back then, you didn't have the money to run in and get something for yourself. You got what your mother needed and that was it."

Yesterday, a man named Ritter Brauer came in for some plum tomatoes and romaine lettuce. The Wagners have never carried either, but told their old friend to come back after lunch.

Before Mr. Brauer returned, Wags Wagner had driven down to Cross Street Market to satisfy his customer.

Some customers take such blessings for granted. The store is open from 7 a.m. to 6 p.m. Tuesday through Saturday and locks up after a half-day Monday. When the Wagners' daughter was getting married a few years ago, an elderly woman caught Mr. Wagner as he was closing to attend the rehearsal dinner.

Told the store would be closed for a few days, the old lady screwed up her face and said: "That's nice, your daughter's getting married and all. But what about my half-pound of ham baloney?"

Neither the man who supplies the Wagners with meat nor the man who keeps their knives sharp know of anyone else butchering meat in Baltimore from a small, neighborhood storefront.

"When I came along 47 years ago they were on every corner," said Bob Jewell, owner of the Heil meat company.

"My great-uncle Lino Vidi was serving that store back when we took the grinding wheel to the customer," said Frank Monaldi, a third-generation knife sharpener. "We do five knives a week for Mr. Wagner — a meat cleaver, two big butcher knives and two boning knives."

With a keen knife, a good round of meat, a grinder he calls his "money-making baby doll" and a pocketful of wisecracks, Mr. Wagner knows how to keep the neighbors happy.

For years he's had the same running joke with a guy who always asks for pork chops and always says, "Make 'em lean." To which Mr. Wagner has no choice but to reply: "You want 'em to lean to the left or to the right?"

The demand for red meat is down, he says, and people are buying more chicken.

When Mrs. Wagner was a little girl, her grandparents slaughtered chickens in the back yard and plucked them at the kitchen table. "You thought nothing of it," she says.

Even the cuts of meat have changed with the times.

"The old timers come in asking for shins to make stew," said Mr. Wagner. "Some want the shins cut up, others get it whole, but the newer crew, they wouldn't know what to do with a shin."

Trained as a printer at the old Mergenthaler High School at Greenmount and Eager streets, Mr. Wagner quit the trade in 1962 when his wife's father became sick. Soon, they had sold their house in Northwood and were living back in the old waterfront village, where Mr. Wagner's father-in-law taught him to cut meat.

It didn't seem so good at the time, they say, but turned out to be the best thing that could have happened to them.

"We don't have a lot, but we raised our kids here and gave them a good education," says Mrs. Wagner. "Right, Wags?"

"You got that right," says Mr. Wagner, looking up from his cutting board. A man comes in and Mr. Wagner wipes his hands on his apron and scoots behind the counter, saying as he moves: "What can I do for you, pal?"

May 17, 1995

Golden touch is paying off

TO GET WHERE HE WANTED TO GO, YOSIE MAKIAS ONCE CONVERTED OUNCES of gold into hoop earrings studded with 70 quarter-karat diamonds: grand schlock to ornament the girlfriends of drug dealers.

With the money Mr. Makias earned at inner-city gold stores — shops in Baltimore and Philadelphia where the owners didn't care where cash for a sale originated — the jeweler from Jerusalem bought his own tools, opened a workshop and aimed his talents higher.

"I sold my soul for a while," says Mr. Makias, without shame or regret over the money he indirectly made off the drug trade. "I did it until I could do what I was born to do."

At 1706 Fleet St., just off Broadway in a shop two centuries old, he now pursues his birthright, the creation of ceremonial Jewish art from scraps of silver and gold.

With Baltimore's humidity tarnishing the work before it's finished, Mr. Makias molds and casts silver goblets beaded with gold, carves doorway scrolls, makes four-sided, spinning Hanukkah dreidels "from scratch," Sabbath candlestick holders with lions bearing the Star of David, charity boxes, ivory fingers at the end of silver Bible pointers, and wedding rings with these words in Hebrew: "Me for my beloved and my beloved for me."

In the shop up front, near old teapot clocks and Sunday china from couples long dead, he sells his art from a case. Upstairs, he lives in three small rooms with his second wife, the former Mary Beth Plansky of Pikesville.

Working in a lime-green building he bought last August for $67,000 and fixed up with stuff other people didn't want, doing simple jewelry repair and selling original work that brings between $200 and $2,000, Yosie Makias has made it in Fells Point for the past year.

"You build something out of nothing," he says. "With jewelry you make money; with the Judaica, I'm hardly making my money back."

He points to the $385 tag on a 4-inch-high dreidel that turns on a silver base and says: "If they play with it and have fun, that is my reward. It is my way of saying thank you to God, thank you and thank you again for being able to make a living with the talent He gave me."

The oldest of 12 children and the grandson of a shepherd who left Morocco to start over in Jerusalem, he was born on Mount Scopus in 1945 and showed artistic talent in grade school. Heartened to see his drawings celebrated, he was tutored at Jerusalem's Bezalel art school and later mastered sculpture. After leaving school, he worked with his father in advertising, fought in the Six Day War, and made jewelry.

"And then I discovered Jewish ceremonial art," he says. "It was rewarding to conquer the metal and bring out what is in your imagination." His first works were silver biblical figurines of David, Moses and Samson.

In late 1985, with $680 and a tourist visa in his pocket, Mr. Makias landed in New York "with dreams of America and English I learned from comic books," and took a room at the 34th Street YMCA. He picked up odd jewelry jobs, found out how easily employers can exploit a greenhorn and soon moved to Baltimore when his boss opened a Howard Street store. There, he made gold ropes and nameplate necklaces. On the advice of a cousin, he moved to Philly to do the same work for twice the money, for four years in the late 1980s.

The excesses of what passes for class among narcotics gangsters allowed him enough money to go into business for himself. Marrying Mary Beth Plansky after she answered his personal ad in the *City Paper* — "38-year-old professional jewelry designer/recently arrived from Israel/looking for someone to show him the town" — allowed him to stay in the United States.

After several years in his wife's Ellicott City jewelry store, the couple made a go of it on Fleet Street.

While his art exalts Judaism, Mr. Makias' own faith is a hodgepodge of observance. He closes his shop each Saturday for Sabbath — "It has proven itself for the good, never have I doubted that I have less business," he says — but does not keep a kosher kitchen. He reads commentaries on the Torah, but only attends synagogue on a handful of holy days.

Because his ceremonial objects don't conform strictly to the specifications of Jewish law, his customers tend to be Reform and secular Jews. The Orthodox, he says, go their own way.

At sundown tomorrow night, when Orthodox adults begin a 24-hour solemn fast to commemorate Tisha Be'Av, the destruction of the first and second temples in Jerusalem and the expulsion of the Jews from Spain in 1492, Mr. Makias will be eating and drinking as usual.

"I haven't fasted since I was a boy in Israel," he says. "When you are young and you see what everybody is doing, you do it. I remember those days now, but I let them pass."

August 4, 1995

Store thrives on a mix of merchandise

THE ALLEY ROWHOUSES AROUND THE CONKLING SALVAGE EXCHANGE AND FOAM Center in Highlandtown are fitted with staircases so twisted and narrow that it's nearly impossible to drag a box spring and mattress to the bedrooms upstairs.

"So they've got to use foam," says store employee Adam Smith.

And so they come to the Salvage Exchange, where a big sign at the corner of Conkling Street and Claremont Avenue promises "Everything from Flypaper to Flying Machines."

Before getting to the piles of foam at the back of the store, customers navigate aisles of fake flowers — 95 cents a bunch — whose constant blooms wind up adorning local tombstones; plastic piggy banks fat enough for 10 times the coins it costs to take one home; spatulas and paint brushes and wooden sauce spoons; framed posters of tough guys and cowboys; socks for 69 cents a pair; and a carnival of bric-a-brac to decorate the parlor windows of East Baltimore's most whimsical grandmothers.

Years ago they sold bikes and wagons on the layaway plan, but those days are gone.

"It's always changing. Except for foam and flowers, we're not trying to sell anything forever," says Stanford Schneider, 69, whose life has been the store since he was old enough to sell three pairs of shoelaces for a nickel and mismatched socks — better than no socks in Depression days — for a dime.

Mixing up the inventory at a neighborhood store is the trick to moving truckloads of low-budget quirks like spatulas, Schneider confides. If folks see something on special one day, they pounce on it in the belief that it might be gone tomorrow. In this way, says Schneider, the Salvage Exchange grosses about $20,000 in sales a month, most of it from flowers and foam.

"My aunt and uncle [Sarah and Mike Lipman] started here in 1934. It used to be a bakery. They lived on the second floor where we store all the Christmas merchandise and took baths at my aunt's house on Chester Street because the store didn't have a tub," says Schneider, standing in shafts of sunshine pouring through the store's plate glass windows, remembering days when "families worked together and cried together."

"After they got married in 1918, they owned shoe stores and variety stores, ma-and-pa places. He'd open up in the morning while she cooked breakfast. When he came to the kitchen to eat, she'd mind the store."

The Lipmans worked their way up to a store at Lombard and Dean streets that sold furniture on time. They were doing well enough to take out a mortgage on the building when the Depression hit.

Schneider says that as his customers became destitute, Uncle Mike — "a ham actor who wrote poetry and would sing you a song at the drop of a hat" — forgave their debts, turned in the store's keys to the bank that held the mortgage and went to live with his in-laws on Chester Street.

By the summer of 1934, Mike Lipman propositioned the same bank that had financed the failed furniture store: Let me clean and repair the old bakery up for auction at Conkling and Claremont in exchange for six months free rent. If I can make a go of a business there, we'll talk about a lease. If not, you'll have a more attractive piece of property to auction off for your trouble.

Sixty-four years later — with nary a flying machine having sailed in or out — Mike Lipman's bright idea of selling "whatever came along" is still ringing up sales.

The neighborhood has changed — graffiti and trash mar once spotless streets around Our Lady of Pompei Church, the old-school Italians who brought homemade lunch to shop owners have died, most of their kids moved to the suburbs and renters threaten to outnumber homeowners.

But the Salvage Exchange stays afloat on flowers and foam.

And Stan Schneider, a kid whose father died when he was 5 and came of age in a store run by an aunt and uncle who had no children, keeps the doors open.

"I had an opportunity to go to college, could have done anything I wanted, but I liked the business. I liked people and I liked this neighborhood," he says. "There's not too many places you can go and get foam cut the way you want. We sell it for boats and campers, recreational vehicle cushions and mattresses. Bring in your slipcovers and we'll measure and stuff them. I can't make it on the neighborhood trade alone anymore, but people come from all over to buy our foam."

About a decade ago, it appeared that Stan's son — a clever, creative man named Jay who brought an elegant touch to the Salvage Exchange — would take over the business and run it with Smith, who is the proprietor's long-time trusted right-hand man.

Jay Schneider died of AIDS in 1990 just shy of his 32nd birthday. Ever since, Stan and his wife, Sylvia, have volunteered at the Johns Hopkins AIDS center and give talks to young people and seniors about the disease.

"The plan was for me to retire and Jay would take over," said Schneider. "It didn't work out."

Now, Smith is poised to become the decision maker who puts out Nativity scenes for sale each December, Easter bunnies in spring, everyday glassware and as much foam as Baltimore can handle.

"Mr. Stanford will run it as long as he can keep on coming in here," says Smith. "I respect him, I'm loyal to him and I make a good living. And he says I don't need to know everything just yet."

May 26, 1998

Parked at Used Car Heaven

KEN MARSHALL — CHIEF EXECUTIVE OFFICER OF A BUCOLIC PATCH OF Baltimore known as Used Car Heaven — falls back on the Roman Catholic education he got at St. Wenceslaus parish to explain the theological nuances involved in the sale of used cars.

"Used Car Heaven — that's my own origination," he explains. "That's because I only handle good cars and you only go to heaven if you're good."

Marshall seems to have forgotten the part of his catechism that says you go to someplace a little warmer than heaven for telling fibs.

If Ma & Pa Kettle were going to abandon the family jalopy, they'd do it at the "little rag bag operation" in Southwest Baltimore where it's anyone's guess as to how many of the cars actually run.

"Probably half don't run," ventures Marshall, still spry enough at 75 to leap off the dented hood of a junked compact at the back of the lot after tying up a string of tattered pennants.

It's hard to tell which half Marshall is referring to on the three-quarters-of-an-acre lot in Morrell Park crowded with gutted pickup trucks attached to vandalized campers, Ford Grenadas with paint jobs that look like they were rolled on and rusting economy cars with missing dashboards.

"Definitely the eight up front run," he says. Marshall takes a 1985 Cutlass Supreme — $550 or best offer — out of the front row to prove his point. Before the engine will turn over, he has to change the battery.

"I scrape out a living, but to be perfectly frank with you, I ain't been making no money here. That's why you see me stuck with this bunch of mangy pieces of junk," says the Chuck Thompson look-alike who offers no warranty on his products.

Every weekday before the sun comes up, Marshall leaves his Overlea home for his livelihood in the 1900 block of Maisel St., just off Washington Boulevard near the old Montgomery Ward warehouse. He stays until noon, then goes home and gets in his pajamas to watch TV and answer mail.

Marshall has done his horse trading on the same lot for some 40 years, ever since selling his last new car for Landay's Nash on South Paca Street, since the days when Maisel Street was a residential neighborhood before the

Gwynns Falls flooded one too many times in the early 1970s and the city demolished the rowhouses there.

"This has always been a live street," he says, waving to a steady parade of truck drivers, friends and strangers who cruise the narrow artery that connects Morrell Park with the Mount Winans neighborhood. "It might look like it's out of the way, but you'd be surprised."

Marshall says he sells about two or three cars a week. He scraps more than he sells.

"You junk 'em for $40 or $50, but the price goes by weight and not only can't you tell one new car from another because they all look alike these days, they don't weigh as much as they used to," Marshall explains. "I got a guy with a tow truck who uses the back of my lot and if we get a car that ain't no good, he'll wait until he gets eight or 10 of them and junk 'em all in the same day."

One of the Maisel Street houses that was torn down was used by Marshall as an office. The old front walkway is still there, right next to the small office trailer Marshall uses and the colony of stray cats that survives behind it on his benevolence.

"They're my friends. If I had to be anything other than a human being, I think I'd be a cat," he says, bending to fill a bowl with milk. "They're such wonderful creatures and they have nine lives."

Which is at least seven more lives than Marshall's cars seem to have. Hooligans have burned him out of three earlier trailers and once set a half-dozen of his cars on fire at once.

The inside of his trailer is festooned with boxing promotions and horse race posters ("I like to bet, but I ain't no racetrack degenerate," he says), snapshots of children and grandchildren and fishing trips, a crucifix, an up-to-date used car dealer's license issued to Kenneth J. Marshall and Catherine F. Marshall, and a sign that counsels folks to: "Be happy. For every minute you are angry you lose 60 seconds of happiness."

A phone inside the trailer rings over the sound of an AM radio station playing Billy Eckstine and Sarah Vaughn. Marshall, a little hard of hearing, starts barking into the phone.

"What can I do for you?" he asks. "Does it run? What year is it? How's the body? Whaddaya want for it? About $100? How about $50? Bring it over."

Marshall gets his inventory from a classified ad that runs in the paper every morning under "Autos Wanted." In the world of used cars, a cheap buy is about $1,000. At Used Car Heaven, you can get a Ford Fairmount for $250, a Chevy Citation for about the same.

"I might get 100 calls before I buy two cars," says Marshall. "A lot of people call up but never show up. Sometimes I'm busy as the devil, other times it's slow as molasses, but I have a third sense when money drives by. By the time the dealers are coming to me, I know they're hungry because they only call me to unload cars when they can't do nothing else. People have a way of knowing when you're down and out."

Now and then he'll pick up a car from Victor Doster of Vic's Auto Sales at Monroe Street and Wilkens Avenue.

Says Doster: "Kenny's one of those people who won't change with the times. He still thinks it's the '50s and '60s. I wished it was, but things don't work that way."

Marshall says he's semi-retired now, but likes hanging around Maisel Street; enjoying the mornings, keeping the roadway clean and feeding his cats. Walking through the woods behind his lot to the flowing falls, he picks a worm from beneath a rock, tosses it into the stream and watches as a fish darts over to chomp it.

"Even though you're in the city, it's like being in the country," he says. "I have a lot of wildlife around here — it's not unusual to see raccoons and fox, squirrel and rabbit. There even used to be pheasants when the grass was tall around here."

Not to mention the illicit lovers and drug addicts.

"But," Marshall explains, "you're going to have that everywhere."

August 8, 1998

Chapter 13

Letters Home

For an innocent abroad in San Francisco, lunch has its price

SAN FRANCISCO — RELIGIOUS ZEALOTS ARE POSITIVELY DRAWN TO ME. Since the time I was old enough to go to shopping malls by myself, some one or some group has assumed the responsibility of showing me the light.

If nothing else, I have learned that the light is available in different colors.

It's probably because I have a hard time being rude to strangers. (Being rude to friends is no problem.)

It happened again on the first day of my California vacation this part summer. I was sitting on a ledge in San Francisco's crowded Union Square at 10 in the morning, pretending it was 1967 and generally minding my own business.

A couple of clean-cut young adults approached, color in their cheeks and gleams in their eyes. A boy and a girl.

"Don't tell me," I said as they were winding up for the pitch, "You're Christians, right?"

"No, not really. What makes you ask that?"

"Well, you look too wholesome to be perverts or dopers. Moonies, right?"

"No, not at all," said the girl. "We're friends of God."

The boy spoke up before I could ask the girl what God was up to these days. And he asked me where I was from. At one time, he lived in Baltimore while attending City College. We talked about Earl Weaver for a few minutes and then the girl pulled out a little notebook.

"Do you like pizza?" she asked.

"Sure."

"Why don't you join us for lunch today? We'll tell you all about what we're all about." She wrote down their names and address and handed it to me.

I said that if nothing came up, I would make a sincere effort to be there.

"What a nice person," said the girl in an effort to close the deal, her gleam getting brighter by a few degrees.

As they left I realized that I didn't succeed in finding out what exactly which religious crock-pot they were stewing in. Walking away in the other direction I wasn't sure if I was going to join them for lunch or not.

I do like pizza.

Four blocks later my fate was sealed. I turned a corner and there they were — smiling.

"This isn't just coincidence, Rafael," said the boy.

"Yeah," I said, a bit spooked. "See you for lunch."

I arrived at the address on Bush Street at 11:30. Waiting in front was a girl with kind of a pumpkin face framed by many curls. Her name was Suzi. She was from Los Angeles and had also been invited to lunch, but by a different couple.

The difference between Baltimore and L. A. is that where I was curious and trustful, she was curious and very suspicious.

"I've met these kind before," she said, ringing the bell. "We may not pay for anything, but this isn't a free lunch."

Inside, a guy with an English accent asked us to register and take off our shoes. Once we did, we were told, "Go right on up."

It was one of the largest rowhouses I've ever seen, with deep wood paneling and fine carpeting everywhere. From behind two large, wood-framed glass doors with sheer curtains, came strains of "He's Got the Whole World in His Hands."

Suzi and I shrugged at each other and went in.

Seated on the floor around a huge coffee table were about 20 people. Suzi and I sat down and were motioned to join in the singing. After the song was over a woman from New Zealand stood up, introduced herself as one of the leaders and asked that we go around the room introducing ourselves and giving our hometown.

Except for the New Zealander and a few others, everyone present had been invited to lunch that morning. And everyone invited to lunch was a tourist.

After the introductions, we were told that the only thing that would be asked of us would be to watch a slide presentation after lunch.

First lunch. It wasn't much on variety — soup, salad, sandwiches and corn on the cob (the promised pizza never appeared) — but there were gluttonous amounts of everything. The volume, I would learn later, was key to what our hosts were all about.

In the middle of my second helping I was spotted by the guy who had invited me, Greg. He didn't want to talk about Earl Weaver.

"Do you like what's going on here?" he asked gently.

"It's really encouraging," I said between chomps of corn. "What's going on here?"

"Basically we're for good will. Whatever a person's talent, and everyone has some, we believe it should be used for the benefit of others. That's why we're called the Creative Community Project."

"That's it? No doctrine? No rules?"

Greg shifted around a bit before answering. "Well, not really. We have a leader, but he won't be around until tonight. He can really explain things better than I can."

Up to this point, the CCP had been different from every other religious group I'd ever met. No preaching, no guilt trip, no quotations. Whatever their doctrine, the initial approach was casual and uplifting without a trace of potential conversion.

"What's your talent, Greg?"

"I drive a tractor on our farm."

"Oh ... your farm."

"That's where all this food came from. You'll learn more about it during the slide show. What are you doing for dinner?"

"What do your parents think about all this, Greg?"

"It's not what they thought I would do after college. Have some more corn."

Around the room I noticed the number of commune members had slowly begun to equal the number of tourists. The members positioned themselves well, about one member in front of every two tourists.

The lady from New Zealand stood up and asked for the lights to be turned off and the shades lowered. I got up to pull down a shade, and when I sat down it was in a corner by myself. I didn't want to be smiled at during the slide show.

The show had one subject — The Farm.

Located about 25 miles outside San Francisco, it was very hilly and not ideal for farming.

In the slides of the farm we saw people singing, praying, working, laughing, eating, praying and singing.

God, Jesus, Allah, Buddha — none of these people was mentioned at all. A bearded English professor shown lecturing in one of the slides was referred to as the leader but he wasn't propped up with holy adjectives.

Heaven was mentioned a few times, especially during particularly picturesque scenes.

One fact about the farm was awesome.

On it, the CCP produces 50,000 pounds of food monthly. Most of it is given away to the needy, part of it is used to feed the curious tourists, and the rest is consumed by the commune.

As soon as the slide show ended, Greg inched his way over to my corner. Other members turned to face the tourist nearest them.

"Now what do you think?"

"What am I going to say? It looks great. Who can be against feeding the hungry? I'm all for good will."

"Why don't you come out to the farm?"

At that moment, I caught the back of Suzi's curly head out of the corner of my eye. I strained to hear what was being said to her.

"Well, Suzi, why don't you come out to the farm?"

I turned my attention back to Greg and said I couldn't go. I said I didn't fly 3,000 miles to see a farm. I asked why they needed me. Why couldn't I spread good will as an individual?

"Can you produce 50,000 pounds of food by yourself?" he asked.

"No," I said, "Why is it that talking and sharing ideas is never good enough for you people? Why do I have to give up what I've got to be like you? Why must I join? Why can't I just applaud you?"

"I thought you were different, Rafael."

"I thought you and the CCP were different."

"But you're not."

"And you're not."

I got up to leave and Greg said he'd carry my suitcase to the bus stop. He finally gave up on getting me to the farm and concentrated on getting me back to Bush Street for dinner with the bearded English professor.

I promised to come back in three days.

Three days later I was eight miles away in Berkeley.

A couple of young adults approached. A boy and a girl.

"Don't tell me," I said. "You want to feed me and take me to a farm, right?"

"What a nice person!" said the girl.

October 15, 1979

'Just a few words, fixed just right'

Marion, Va. — I am standing at the window of Room 307 of the Lincoln Hotel on Main Street here in the Blue Ridge mountains, looking out at the world and pretending I am George Willard, a reporter for the *Winesburg Eagle*.

"The young man's mind was carried away by his growing passion for dreams. One looking at him would not have thought him particularly sharp…"

I don't know who may be looking at me, as I stare out the window; maybe some folks on the far autumn hills, or the ghost of the man who wrote of dreams and passion in "Winesburg, Ohio," the book quoted above, the book that brought me here.

After traveling seven hours south from Baltimore, most of it at high speeds on Interstate 81, I am here to gather the power of a dead man's spirit from his former haunts; from gravel country lanes, desks where he wrote, and the memories of old folks who knew him.

I am here, where I know no one, to take a weekend walk with Sherwood Anderson — beyond the printed page, to know better the man who dug a sharp fork into American literature in 1919 with the groping beauty of "Winesburg."

"Nothing quite like it has ever been done in America," wrote H. L. Mencken, reviewing the book of simple stories in *The Smart Set*. "It is a book that, at one stroke, turns depression into enthusiasm… brilliant images of men and women who walk in all the colors of reality."

Moving to Marion for good after a summer visit for cool mountain air in 1925, Anderson eventually honored the Bard of Baltimore by renaming a town junk lot "Henry Mencken Park." He stayed here on and off, buying and editing a pair of local papers and writing on a farm he called "Ripshin" in the hills south of here for the next, and last, 16 years of his life.

Anderson's body lies in a graveyard overlooking the town called Round Hill Cemetery, about as steep a cemetery as you'll ever see. He is buried beneath a curved modern stone declaring:

"Life is the adventure, not death."

No one needs a tombstone to know this truth, so I stand at the window of the old Lincoln Hotel and pretend I am George Willard, the hero of

Winesburg who defined reality with words, an excited young man with a need to know.

But instead of catching glimpses of Myerbaum's Notion Store, Sylvester West's Drug Store, Winney's Dry Goods and other small-town businesses that were part of Willard's beat as he ran from story to story for the *Eagle*, I am faced with the modern Dominion Bank and the Appalachian Realty company at the other end of Main Street.

In very different ways, both buildings and a pair of very different men who walk the floors in them would supply me with some Sherwood Anderson secrets.

Don Francis, senior vice president of Dominion Bank, whose office holds first editions of all Anderson's 26 books, was the first to take me to Ripshin. At 7 a.m. he picked me up in the lobby of the old Lincoln, built in 1927, the year Anderson purchased the *Smyth County News* and the *Marion Democrat*, and treated me to eggs with biscuits and gravy at the local diner.

After breakfast, speaking with gentle authority as we wound through orange and gold hills wet with gray morning rain on our drive to nearby Troutdale, Mr. Francis said his fascination with Anderson was more historical than literary.

"I'm not a scholar; my objective is to help local people know a little bit more about his achievement," he said, pulling alongside a green metal mailbox stuffed with cobwebs at the gate. "When I was transferred to Marion by the bank in 1970, I didn't understand why no one had capitalized on the connection in a cultural way."

Mr. Francis had a key to the house and writing cabin from the relatives of Anderson's fourth and last wife, Marion native Eleanor Copenhaver, and as he told me of the town's annual Sherwood Anderson Short Story Contest, I poked around the stone and log country estate that would seem more in tune with the French countryside than the hills of Virginia.

Mr. Francis stood by patiently while I looked around for I don't know what. Something I couldn't see, I guess. I was scribbling fast and looking at a lot of things — Anderson's bed, Japanese translations of his books, a wooden model of his tombstone by Wharton Esherick, the sculptor who designed it, and private, signed pictures of such folks as Katherine Anne Porter and Max Eastman.

"Thomas Wolfe was here and complained about his bed not being long enough," said Mr. Francis.

On the way out I went into Anderson's writing cabin, a place built for nothing else, and smoothed my palms over the top of a desk built right into the wall.

"He was gone from here so much that when he came back it was almost like visiting," said Mr. Francis. "Even after he built this place he'd hole up in a hotel room somewhere to do his best work." I stood at the desk, staring out at Ripshin Creek bubbling in the rain outside the window, and thought about my room back at the Lincoln and the little desk under the window there.

That night, Mr. Francis introduced me to two of the dwindling number of folks in Marion who knew Anderson: Kathryn Weindel, a secretary to one of his best friends, and Joe Stephenson, a printer retired from the papers Anderson owned.

"He was the kind of guy who'd stop to think at the checkout turnstiles of the Piggly-Wiggly and other people couldn't get by," said Ms. Sweindel, who remembers typing a few letters and bits of manuscript for Anderson. "Other than that, he was just another man in a gray business suit as far as most people were concerned."

Joe Stephenson, 87, ran a Linotype machine at the *Smyth County News* for 64 years and had more vivid memories of the man with "them black eyes that'd look right at you," and said that if he'd been more aware of his boss' fame, "I'd have taken down some notes."

He remembered Anderson, "a racetrack man and a man who drank his part," coming into town to have the boys in the print shop slice up big stacks of blank newsprint to use as writing paper; Anderson, "who got people to send money from all over the country to buy matching band uniforms," telling him to go pick out "a suit of furniture" as a wedding present; and he remembered a big bonus from Anderson every Christmas: "... he gave us each a turkey and 10 bucks apiece," said Mr. Stephenson of the man Henry Miller said "could become ecstatic about a knife and fork." "We'd all like to fall down in the office when he gave us that," Mr. Stephenson said. "Nobody ever give us anything like that, not even my daddy."

The next morning, a man from a book-choked loft above the Appalachian Realty company appeared in the lobby in the Lincoln looking for me, having heard I was kicking around Smyth County on the Anderson trail. The man was John Mason Rudolph, a rare book dealer from Baltimore who arrived in Marion in 1986 to comb through the last remnants of the Anderson estate after the death of Eleanor. He never got around to telling me why he never left Marion.

Mr. Rudolph talks in fast Baltimorese, the voice of a slick-haired sport from the corner who verbalizes everything that passes before him in the language from Broadway and Thames Street in 1950s Bawlmer dialect peppered with vulgarities that "don't mean nothin'."

He is hunched over the wheel of a battered Chyrsler Le Baron station wagon and winds the same Route 16 south to Ripshin that Mr. Francis drove the day before, only today, Sunday, is clear and bright. He reminds me of a middle-aged Dean Moriarity, Jack Kerouac's saint-boy of the highway, glad to be in motion with somebody to talk to besides himself.

"Anderson was running away, he was running away all his life," says Mr. Rudolph, small eyes darting back and forth between the beautiful hills and the road. "He kept looking for that utopic [expletive] thing that ain't there. We're all kindred spirits like him. He wanted it like we all do. He was a real person. He liked to play croquet up there all [expletive] night."

We get to Ripshin and start taking pictures of each other. Me jotting notes on a wooden lounge chair, John jotting notes on a wooden lounge chair. Me sitting on a stone wall. John sitting on a stone wall. I find out that Mr. Rudolph is a writer, a desperate writer with a sick story to tell who says he's walked every street in Marion and doesn't have anything to say to anybody there.

"I really didn't plan on getting into literature," he says. "I was too busy making money. I'd make a big kill on a rare book and go straight to the track. But now I know that your writing is like your fingerprints, like your voice, it's you. You write the [expletive] way you write."

We pick red and gold leaves from the trees and give away Ripshin postcards to people in a passing car — a mom and dad with a retarded son and beautiful, big-eyed daughter in a back seat who want to know if somebody famous lived in the house. We walk around and around the house, picking up stones and telling stories.

"I'm gonna get out of the way of my life and write it all down," says Mr. Rudolph. "But if you don't get 'em hooked on the first pages you lose 'em. You start with a little scene and start to unravel it. These little [expletive] stories with a protagonist and a cockroach climbing the wall. You do it till you get your big slice of life, whether it's right or wrong. You can't be thinking of the whole novel, just the next sentence, and then the next paragraph.

"And you gotta have some kinda character," he says. "You might not be crazy about him but you gotta like him a little bit and he's got to see what ails other people and not just himself. He's gotta see pink clouds now and then, not just gray clouds. I feel a part of those people now — Wolfe and Turgenev and all those [expletives] — just like I feel a part of this Earth looking at these trees... Sherwood Anderson is just one person among many. We're all searching for love and we're always here in some kind of way."

Mr. Rudolph keeps talking and talking hunched over the wheel now as we drive back to town. While listening to Mr. Rudolph's words and thinking about the ghost I came looking for in Marion, I'm reminded of an old man named Ralph Repass whom I met early that morning in the lobby of the Lincoln Hotel.

"Anderson was one of these that could take a little ol' short sentence and paint the most complete picture," said Mr. Repass. "Just a few words, fixed just right."

November 20, 1988

'So big and so humble'

WACO, TEXAS — THERE ARE THREE SPOTS EVERY WANDERER OUGHT TO VISIT when passing through this central Texas town: the Dr. Pepper Museum, the Texas Ranger Hall of Fame and the little room at the back of Eddie Fadal's house.

We couldn't stay long enough to see the first two, but we made sure we had time to drop in on Eddie.

"I'll never forget for as long as I live," he said, standing in the middle of his special room on Green Oak Drive and holding his right hand in the air with fingers spread wide. "I'll never forget the day Elvis held his hand up like this in front of a room full of people and said: 'Eddie's one of the five best friends I ever had. He doesn't need me, he doesn't use me and I can't give him anything.'"

Eddie Fadal's Elvis Room is a tribute to that friendship.

And because of the retired disc jockey's personal connection to the King of Rock 'n' Roll, people the world over have made the trip to his suburban rancher just beyond Lake Waco — a gang of tourists from Austria; Anne Arundel County's Ace Anderson and his teen-age son, Elvis; and your correspondent, on his way to the Grand Canyon with his 9-year-old boy.

The guest book is full and growing, and the garage holds five large filing cabinets with mail Eddie gets from fans in Italy and Greece and Japan and most every country in between, fans who have read about Eddie Fadal in their Elvis newsletters.

"They see me as a link to him," said Eddie, 66, who befriended Elvis in 1956 while working for a local radio station when Presley performed in Waco.

The friendship deepened when Elvis was stationed at Fort Hood in nearby Killeen and visited the Fadals on weekends. It was a time when the singer was certain that the Army would end his entertainment career and was grateful for a home away from home.

"That's the hook," said Eddie. "The fans know I knew Elvis in his private moments in an old house on Lasker Avenue. And they want me to tell them what he was like."

To Eddie Fadal, Elvis Presley was nothing if not "lonely and sensitive."

I met Eddie in the Meditation Garden at Graceland last August while covering the 14th anniversary of Elvis' death and found him to be gentle, generous with his time and knowledgeable.

And about a week ago, while driving from Johnny Winter's hometown of Beaumont, Texas, northwest across the Lone Star State toward the Grand Canyon, I remembered Eddie and decided to stop by.

You don't know of Eddie's connection to the King when you enter the home where Eddie lives with his wife LaNelle. There are no traces of Elvis in the part of the house where the Fadals take their meals or watch television, no signs of Presley in the bedrooms or bathrooms.

We were seated in the dining room, and Mrs. Fadal — the woman who couldn't burn the bacon black enough to please Elvis — served us coffee and hot cinnamon buns.

As Eddie and I began chatting about the Elvis community, how various fan clubs split off into warring factions like fundamentalist churches arguing over who loves Elvis the most, my son Jake began to ask the blunt questions of a child.

Why was Elvis so fat?

Why did he eat fried peanut butter and banana sandwiches?

How come there is so much junk with Elvis' face on it?

Eddie smiled, looked at Jake with his big, kind eyes and was silent for a moment.

I tried to explain that Mr. Eddie knew the real Elvis, the human being, not the cartoon that Presley has become. I told Jake that Mr. Eddie knew the flesh and blood, not the plaster Elvis head we put in the window of our Highlandtown rowhouse at Christmas. I said Mr. Eddie cares for Elvis very much.

"Mr. Eddie knew Elvis as a friend," I said. "You might be hurting his feelings. Do you understand?"

"I think he does," said Eddie, getting up from the table. "Do you want to see the room now?"

We entered a room no bigger than a typical Cockeysville den and no different except that it is crammed from ceiling to floor and wall to wall with rare Elvis artifacts that Miss Bonnie's Elvis Bar on Fleet Street would be proud to own.

Eddie put on some Elvis music as we entered, and the room was immediately filled with Presley's voice.

At the center of everything is a long green sofa from the early 1950s, where Elvis would take naps. "He'd just stretch out and close his eyes, setting his head right there on the arm rest. He never used a pillow."

The sofa was covered with teddy bears, and on every side were piles of books and buttons and posters, original photographs of the Fadal children with Elvis, a record album made in the Fadal home and the microphone Elvis used to record it. There's the original contract between Elvis' manager, Col. Tom Parker, and the local civic center where Elvis appeared in the early days. There's a framed three-page Western Union telegram sent by Elvis from Germany when Eddie's mother died.

Eddie is proud that he never accepted expensive gifts from Elvis. "I could've had anything I wanted back then," said Eddie. "I didn't take any of it because I wanted to be a real friend. Everybody he met had their hand out. He tried to give me a purple Cadillac once, and I said: 'Elvis, there's no one way I'm going to drive a purple Cadillac through the streets of Waco.'

"All the time as I travel around to the different fan clubs, I hear stories about how healing his music is for people. Those stories are from the heart, and I hear them all the time," said Eddie, staring over at the couch where the King used to nap. "And as I sit here and listen to the music and think back to those times — he was so big and so humble — a feeling just comes over me."

July 23, 1992

In search of the blues

HOLLY SPRINGS, MISS. — TWO OR THREE TIMES A MONTH, THE PHONE RINGS in R.L. Burnside's little farmhouse on Highway 4; calls from strangers asking if they can stop by to talk about the blues.

The last time Mr. Burnside's phone jumped with a curious ring, the callers were pilgrims from Baltimore.

"Sure, I remember you," said the 66-year-old guitarist who learned his lessons by watching Mississippi Fred McDowell and Muddy Waters. "Come on over."

I had met "Rule" Burnside once before, when he played at the Cat's Eye Pub on Thames Street in May 1986. Back then he had said: "I think the blues are beginning to come back a little bit."

Maybe. Hopes for a blues revival flutter beneath the chaos of mainstream music every six or seven years. As they come and go, artists like Mr. Burnside endure, hauling the blues around the world for those who care to listen.

Rule Burnside will be bringing the blues back to Baltimore when he plays the gilded juke joint known as the Walters Art Gallery tomorrow at 8 p.m.

Since Mr. Burnside's last visit to the jewel at the head of the Patapsco, his music has grown stronger, while year after year his peers have been dying in twos and threes.

When I interviewed Albert King on his 68th birthday in New York City last April, we talked about the death of bluesman Johnny Shines, one of those rare blue birds who actually traveled and played with the fabled Robert Johnson.

Around the wood-burning stove in the living room of R.L. Burnside's two-story white frame farmhouse, we discussed the December death of King.

"I saw Albert two weeks before he died, in Memphis on Beale Street," said Mr. Burnside. "I go up there to sit in with my son Dwayne sometimes. He plays at B.B.'s [B.B. King's] club. Sometimes we all jam. Albert was there and he looked healthy. I had talked to him that Wednesday night, but Friday he said something about his heart. His breath was short. He told Dwayne to get him an Alka Seltzer," Burnside said. "And the next Monday he died."

Asked to identify what was special about Albert King's music, Mr. Burnside said: "He could sing the blues good and he was a good guitar player."

As is Mr. Burnside, who plays both electric and acoustic guitar and counts

Albert's "Born Under a Bad Sign," popularized in the hippie era by Cream, in his repertoire.

The great fun of seeking out bluesmen in their own backyards is asking if they would play a song or two.

"I'd rather not," Mr. Burnside said, smiling and picking up his guitar.

He is a classic Delta-style guitarist in the tradition of Robert Johnson and Fred McDowell, whom R.L. honors as his mentor. He lived in the electric blues of Chicago for a few years in the 1950s, where he picked up slide guitar by watching Muddy Waters. But, "I like the old-time blues best."

The old-time blues is what my friend and I got as he launched into "Jumper on the Line," a song he performed in the documentary "Deep Blues," which was shown earlier this month at the Orpheum Cinema in Fells Point.

Now what do you think a title like "Jumper on the Line" means?

I thought maybe it was about fishing. It is, sort of.

Mr. Burnside, eyes wide in the joy of making others happy, sang out in a high voice: "See my jumper, Lord, oh hangin' on the line... yes, I see my jumper, oh lord, a hangin' on the line.

"When I see my jumper, you know there's somethin' on my mind."

Call it espionage of the heart. In blues lore, if a married woman hangs her housecoat or "jumper" out on the clothesline, it's a sign to her lover that the coast is clear.

R.L. had some competition from a TV set in another room, and several of his 12 children came and went. A few were working on a derelict Ford Pinto in the front yard. His wife Alice sat beside him, rubbing her temples as her man showed off the way he earns a living.

Mr. Burnside played three songs before quitting, picking the notes with the nail of his right index finger and strumming chords with his thumb.

Once in a while, as he sat on the sofa across from a big blue and red poster of a Paris blues festival with his name on it, Mr. Burnside banged on the wooden guitar as though it were a drum.

There was one more thing I wanted to give this generous man before leaving, but first I had to see if the gift was appropriate.

I wanted to know what R.L. Burnside, a former sharecropper whose music is a direct link to the most primal of American art, thought of Elvis Presley, another Magnolia State native who is accused of stealing that art.

As I posed the question, there was music spinning in my head: Elvis hits interpreted by the late Albert King on an album with the eerie title "Blues for Elvis."

"I like Elvis, yeah man, yeah," he said. "I think Elvis helped the black people. I believe it now; I sure enough do."

And so the image of R.L. Burnside that stayed with me, as I backed out of his front yard to drive to the grave of Elmore James an hour's drive south, is that of a grinning man in a red flannel shirt and work pants.

And he's holding up a sheet of Elvis stamps from Baltimore's Gough Street post office.

It seems there is no room for resentment in R.L. Burnside's blues.

"I never figured it would come to this," he said. "Me — a poor man growing up on a farm, playing music all over the world. I never thought I would go the places I've been… The blues have helped me a heap. I've been lucky there."

February 26, 1993

'He's not a rock star'

BANGKOK — THERE I WAS WITH EIGHT NOBEL PEACE PRIZE LAUREATES. What a crowd of high-rollers!

It was like being in the parlor of a Highlandtown rowhouse with all four Beatles, Elvis, Little Richard and the Everly Brothers.

Like trudging to the top of the mountain to ask an aged guru the meaning of life.

Except that the pilgrimage was made by elevator to the top floor of the five-star Dusit Thani hotel, up a narrow staircase and into the tight quarters of the Foreign Correspondents Club of Thailand where wisdom was offered to some 50 reporters from around the world.

The marquee names were Archbishop Desmond Tutu of South Africa, who won the peace prize in 1984, and His Holiness, the Dalai Lama of Tibet, honored in 1989.

Also present were Oscar Arias Sanchez, the former president of Costa Rica, who won in 1987; Northern Ireland's Betty Williams and Mairead Corrigan, who shared the prize in 1976; Adolfo Perez Esquivel, of Argentina (1980); Ross Daniels, representing Amnesty International (1977); and Donna Kyle Anderton, who appeared on behalf of the American Friends Service Committee (1947).

They gathered to appeal for the release of 1991 Nobel peace laureate Aung San Suu Kyi, the Burmese opposition leader under house arrest since 1989. Her captors, Burma's brutal military junta known as the State Law and Order Restoration Council, have killed and tortured thousands since seizing power from a fledgling democracy in 1988.

After opening remarks calling for a global arms embargo against Burma, all but one of the laureates strolled away, leaving behind a serious but easy-going man of 60 in a saffron robe, burgundy scarf and designer spectacles.

A man, the moderator said, "who needs very little introduction."

Hello, Dalai.

Despite the relative importance of his Nobel brethren, the Dalai Lama was the big cheese in Bangkok, the one whose mere presence caused formal protest from the People's Republic of China, which rules Tibet and forced his exile to India in 1959; whose arrival agitated the Thai military, which has ties to the junta in Rangoon and saw nothing to gain and much to lose by hosting the peace mission; who, as a Buddhist celebrity in a nation of Buddhists, was mobbed everywhere he went.

For 27 hours in February, the banished spiritual leader of the Tibetan people was just about the only thing people were talking about here, his every move front-page news.

Said one local monk, upset that crushing crowds prevented him from making eye contact with His Holiness: "It's too much, very inhumane. . . . He's not a rock star."

Indeed, the press conference was so jammed with reporters, cameramen and media groupies that my best view of the Dalai's kindly face was through the upside-down V made by the legs of a photographer standing on a chair in front of me.

Holy as he may be, he knows well the carnal world in which the media whirls.

Gone, he said, are the days when a monk can seclude himself and his secrets inside a temple.

While he argued for spiritual solutions to material dilemmas — saying that human compassion should not be seen as a philosophy only for the religious — reporters persisted with questions of juntas and guns and gummed-up balls of geo-political yarn.

He implored: "Media — when I talk of these things, it may seem boring. You want me to talk of the Tibetan issue, of the discomfort my visit has caused . . . of my own tragedy."

But, he said, there must be talk of greater truths.

And then he shared opinions on fantastic subjects seldom aired at press conferences. I could not imagine such a dialogue taking place back home, even at a conference of Catholic bishops or a congress of rabbis.

In capable English, this Holy Knight of Mirth said: "What is human rights? The purpose of human rights is happiness. Everyone survives because of hope for the better . . . whether we are religious or businessman. Essentially we belong to one world, one family. If we do something in the wrong direction, we all suffer."

Rangoon's military leaders should realize, from a practical view, he said, that they cannot hurt the Burmese people without hurting themselves and all of Burma.

"And so," said the Dalai Lama, "motivation is the key factor of every human action. Motivation is the key factor for our future. Human compassion, human love, human feeling . . . in order to have a better world we must cultivate these good things within ourselves."

The next morning the headlines in the English-speaking dailies barked: "Impose arms embargo — Dalai Lama."

Fine.

Do it.

But while Burma is just a few hundred miles from where I am now, it is a million miles away in my mind.

As the Dalai Lama spoke of the suffering there — the thousands slain at pro-democracy demonstrations, the drunken soldiers who beat and kick people unconscious during downtown torture sessions, the families who cringe as government thugs shoot their chickens for fun — I wondered how Buddhism might address the daily death and torture in Baltimore.

I wondered if a savvy voice such as the Dalai Lama's might be the one to touch the hearts of 15-year-old boys with handguns; the kids with beepers and gold and poison powders.

Smart children who might have a future if only they could conjure a vision of it beyond the glamour of money and death.

When convicted killer Dontay Carter was captured following his January escape from a courthouse bathroom, the wily teenager crowed that his manhunt got better press play than a reception for American mayors hosted by Kurt Schmoke.

A thrill for a moment.

Dead, like so many victims.

To the curbside cartels of guns, drugs and money from O'Donnell Heights to Poplar Grove, I ask simple willingness: ears for the words of a man with an orange robe and a shaved head.

"Weapons and narrow minds together are very dangerous," said the Dalai Lama. "The true source of happiness is within ourselves."

And I quote him again to clergy and lay folk in scores of Baltimore churches where I have taken tragically redundant notes during a dozen years of funerals for murder victims.

I recite him for anyone who has spent 10 minutes working to Stop the Killing.

Asked if a gathering of eight Nobel Peace Prize winners calling for justice in a loud, passionate and very public voice might effect change, the Dalai Lama said: "I don't know. My basic belief is whether the goal was achieved or not, we must make the effort."

March 28, 1993

'A powerful legacy'

LEXINGTON, MISS.— TRYING TO DESCRIBE THE MUSIC OF ELMORE JAMES, someone said the other day, is like trying to describe a primary color.

A color that screams your name as you walk by.

That cries all night long.

And bleeds.

Not just on you, but through you.

All the way through to the other side.

The color is blue.

Electric blue.

And it came down in buckets when the great Elmore James opened his mouth. "When Elmo played the blues you could feel a chill going over you," remembers guitarist Jimmy Spruill, who made records with James in the 1950s. "He made you feel like your mother just died: sad and miserable and doubtful."

From the late 1930s, when he began his rambles through the American South with Robert Johnson and Rice Miller, until his fatal heart attack in 1963, Elmore James used his voice and a slide guitar to paint lusty narratives with the primary colors of sadness, misery, and doubt.

"The sky is crying," he often sang, "look at the tears roll down the street."

The sky above the Newport Missionary Baptist Church graveyard is graced today with a pale, afternoon moon; a sky that is pleased on this warm and quiet Tuesday in February, carrying gentle winds of an early spring through fields of pine.

Down below, Elmore James lies in his 30th year of silence.

He is here, somewhere in this churchyard of rolling hills and crumbling tombstones off of Highway 17, but I am not sure just where because his grave went unmarked until late last year.

Last December, a handsome stone of ebony granite was erected at the cemetery entrance by Elmore's fans. No one is around on this bright afternoon to tell me if the man who could make an electric guitar sound like a tomcat being skinned alive is actually beneath it.

A black pick-up truck rumbles down the gravel road in front of the church, and the driver waves as he goes by. Nothing stirs but the wind until the pickup comes back the other way and the driver waves again.

The stone sports a bronze relief of a bespectacled James in suit coat and tie; a small, metal "slide" tube envelopes his pinky finger as he grips a six-string guitar; Elmore staring out across the quiet Mississippi countryside where he grew up as a farmhand.

Every man is the King of Something, if only his own lonely wanderings, and Elmore is memorialized as "King of the Slide Guitar."

Because the three-foot-tall monument is so far removed from the rest of the graves (it's the first one you meet, alongside a wooden sign welcoming people to the church), I wondered if the exact location of Elmore's body has been forgotten and they put his marker out front so pilgrims wouldn't miss it.

The other graves — "Queen Davis, Born 1850. Died Nov. 16, 1918" and "Omega Owens, Born July 26, 1908, Died August 11, 1970" — are out behind the church, a good 50 yards from the bluesman's headstone.

I stare at Elmore for a few minutes, the eerie, Hawaiian twang of his guitar looping through my mind, and walk around behind it to find an inscription chiseled on the back: "Born in Holmes County, Mississippi, Elmore James electrified the Delta blues with his unique slide guitar style, creating a powerful legacy that will remain forever in American music."

The legacy, which continues today through rock and roll, began on the sly.

At the gravestone's dedication on December 10, 1992, a cousin of Elmore's named Bessie Brooks told of a young James, known then as "Joe Willie," singing gospel for the grown-ups, "but when my parents would leave to go visiting he played the blues for us."

By the age of 12, already working in the fields, he was making sounds on wire uncoiled from a broom head and strung on the shack wall.

Such a blues conviction made for trouble with his parents, who only held to the conviction of the Holy Spirit, and soon he went to live with a more permissive aunt.

The Jackson (Miss.) *Advocate* quoted another cousin at the dedication, a woman named Annie Redmond who remembered Elmore making a guitar out of an old coffee can and two wires used to hang clothes.

"When my mother saw how determined he was to play the blues, she started throwing house parties to raise money to buy him a guitar," Ms. Redmond said.

Coming back to the front of the tombstone, I notice that birds have soiled the stone and I retrieve a bottle of glass cleaner and some paper towels from the car and go over the smooth face of the marker like an old Polish lady in Canton getting the streaks out of her front window.

After putting the cleaning stuff back in the car, I come back with a tape player and set it in the grass next to the stone.

I push a button and Elmore comes alive, the stillness broken, his voice booming deep blue philosophy across the countryside: "When things go wrong... so wrong with you... it hurts me too."

It took me back to a Southside Chicago funeral parlor in May of 1983 when a loudspeaker above an open coffin allowed Muddy Waters to sing at his own funeral.

The music that sails across this Mississippi churchyard comes courtesy of Elmore James by way of Capricorn Records, which last summer released 50 of Elmore's singles from 1959 to 1963 in a two-CD set titled: "King of the Slide Guitar."

Phil Walden, Capricorn's president, was one of the many who helped raised the cash for Elmore's tombstone.

Elmore's voice shadows me as I walk among the other graves, knowing little about his boneyard brethren except what information will fit on a grave marker: "Wash Brooks, March 16, 1872 to October 30, 1925... Asleep."

The thunder of Elmore's voice and the sting of his guitar recall a poet's description of strong coffee: "Black as night/strong as sin/sweet as love/hot as hell."

Elmore James died on my fifth birthday — May 24, 1963 — nine months before the Beatles appeared on Ed Sullivan and my life changed forever.

Those bright boys with bangs led me to the dark thrills of the Rolling Stones who opened the door to Johnny Winter who introduced me to Muddy Waters who carried me to Elmore James and a little graveyard down at the end of Newport Road in Lexington, Mississippi.

I don't remember my parents interrupting my birthday party to break the news: "Ralphie, we're sorry to have to tell you this, but Elmo has passed."

I wouldn't come to know the voice of Elmore James for another 15 years.

No one who loves music should wait so long.

As I take a last glimpse of Elmore's grave, the bluesman moans from the tape machine: "I believe... I believe... I believe my time ain't long."

The sun is dropping behind the pines and it is time to drive toward it.

May 2, 1993

Turning misery into song

STOVALL, MISS. — I AM STANDING ON THE SPOT WHERE MUDDY WATERS lived before he quit Mississippi for Chicago, staring across a verdant sea from the splintered foundation that once held the great blues singer's plantation shack.

The landscape is serene, the moment surreal with the knowledge that Muddy's cabin is touring the world. And though it seems as if all the pain and beauty of Mississippi is within reach, my thoughts fly north to the Park Heights Avenue home of an 80-year-old rabbi.

Riddle me this: Is it possible that the blues will set you free?

A few summers ago, in a brutal Baltimore August where any reporter foolish enough to make eye contact with an editor could wind up asking innocent people if it was hot enough for them, I would quietly disappear from the newsroom to take down the history of this particular Hasidic rabbi.

It was a fantastic tale of painful and valiant faith — "He is a big, big book! A whole life for you to read," promised the rabbi's wife — and I was keen to get it in the paper until the old man set down the rules.

I must give my word to either keep his name out of the article completely, or, when the writing was done, hide the story in a drawer until he had been dead for 10 years. It was, he said, a matter of modesty. I agreed.

And every time the temperature went above 95 degrees, I'd duck out of the office and make a beeline for the ramshackle Cape Cod-turned-synagogue for another installment in the tales of the Hasidim.

Known among Baltimore's Orthodox Jews as a peacemaker adept at mending broken relationships, my subject said he was the son of a rabbi, the grandson of a rabbi, the great-grandson of a rabbi, and on and on; rabbis begetting rabbis all the way back before the advent of Judaism's Hasidic movement in the mid-18th century. Born in Czechoslovakia between the Great War and the Good War, the rabbi said his earliest memory was the celebration, at age 3, that accompanied the shearing of all his hair except for long sidelocks. By 5, he would begin a formal, lifelong study of the Torah.

It was a community-wide upbringing in religious ritual "so natural I wouldn't consider myself successful if I didn't become a rabbi," and through it he grew wise to erratic beatings of the human heart without ever owning a television or stepping inside a movie theater.

"The main thing is to love people, to speak nice to them even when they're not so nice," he explained. "It's hard sometimes."

He remembered how the circus wagons would pass through his village once a year and, like the Yeshiva boys who love God but can't break free of baseball box scores, how tempting it was to peek at the acrobats and the animals.

"I could go and look if I wanted," he said, "but I wouldn't be praised for it."

Though today there are Orthodox Jews who encourage the joyful escape provided by dancing bears and juggling clowns, it is still rare. It certainly was not the case when the rabbi was a young boy in eastern Europe. He came to accept this frowning upon the frivolous in the same spirit that Hasidic Jews aspire to "accepting everything in a happy way, to believe that everything is from God."

And then the Nazis passed through his village and emptied it of Jews.

Sent to his first concentration camp in his mid-20s, he lost three siblings. His mother and father. A wife and all five of their children. The last stop was Auschwitz.

No mercy, not for a moment

"We prayed constantly," he said. "Our prayers were like the Psalms of David, not knowing what to ask for, only to save us. Our hope was so strong, but there was no mercy, not for a moment."

To vanish from the newsroom and fall before the next installment of this story became my secret vocation that August. Straining to discern the rabbi's gently broken English over his wheezing air conditioner had the feel of gathering stones that other people couldn't see.

One humid afternoon, I raced up Park Heights Avenue without noticing that I was more appropriately dressed for the Ramones than a holy man. Over torn blue jeans and ragged gym shoes, I wore a black T-shirt showing a black man holding an electric guitar.

As I picked up his story after the liberation of the death camps (recently married a third time, he'd been blessed with children and grandchildren from a second wife who'd passed away), the rabbi noticed the musician on my shirt and asked his name.

"It's B.B. King, rebbe."

"Who is B.B. King?"

"He sings the blues."

"What is this blues?"

While I can fall as blue as the next middle-class crybaby every now and again, I found myself explaining an experience I only know through words that rhyme.

"The blues are songs American slaves made up from their suffering," I said. "How their souls cried while they were worked to death. The way they watched their people die without being able to do anything about it. Making songs out of the misery helped them get through another day."

The rabbi considered the face on my T-shirt for a long moment — as if by staring into B.B.'s eyes he could see beyond the cotton fields to the ash storms of Auschwitz. Finally, he turned his lights on me.

"In the camps," he said, "we sang the blues."

Perhaps it is only death that sets us free.

(I'm convinced that our tears are always for ourselves, that the dead do not sing the blues for us.)

In the world to come — that blessed realm yearned for by all believers faithful to the struggles of this world — the rabbi anticipates answers to evils that 50 years of puzzling have not solved.

"Our souls will be so elevated, we won't have to ask, we'll know," he said. "Every soul is a spark of God that goes back to the place where it came from. In the world to come, our souls will understand hundreds of thousands of stages beyond what we understand now."

But on this planet, we must decide moment by moment which way to turn at the crossroads. In the absence of holocausts, it is this choosing that so often determines how blue the rain.

"As long as we are alive, we have a choice to correct the way we live," said the rabbi. "That is for us to do here and now."

September 2, 1997

Chapter 14

Blues, etc.

Elvis' inspiration

NEW YORK — SOME STORIES DON'T GET TOLD FOR A LONG, LONG TIME.

One of the geniuses behind the revolutionary music of Elvis Presley was a small, poor-sighted black man who wrote songs in his Brooklyn attic and mailed the demonstration tapes to the King in Memphis.

Otis Blackwell, now 50, never met the man who spun gold with the titles he borrowed "from cartoons and love comics." Among those novel compositions that Elvis turned into industry standards were "Don't Be Cruel," No. 1 in 1956; "All Shook Up," No. 1 in 1957; "Return to Sender," No. 5 in 1962; "One Broken Heart for Sale," No. 11 in 1963, and others.

Presley's and Mr. Blackwell's vocal styles were, and remain, spookily similar — so much so that Presley's management would mail Mr. Blackwell tapes of songs other people had written for him (like "Teddy Bear"), and pay Mr. Blackwell to record a demo and mail it back.

"I was surprised when I heard ['Don't Be Cruel'], because it was just like I had done the demo," said Mr. Blackwell behind dark green sunglasses that protect his fragile sight. A bit close-lipped because the dentist had just yanked a few of his teeth, he recalled hearing Elvis's version on the radio for the first time. "I said, 'Jesus, man, he sings like me, or I sing like him.'"

As the hits mounted, Presley became fondly indebted to Mr. Blackwell, and in true Elvis fashion, wanted to express his thanks on a grand scale. Mr. Blackwell, however, was more comfortable in the back seat.

Dwarfed by the exaggerated figure Elvis lorded over the world ("When Elvis started singing like Otis, Otis forgot singing," said one source), Mr. Blackwell resigned himself to writing in the shadow of the King — no matter how hard Presley tried to drag him out.

Elvis sent limos to Brooklyn to pick up his "little good luck charm." Mr. Blackwell locked the door.

Elvis threw surprise parties in honor of the man who spent a mere two hours cooking up "Great Balls of Fire" for Jerry Lee Lewis. Mr. Blackwell stood him up.

Elvis invited Mr. Blackwell to Hollywood to be wined and dined, and even asked him to play guest roles in a couple of movies. Mr. Blackwell respectful declined.

"Elvis and I both had a thing going that was super," Mr. Blackwell said from his gray office in the 400 block of Fifth Avenue. "Call it superstition, but I wanted to keep it."

He also said it is untrue that his employer, Presley Music, actually paid him not to perform. "I had really decided just to be a writer."

By 1977, Mr. Blackwell felt it was about time to meet the man who insured that the royalty checks would roll in for the rest of his, and his children's, lives.

He sat down, tailored a white gospel song about family and friendship called "In Our House" to fit only Elvis, and made plans to present the song to Presley in Las Vegas.

But by then, after years of Mr. Blackwell trying to keep the magic alive by hiding, it was too late.

"I was in the studio when I got word he had passed," Mr. Blackwell said. "It shook me up, really ... just like it did everybody else.

"Here's a dude, he was like a god, not supposed to get sick."

Otis Blackwell began writing songs when be was about 15, and by age 17 had signed with JD Records in New York.

"They were blues," he recalls. "I wouldn't know what the hell to call it; it was just blues."

By the early Fifties he went on the road, entertaining black audiences at rent parties, rural fish fries and, once in a while, a hole-in-the-wall bar passing as a nightclub — the type of lifestyle folk historians commonly weave into myth.

Mr. Blackwell says it was miserable.

"I had one hit [circa 1952] called 'Daddy Rollin' Stone,' but on the road, I didn't dig it worth a hell. It was race joints, barns, garages, sawdust joints. I didn't dig entertaining, not for that."

So he packed it in and retreated to his Brooklyn attic and writing desk — an upright piano on which he had taken 50-cents-an-hour lessons as a kid.

"If you didn't have nothing to sleep on growing up, you had a damn piano," he recalls. "Everybody had an upright."

He supported his efforts by pressing coats and dresses on a steam iron in a factory, and on Christmas Eve 1955 he took a half-dozen songs to Shalomar Music.

One of Mr. Blackwell's presents for Shalomar that year was "Don't Be Cruel." Then "Fever," co-written with Ed Cooley, produced a hit for four different artists, most notably Little Willie John in 1956 and Peggy Lee in 1958. Both sold over a million copies. And "Handy Man," originally a rhythm-and-blues hit by Jimmy Jones, went to the top 10 for 20 weeks in 1977 for the folk-rocker James Taylor. It rose as high as third.

Though they and others sold well, none left its mark on the course of popular music like the songs he showed Elvis how to sing.

After all the ghoulish schlock foisted on Presley's fans since his death, it turns out that the greatest Elvis imitator of all time is the original. To listen to a tape of Mr. Blackwell is to listen to the voice of Elvis, complete with shadowy echoes and rockabilly hiccups.

"Otis will not allow you to say Elvis copied him," asserted Jonathan Stathakis, vice president of Television Theater Company. "The way Otis looks at it, they influenced each other."

Two television sets in his South Park Avenue office played video footage of Mr. Blackwell's first serious performance, outside of one-night stands, in about 25 years. TTC, a 16-month-old operation, has produced two 65-minute video shows from eight hours of blues footage shot last August at a club called Stages in Chicago.

"Before the show, none of us knew who Otis Blackwell was," Mr. Stathakis said, echoing the reaction of nearly everyone intimately familiar with his songs, but totally ignorant of the man himself.

Titled "The Blues: Living Legends," the two shows were financed by RKO Enterprises and are being marketed nationally to independent cable carriers.

The tapes also include performances by and interviews with Willie ("I Am the Blues") Dixon, Koko Taylor, Albert Collins, Jimmy Witherspoon, and Son Seals. All are blues stars except Mr. Blackwell.

"You know I'm about rock and roll, not about blues," Mr. Blackwell recalls telling Mike Millius, publishing agent for MCA Records who tracked him down in Brooklyn and brought him to the attention of Niles Seigel, an RKO consultant.

"Millius said, 'Well, we'll call you a legend then.' I said why not? It paid good money for two days work — I'll take it; don't matter what you call me."

Mr. Blackwell was nervous about playing piano for an audience ("I have never played a piano in front of anybody except guys I was working on songs with"). But he was forced into it when he was told there was no keyboardist for him.

Mr. Millius said finding Mr. Blackwell for the project was almost as difficult as talking him into it, though Mr. Blackwell now says, "It's really the time to do it, before I grow old with a beard and have to walk with a cane."

"I found these old songs [demos] of his, and finally drew out of him that he had eyes to be a singer," Mr. Millius said.

"He had spent a lot of time hiding from Elvis — the little black frog and the big white prince. But after a couple weeks I finally got a line on him through ASCAP [the American Society of Composers, Authors and Publishers].

All of which brought Mr. Blackwell to the mecca of the music industry: Pasadena, Md.

For the past two months he has been quietly breaking in a new act at the Desert Lounge on Mountain Road, picking up the house band, Savannah, as his backup, along with a Manhattan pianist, Andy Rosen, who has said, "There's nothing I wouldn't do to be near a piano to play with him."

He picked the club because it is managed by one of his oldest friends in the business, Chuck Webber.

"I've been after him [to perform] for the past eight years," Mr. Webber said. "I booked him into a few small rooms in Florida and Georgia, and when he started getting standing ovations he said, 'Hell, why not?'"

Recently Mr. Blackwell entertained a crowd at the Desert with a story of the typical reaction he gets when taking credit for writing some of the biggest hits in the history of rock and roll.

"I had one girl come up to me and she asked, 'You wrote all those songs?' I said, 'Yes, dear, I did.' And she said, 'You're full of s—.'"

Well, if the girl meant fertilizer, Otis Blackwell is filled with the rich soil from which popular standards blossom.

Otis Blackwell and his work will certainly be around tomorrow. More specifically the Desert Lounge every Friday and Saturday night in November, where he will perform his hits and a passel of new material.

November 19, 1982

Broom Man has a handle on the blues

LELAND, MISS. — THEY CALL HIM THE BROOM MAN.
There is no documented tradition for the folk art of Cleveland Jones. He plays the blues in a style like no one before him and no one since.

The 71-year-old retired sharecropper has mastered a sophisticated musical instrument found in every American home — the broom.

Unwrapping a brown paper bag to sprinkle a handful or two of delta dirt on the plywood stage of the recent Delta Blues Festival in nearby Freedom Village, the Broom Man began to rub, grind, and scrape his broom pole across the dirt to get a deep, resonating rhythm he likens to "a bass viola."

Using his right hand to move the pole across the floor, the fingers on his left hand dance like fleshy black pistons near the head of the broom, as if it were the fretboard of a guitar.

Dressed all in white from his taxi driver's cap to his shoes and socks, the Broom Man's eyes rarely leave the floor as he draws broad sweeps, short stabs, and intricate circles with the pole to get the sound he needs to support the guitar work of his partner and friend, James "Son" Thomas.

The harder he presses down, the lower the tone, an earthy, hollow but rich "waump, waump" sound.

Watching him are 35,000 blues fans. "That's history folks," announces a festival emcee as Broom Man leaves the stage with Son, rhythm guitarist Uncle Joe Cooper, and harp man Walter Linniger.

Because most of his peers have passed on, the Broom Man says that Son Thomas, who lives a half-dozen miles away from him along the railroad tracks near downtown Leland, "is the only somebody I play with now."

Cleveland Jones makes an appearance with Son each year at the Delta Blues Festival, has traveled to Dallas with his broomstick for a show, and in 1974 worked the American Folk Life Festival in Washington.

He always brings his own dirt, and said he's ready to travel anywhere to play if he's invited. "I only go when they send for me," he says.

A few days before the festival, the Broom Man sat on the porch of his home, a decrepit, wooden shack that sits just a few yards off Highway 82 between Leland and Greenville, and talked about his life. He has rented the hovel for 13 years from a man who refuses to sell.

In the breezy early Mississippi evening, cars and trucks zip by at 55 mph or better. Some drivers wave or honk. Cleveland raises a wrinkled black hand as they pass, and brings it down to shoo flies that settle on his nose, ears, and head.

With the Broom Man is his wife of 42 years, Mattie H. Jones, a sweet woman who says she is "as old as my tongue and a little older than my teeth," her tongue being 67 years old.

Mattie completed the 11th grade, 11 grades more than her husband. What Cleveland can't remember or articulate about his life, one lived by a shy man who apparently knew little but work and music when there was time left over, Mattie fills in.

"This house is raggedy," says Mattie, "but I like it better out here than I do town. I ain't never want to be rich, just happy to live without having a big strain."

"You ain't never going to be rich no way," says Cleveland.

Early on in life, the Broom Man says, he realized he "ain't got no voice to sing" and tried "to play guitar but I couldn't fool with it and left it alone. Couldn't do the harp either."

But when he was just a boy of 11, already working in the cotton fields, Cleveland looked at a broom in a new way, "and just took it up, put it in my head and went about my business with it. It took me two or three months to get the feeling of it, and I been doing it for years to come, years to come.

"I started hearing the blues when I was about 11 years old, when I started working the fields. I've been having trouble ever since. A man tries to make a living and he can't. All they got down here is farms in Mississippi. We growed corn and picked cotton till they took all the mules away" and farm work became mechanized.

"I went to school twice and they kicked me out in the field to work. I come up the hard way, but it seemed like it was good ole days in them times, everybody had a little something, raised up chickens and hogs. I didn't have no wife at the time and got to rambling. I come to Greenville in 1935 and been here ever since.

"I ain't never been in the service," he said, when asked if he had any experiences outside the Delta. "I couldn't read or write, so [the World War II draft board] cut me off. They kept me working all the time, wouldn't even let me go to the war."

In his time, the Broom Man says he witnessed live performances by such blues greats and folk legends as Charley Patton and Blind Lemon Jefferson, Howlin' Wolf ("I went to school with him," says Mattie), Muddy Waters, Sam Chatmon, and Rice Miller, better known as Sonny Boy Williamson No. 2.

The Broom Man never followed any of these men out of the fields and into show business, and as far as he knows he has never been recorded.

Bill Ferris, folklorist and director of the Center for the Study of Southern Culture at the University of Mississippi, made a black and white Super 8 film of the Broom Man, Son Thomas, and some of their friends playing blues at a corn whiskey juke joint in 1968, and mentions Cleveland Jones in his book, "Blues from the Delta." The film is on file at the archives on the Oxford campus.

Mr. Ferris, one of the most knowledgeable and sensitive of all blues historians, reports that other than Cleveland Jones, he has found no record of the broom in folk music.

"He's the only one I knowed can do it," said Son Thomas, who has crossed paths with scores of country bluesmen in his 59 years.

September 27, 1985

Frank Zappa: "I never set out to be weird"

IT WAS THE POSTER OF FRANK SITTING ON A TOILET BENEATH THE LEGEND "Phi Zappa Krappa" that did it.

The year was 1968, summertime, and I was a 10-year-old fifth-grader on vacation with my family in Ocean City. With long-haired, freaky hippies and psychedelic music grooving everywhere, it was hard to act hip wearing Bermuda shorts and a peach-fuzz wiffle haircut.

But the image of this strange, nearly nude man hanging from a Boardwalk souvenir shop provided yet another opportunity to jab the rock' n' roll needle into my parents' sensibilities.

The poster — and the brush fire of scatological rumors about Zappa that grew fat and far beyond such indiscretions as being photographed on the john — went a long way in turning my head.

It went that much further in turning my mother's stomach. "You can forget about buying that one," said Mom.

Four years would pass until I finally became turned on to Frank Zappa, whose eccentric labors in contemporary music will be "legitimized" this Thursday night when members of the Baltimore Symphony Orchestra perform one of his compositions at Westminster Church, Fayette and Greene streets.

Like most other Marylanders digging into Zappa's long, varied career for clues to the man behind the sound track, one of the first things I was told by those in the know was that he was a local boy.

The truth usually stopped there, with the mangled information passed on something like this: "Frank went to my high school, man. Oh yeah, he graduated from Glen Burnie High. He used to party up there all the time."

"He grew up in Catonsville. My sister said he went to Catonsville High School but got kicked out for being weird."

"Hey man, like Zappa grew up in Essex. It's true. His father worked at Bethlehem Steel."

Those succumbing to the lure of such lore have not exclusively been teen-age boys hot for Zappa's naughty lyrics and the lusty squeal of an electric guitar.

Dig the following true confessions of State Sen. John Pica, a Democrat representing Northeast Baltimore and longtime Zappa fan.

Mr. Pica, eager to make small talk with the composer last March 18 when Frank visited Maryland's General Assembly to help argue down an obscenity bill aimed at sanitizing rock 'n' roll, trotted out his own version of the old myths.

"For years I thought he was a Hamilton boy who went to Towson High School, until I asked him myself," said Mr. Pica. "I had always thought he grew up in my district, and he didn't."

Such tales — "complete fiction" would be a favorite Zappa description — go on and on, with the locales ranging from one side of the state to the other.

The myths only added to the mystique of an adamantly anti-drug performer who is forever accused of being on some sort of substance to create his sounds, and who, for two decades, has had to put up with such lies as those insisting he once ingested human excrement on stage and that he is the son of Mr. Green Jeans from the old "Captain Kangaroo" show.

"I never set out to be weird," he said. "It was always other people who called me weird."

"Frankie probably doesn't even know this, but at his birth he almost didn't make it," said Maria "Aunt Mary" Cimino, the 85-year-old sister of Rose Marie Zappa, Frank's 74-year-old mother.

Aunt Mary is sitting at the dining room table in her apartment next to Seton High School on North Charles Street. Spread over the table are old family photos and newspaper clippings about her famous nephew, the earliest from the time he won a fire prevention poster contest in the ninth grade.

"The doctor had delivered about nine babies that day and didn't want to do any more so he gave Rose Marie some kind of drug to retard her labor," she continued, noting that she had a front-row seat at Mercy Hospital for the entire episode on Dec. 21, 1940.

"The baby was born breech and it was going from bad to worse," she says. "At one point it looked like they might lose mother and child; Rose Marie needed a blood transfusion.

"When the nurse finally brought him out he was limp and his skin looked black. Rose Marie's husband was crying that the boy wouldn't live, but Frankie fooled him — he made it."

Today, 20 years and nearly 40 albums after his Mothers of Invention made its debut with the rocking satire of America called "Freak Out," Zappa has made it in terms understandable to any American businessman.

That is, he succeeds in marketing his music and related projects to the tune of six digits a year while maintaining complete control over every aspect of his work from conception to consumption.

His home contains a $2 million recording studio, and a universe of Zappa products — from T-shirts to videos to deluxe packages of his vintage albums — are available through a mail-order business run by his wife, Gail. They have four children.

Zappa's fans — global, legion and as diverse as the musical styles he draws on — provide the cash and attention that allow Zappa artistic and business independence without the noose of fickle pop fashion.

"He's into playing what he wants and not what people would like to hear," said Richard Gill, a 28-year old tuba major at the Peabody institute. "He's contributed more to music by what he is than he could have by... going to a conservatory... or playing lounge music all his life."

Despised by some as a puerile pervert, loved by others for his guts, wit and guitar virtuosity, Zappa is acknowledged by both sides as an articulate, informed man of uncommon intelligence.

"I'll put my brains up against anybody, any day of the week," he said. "I don't wear a suit all the time, but I can put one on when I have to."

His most recent opportunity to do both flashed across the nation's consciousness earlier this year when Zappa appeared before U.S. Senate and Maryland legislative committees to give biting arguments against the labeling of rock 'n' roll records considered obscene by conservative groups.

"We've got a bear by the tail here...," muttered Sen. Ernest "Fritz" Hollings, D–S.C., in an aside during Washington hearings where Zappa compared the proposed censorship of rock to "treating dandruff with decapitation."

"He's self-made and can talk to anybody," declared Frank's mom in a interview from her North Hollywood, Calif., duplex. "He doesn't mince words, does he?"

Still contemplating a generation's worth of Zappa photos on her dining room table, Aunt Mary wonders how a baby "with such beautiful eyelashes" grew into the outspoken hairy '60s freak of rock fame.

"Sometimes," she said, "I look at them, and I say to myself, 'Is that Frankie?'"

After leaving the maternity ward, Rose Marie and the infant Zappa went home with Frank Sr. to live with Rose Marie's family, the Colimores, in a West Baltimore rowhouse at 2019 Whittier Ave., at the corner of Monroe Street. To this day, a fig tree planted in the back yard by the Colimore family continues to bloom.

Frank Zappa's local roots, on both sides of his family, have their beginnings around Baltimore's old industrial waterfront.

Rose Marie's father, Charles Colimore, was a small-business man and native of Naples who owned a lunchroom called Little Charlie's at 122 Market Place near Pratt Street, and an adjacent confectionery.

Careful to point out that he is far from a family historian — he reportedly can't remember the year his father died — Zappa remembered his paternal grandfather as a Sicilian immigrant and pier-side barber who made a living separating stubble from the rough-skinned jowls of seamen.

"One of my father's first jobs in life, he must have been about 6, was standing on a little wooden box in his father's barbershop. He got paid a penny a day to put lather on the faces of sailors," said Zappa during recent interviews in New York.

"What they said about my [paternal] grandfather was that he never took a bath, used to drink a lot of wine and started every day with a full glass of Bromo Seltzer," said Zappa. "And because he didn't take a bath, he wore a lot of clothes, and put cologne on. He had a terminal case of ring around the collar, one of those kind of fat Italian guys who would sit on the porch."

The Zappa family only lived at the Colimore home for a short time, probably less than two years, according to Aunt Mary, who remembers the year of Mr. Zappa's death as 1973.

Mr. Colimore died in 1941, his wife sold the house not long afterward, "and we all went our separate ways," said Mrs. Zappa, a 1931 Seton High School graduate.

Mr. Zappa, one of four children to survive his mother's 18 pregnancies, was teaching math at Loyola High School not long after the birth of his namesake, according to Mrs. Zappa.

When the family left Whittier Avenue they took an apartment in the 4600 block of Park Heights Ave. "I remember it was one of those rowhouses," said Zappa, whose parents often spoke Italian in the home. "There was an alley in the back and down the alley used to come the knife sharpener man — you know, a guy with the wheel. And everybody used to come down off their back porch to the alley to get their knives and scissors done."

While living on Park Heights, Mrs. Zappa and Aunt Mary would take young Frankie to the Lexington and Howard Street shopping districts on the weekends.

"He was about 3 years old and he saw three nuns on the street," said Aunt Mary. "He pointed to them and said: 'Look at the lady penguins.' We looked at him and said, 'Where did he get that from?'"

The bulk of Zappa's Maryland memories "are connected mostly to ill health," he said. "In my earliest years my best friend was a vaporizer with the [expletive] snout blowing that steam in my face. I was sick all of the time."

Mrs. Zappa said that in addition to being prone to severe colds, her son was asthmatic, which kept him in the house a lot. She credits this for the fascination with reading developed by the oldest of her four children.

"The whole time he had to stay in bed and rest he would have all his books on the bed," she said. "He was always creating something or inventing, he never liked sports. Every month something new would come for him in the mail."

Early and wide reading, supported later by independent study at public libraries, satisfied a hyper curiosity that possessed the young boy.

"I never thought it was a bad thing to increase my amount of knowledge," he said. "But my seeking for different kinds of knowledge was being conducted at a time when it was completely unfashionable to be intelligent."

About the time that Frankie was ready to start school, the Zappa family moved from the city to Harford County.

Mr. Zappa, who earned a history degree at University of North Carolina at

Chapel Hill while supporting himself as a barber, had landed a job as a government researcher, and began a career in meteorology and metallurgy at the Aberdeen Proving Ground.

The family settled in a neighborhood of Army housing in Edgewood. Frank remembers the address as 15 Dexter St., located in a now-demolished project.

"We were living in a house that was made out of cardboard almost," he said. "They were duplexes made out of clapboard... real flimsy stuff, real cheezoid."

"In those days they were making mustard gas at Edgewood and each member of the family had a gas mask hanging in the closet in case the tanks broke. That was really my main toy at that time. That was my space helmet. I decided to get a can opener and open it up.

"It satisfied my scientific curiosity but it rendered the gas mask useless. My father was so upset when he found out... he said, 'If the tanks break, who doesn't get the mask?' It was Frankie up the creek.

"I was fascinated by [poison gas]... The idea that you could make a chemical, and then all you had to do was smell it and you die... For years in grammar school every time we had to do a science report I would always do mine on what I knew about poison gas."

Zappa remembers his early home life as "fairly poor," to the point that taking a Sunday drive to see the where his grandfather cut hair have been considered "a rather large waste of money.

"I swear I don't remember a single Christmas present," from the Maryland days, said Zappa, who recalled a trip to the Shot Tower and a rare visit or two to Haussner's Restaurant in East Baltimore.

Once in Harford County, Zappa was enrolled at Edgewood School, which is no longer used but still stands on Cedar Drive. His teacher, Mary H. Spencer, an Edgewood resident, recalls a boy who "was fairly mischievous, but he wasn't naughty."

A colleague of Ms. Spencer's at the time was Cybil Gunther, who holds sharper Zappa memories.

"I had him in the third grade," said Ms. Gunther. "And sometimes when I tell people I had Frank Zappa in class... their mouths just fall open."

She said she taught Zappa at a time "when we had 40 or more in a class and kids could get lost in a crowd. Frank didn't get lost in the crowd but it wasn't music he was into — he was big on drama.

"For any reason I had to leave the room, I could turn to Frank and he would hold the whole class enthralled with something," she said. "I never did figure out what it was, but there never was any trouble with the class because Frank was doing something that never really made any sense to me.

"It was some sort of drama... my impression [of Zappa's act] would be some sort of cowboys and Indians. I don't know that he liked the attention, but he liked doing what he was doing."

Actually, said Zappa, he was attempting to recreate the crashing temple scene from the movie "Samson and Delilah."

Whatever it was, Ms. Gunther was able to hit a clear key into Zappa's career without the benefit of seeing any of his professional performances:

"I always had the feeling that he was doing it for himself," she said. "That it was rather immaterial to him whether people really sat there and listened, but he was happy in what he was doing."

"His papa was a character, too," said Ms. Gunther of the proud man who rode the New World work ethic to become a scientist. "Mr. Zappa wanted to have the whole school screened so that flies wouldn't get in. I think eventually the cafeteria was screened."

Zappa's memories of the Edgewood years include how to make gunpowder, and playing with laboratory stuff — flasks, beakers and vials his father brought home from work.

His interest in arts and crafts would grow beyond the cardboard tubes from roles of linoleum that he used as pillars to be knocked down in his Samson act and became more involved with drawing and the building of puppets.

Through it all he continued to be in poor health, particularly susceptible to flus and viruses. When he was about 7, his parents decided to move to Florida in the hope that a warmer climate and having the child's tonsils removed would help.

"You know what it was like?" said Zappa. "Suddenly I was in a state that was entirely in Technicolor. All my life I'd been seeing things in black and white while living in Maryland. And here I was down there and it was flowers, trees, it was great. It seemed like suddenly, BOOM!, here's Technicolor.

"So then they thought I was OK, we moved back and I got sick again. It was just totally bleak."

On their return, Zappa entered the third-grade and became smitten with a fellow 8-year old by the name of Marlene Beck, "a nice girl," according to Zappa.

"Jesus God Almighty," howled the present Marlene Baer between belly-laughs after being told that Frank Zappa had named her as his original grade-school sweetheart. "I don't believe this."

"I don't remember being his girlfriend but he was a cut-up... kind of like being the class clown," she said. "He was a very nice person, but he was always kind of strange. We were just teeny kids."

As Frankie's illnesses continued, Mr. Zappa decided the family would leave for a warmer climate permanently. This time, said Frank, his father decided to go West. One day he came home with pictures, and said 'What do you think about going here to the desert?' And he shows us more of these cardboard houses... I was going, 'No. I don't want to go there.' But he thought it was nice.

"My father was so nostalgic for where he used to live in Sicily. [The village] Partiniko is about a 45-minute drive outside of Palermo, and the terrain looks like Arizona. It's got that same kind of desert and mountains.

"... Any time he would see cowboy movies or anything to do with the desert he thought it could be a really wonderful place. He thought the desert was great, but I didn't, and my mother didn't either. So he took a job in California at the Naval Post Graduate School in Monterey."

The family — which now included a second son, Bobby, with two more children to follow in California — left Maryland in November 1950, and made the rounds of goodbyes to family and friends.

"It was sad," said Aunt Mary. "Rose Marie thought it would just be for a while."

Zappa said that the family, "remained in the poor category even after we moved to California. We drove across country in a Henry J. There was nothing more uncomfortable than the back seat of a Henry J because a Henry J didn't have a trunk in the back. You got to the trunk by pulling down the back seat to throw your stuff in there.

"That seat was a piece of wood with covering. To spend 3,000 miles riding in the back of a car like that with all your worldly possessions piled on top of you, that is not a terrific experience.

"So my father had these fantasies about California, how wonderful it was, how warm. We took off in the middle of winter and took the southern route, going down through South Carolina.

"There was this black family in the field working. He said, 'Wait a minute!' He stops the car, and goes over to these people and handed them every stitch of winter clothing that we owned, every bit of it: 'Here, take this with our blessings,' and then we left. They were very grateful.

"However, by the time we got to Monterey, which is in northern California, it was raining constantly and we didn't have any coats. My dad thought all of California was like cowboy movies — he didn't know."

On the West Coast, Frank's attention slowly began to turn away from art and toward music. He said he originally began to compose music because he liked the visual images of the notes, and enjoyed drawing them.

This would lead to crude attempts at composing chamber and orchestra music, which he largely taught himself through books.

While boogie rhythms and do-wop lyrics were gobbling up entire generations of young people during the early days of rock 'n' roll, which coincided with Zappa's high school years, he would not merely be another grease mop obsessed with imitating Elvis.

Instead his intellectual adventures on the printed page would put him under the spell of experimental composer Edgar Varese and black bluesmen like Johnny "Guitar" Watson.

Throughout his career such seemingly incongruous mosaics — like his sticking a kazoo into dissonant orchestral pieces — have marked his work.

"I think [the motivation was] a curiosity and tolerance for different styles which some people are trying to legislate out of human behavior," said Zappa. "Others should try this instead of narrowing their viewpoint."

Frustrated by his inability to get his compositions played, he turned somewhat reluctantly to rock 'n' roll, forming his first band in high school and calling them the Blackouts.

"It's not that I happen to dislike rock 'n' roll music and was just doing it to while away the time. I happen to like it," he said. "Musically, I started off when I was 12 playing the drums, started writing when I was 14 and changed to the guitar when I was 18.

"And all the time, until I was 20, I never wrote a rock 'n' roll song. I listened to it, I liked it, I played it, but I never wrote it. The only stuff I was writing was chamber music and orchestra music but I couldn't get any of it played.

"So if you can't get your music played what do you do? Go where the action is...so I started writing rock 'n' roll music."

The Zappa family spent three years in Monterey, lived in Pomona through 1954, spent a year or less in San Diego, and finally settled in the Mojave Desert town of Lancaster where Zappa graduated from Antelope Valley High School on Friday the 13th in June of 1958.

In school Frank did well in the classes he enjoyed, such as music theory, but not so well in the ones his father the scientist believed were important, like math. Acknowledged by his teachers as exceptionally bright but rebellious academically, Zappa was given a diploma despite a lack of required credits.

After graduation, he wanted to see some of the world, and his mother suggested a trip back to Baltimore to visit his relatives. Frank wrote Aunt Mary to get the OK.

"Besides sending thanks, this letter is going to be kind of a questionnaire," he wrote. "The question being, 'Could you find some space for me if I were to come and visit you and Uncle Robert?'...The reason for the trip is twofold. Firstly, I would like to see the East again and all the relatives (most of which I probably couldn't recognize by face at all) back there.

"The second reason is that I think I have invented something new in the way of music (probably not) which I would like to take to the conservatory back there for investigation. If I did come I would not stay long, and I would help out around the house any way I could, so please consider this request and write soon."

Aunt Mary opened her home at 4805 Loch Raven Blvd. to her nephew and soon Zappa was traveling the length of the country on a train. Finally emerging from Penn Station, he said, "My relatives were shocked to see the way I looked. They were all so horrified that I think I was an embarrassment to them.

"I was accused," he said "of rampant drapery." Which is to say he looked like a "drape," a Baltimore term used to describe what Californians, according to Zappa, simply called juvenile delinquents.

Inspired by the fashion of his Mexican friends, the look included pants so pegged at the ankles that one could hardly get his foot through (some hipsters actually installed zippers), longish greasy hair combed in a barely controlled pompadour, sideburns and a wisp of a moustache, a zoot-suit inspired jacket, and Cuban-styled shoes.

In this costume he passed the time in such classic Baltimore pursuits as sitting on the front porch, shooting mosquitoes and meeting relatives. He also wanted, but failed, to meet girls.

"At the time I got back [to Maryland] the girls were very, very Catholic and tended not to be stimulated by people who had [my] kind of appearance," he said.

Zappa also engaged in such non-traditional activities for white Baltimoreans in the late 1950s as taking a bus into the heart of black West Baltimore to search for stores selling rhythm and blues records.

And then there was his appearance with Aunt Mary in the tearoom at Hutzler's downtown department store.

"They wouldn't let me in because I wasn't properly dressed," said Zappa, relishing the memory. "But they said if I wouldn't mind, they had a seersucker coat in the closet that they saved for occasions like this and if I'd wear this they would let me sit down.

"So I put on the seersucker jacket. I'd started smoking at 15, and before we went to this place I stopped at a tobacco shop. I totally love tobacco, no question about it.

"And I went to this place, they had cigarettes of the world, and I bought all these different kinds, including something called...Imperials or something; they were Russian cigarettes [with a little] tobacco and the rest was a long, hollow, cardboard tube in a fancy box. I thought after lunch I would light up this Russian cigarette in the tea room. Have you ever smelled Russian tobacco? Ho-ho, boy — I hadn't.

"It was the most nauseating smell, and the minute I lit it, chairs began moving away while my aunt was trying to be polite. And I'm sitting there with this long, really elegant-looking but vile-smelling Russian cigarette in my hand with a seersucker coat on — ha, ha, ha — having tea with Aunt Mary."

Zappa hoped to travel to New York to visit French-born composer Edgar Varese (1883-1965), an early and major influence, during his East Coast trip, but the older man was not available.

Known as a pioneer of works for electronic sound, Varese, like Zappa, was very fond of rhythmic complexity and unpitched percussion. He is listed in musical histories as "an adventurous explorer of techniques and conceptions far ahead of his time."

Varese would die before Zappa could meet his idol. An insufficient consolation, however, was an introduction to Massimo Freccia, at the time the conductor of the Baltimore Symphony Orchestra, now in retirement in London.

He brought along his "new" music, a foreshadowing of the trademark Zappa pastiche of this and that, culled from here and there.

"I had brought manuscript paper to Maryland and was writing orchestra music at Aunt Mary's house," he said. "I was naive and thought [Freccia] could play it. He looked at [my appearance] and couldn't believe I was writing orchestra music."

Instead of discussing the earnest but somewhat crude Zappa compositions,

Freccia instead quizzed the youngster with questions like: "What's the lowest note on the bassoon?" The relationship ended there.

Returning to California after the two-week visit, he entered and dropped out of junior college, had several false starts of living on his own, appeared on Steve Allen's "Tonight Show" to coax music from the spokes and wheels of a bicycle, and made his every dime from some form of music or musically related entertainment.

In 1964 he hooked up with a group of musicians who would become the outrageous Mothers of Invention.

Zappa's considerable spot in music history — equally revered by those who find him worthy of high praise for the intricate exactness of his classical, jazz, electronic and rock compositions, and those who hold him in contempt for too often applying those talents to the theater of smut — is assured despite total disregard for commercial and critical considerations.

"I like to be able to earn a living from doing what I like to do — without compromise," he said. "I could be way more popular by doing formula stuff — there's plenty of other things I could do that would make more money than what I'm doing. But who could stand to do it?

"There's other people who like doing that, who enthusiastically write love songs, and do choreography and believe in it. Let them do it. I just want to do odd stuff that appeals to me. And if somebody likes it, great, and if they don't like it, that's great too. Just don't get in my way."

Hey, you gotta like a guy with such titles as "Bossa Nova Pervertamento."

And now, almost 30 years later, the BSO — like a handful of other American and foreign orchestras — will finally perform a work by the hometown boy. The piece to be performed Thursday is titled "Dupree's Paradise."

"It's a terrific upbeat piece, very well crafted," said David Zinman, the BSO music director, who called Zappa "the exception to the rock rule.

"It's not an easy piece — it is very tricky rhythmically, but I find it rewarding. It's driving. I've enjoyed his rock music and he was always classically bent."

"I just hope," said Zappa, deadly serious, "that they play it right."

October 12, 1986

From Rock's Aristocracy
to South Baltimore Gigs

"THE MAD ALBINO FROM BEAUMONT" IS JUST BEGINNING TO WARM UP the crowd at Hammerjack's in South Baltimore. Tattoos of flaming monsters and shooting stars ripple blue and green and red on his milk-white skin and his muscles tighten around his guitar.

At the back of the club, roadie Bobby Peterson sells "Johnny Winter... 25 Years on the Road" T-shirts for $20 each with the help of a portable American Express charge plate.

Nearby, a skinny young woman in a puffed white party dress balances her rear-end on a railing, snapping gum and swinging her legs like a little kid on the playground.

"I never ever heard of Johnny Winter before tonight," she says. "I'm just here to drink Kamikazes."

Twenty-five years on the road, and the little girls don't even know your name.

It reminds me of a favorite quote from Winter, once an unknown guitar phenom who signed with Columbia Records in 1969 for a reported $300,000 and went on to play Woodstock and record some 20 albums: "Man, in 1969 I couldn't walk outside of my house. What happened to all those Johnny Winter fans? Did they die?"

For a brief moment 20 years ago, Winter walked among rock's aristocracy, trading on the deep blues of his Mississippi birthplace in Leland and his Texas upbringing in Beaumont for sonic interpretations of songs by Bob Dylan, the Rolling Stones and John Lennon while making all the groovy scenes.

"Musicians always feel [empathy] with other musicians and John [Lennon] was the Beatle I felt most like. I hated it when he died," Winter has said. "He went through a lot of the same stuff I went through, being a junkie and everything, I could relate to him."

Because of drugs, exhaustion and constant touring, many did not expect Winter to survive the early '70s.

But he did, eluding the hellhound who took Jimi Hendrix, with whom Winter played the Newport Rock Festival in Northridge, Calif., in June

1970, and Janis Joplin, who appeared with him at the Atlanta Pop Festival the next month.

"I did not like [fame], I *did* not like it. It scares me to death thinking about getting big again," he once said. "I'm much happier now than I was when I was really big. It's not a real feeling. You don't feel normal. I hated it."

Winter's reward for enduring obscurity, fame, drugs, recovery and the loss of fame while becoming a living footnote to rock history is a spot on the cover of the Beaumont telephone directory.

He has the respect of fellow guitarists and people who cherish his seldom-displayed mastery of Delta blues, and he still carries enough name recognition to play year-round gigs across America at joints like Hammerjack's.

An old brick warehouse that straddles Interstate 95 and will soon sit in the shadow of the new Camden Yards baseball stadium, Hammerjack's is a wet T-shirt palace where it only costs $5 to get in to see a guy like Johnny Winter and an artist's performance is judged by how many empty liquor bottles get thrown away at the end of the show.

Winter played about an hour of highspeed rock and charged up blues last week and ended his show with "Jumpin' Jack Flash" and "It's All Over Now."

Legally blind, he was helped offstage by men pointing the way in the darkness with flashlights.

After the show I sat in an office and waited for the nod from Winter's manager to hop on the tour bus parked behind the club, eager to ask Johnny a few questions. Like why he panders to a core following of motorheads with velocity instead of seducing a new audience with nuance?

There wasn't time for too much conversation but Winter was cordial and patient, complaining about his cramped living quarters on the bus and hoping for the best in his upcoming album deal, which should produce his first album in three years.

"In the negotiation stages everything is always beautiful and we love you and you're the greatest and we're going to support the album and put money behind it," he said. "And as soon as you make the record, it's completely different. These guys are salesmen. You hope for the best."

Winter is a man who can lay the human heart bare by moving a pick and a hunk of metal across the strings of a National steel guitar while moaning and yodeling the blues like the pale ghost of Robert Johnson.

Yet, he says he is a prisoner of high-voltage rock because it seems to be the only thing his audience wants.

"When I do the ballads or some of the pretty stuff I like, it goes right by them. People don't care," he said. "When I was playing bars before I got known, people wanted variety. You had to do a country song, a jazz song… all kinds of stuff. People don't want to hear the softer side and that bothers me because I really miss doing those songs."

A student of all forms of American music, Winter started off playing the ukulele when his father, the mayor of Leland during the Depression, gave him one during the Arthur Godfrey craze.

Then came the guitar, and then came Elvis Presley, whom Winter said rescued pop music from such tofu as "How Much Is that Doggie in the Window?"

"That was the first real rock and roll," he says. "I loved Elvis in the early days. It was just so different."

Just about the same time, in 1955, Winter went to summer camp at the age of 11 and discovered the blues of Howlin' Wolf and Muddy Waters. "That stuff changed my life," he said.

After that he no longer had much use for Elvis, although he did tour Graceland in 1988 while recording an album for MCA in Memphis.

"It definitely showed me that just making it doesn't make you happy," said Winter, remembering the Presley mansion. "I walked through his hall of gold, with all these gold albums just stretching for miles and I thought, 'Man, this guy had everything you could want and it definitely did not make him happy.'"

Today, at age 47, with nearly all of the blues heroes from his youth passing over to the next world, Johnny Winter is more aware of his mortality than he was during the spooky years of his early fame.

Someday, he said, a hot young rocker might come along and do for his career what Winter did for Muddy Waters when he produced the last of Waters albums, earning Muddy his only Grammys.

I will never forget the sight of Winter's limousine pulling up to the side of Waters' Chicago grave in 1983. Johnny wore dark shades and sat in the back with his head in his hands, mourning his good friend, the grand old man of blues.

Once, more than a dozen years ago in a damp, cold room at Baltimore's old Marble Bar on Franklin Street, Waters told me that "Johnny Winter is the only white man who really understands the blues."

Muddy Waters has been gone for almost eight years now and it seems that Johnny Winter hasn't adjusted to the loss.

"I still talk about the young white guys and the old black guys... I enjoyed having idols, older musicians to look up to and most of them are gone now," he said. "I keep having to remind myself, 'Wait a minute, You're not a young white guy anymore. You're an old white guy.'"

February 24, 1991

'The blues are the truth'

When I was 20, knowing little of the blues and almost nothing of pain, I began chasing old black men across America for answers.

Answers to what I didn't exactly know, but because these men made music that spirited me to worlds I never knew, it seemed important to cut their work open and look inside.

Once, in a Route 40 motel out near White Marsh, I asked J.B. Hutto to name that certain something which made his music so magnificent. The slide guitarist was silent for a long moment and said: "Oh well, you know, I just play the blues."

In the basement of the old Congress Hotel I asked Muddy Waters where the blues came from and he said: "Son, the blues come from slavery days when you had to turn the kettle up high and sing down low."

And in the shadow of the Smithsonian Institute's great woolly mammoth I tried to find the bottom line by asking Willie Dixon if he could tell me what is the blues.

Without taking a breath he declared: "The blues are the truth, the blues are the facts, the blues are the roots of all American music."

That was the last time I asked anyone who had devoted his life to the blues to explain the elusive mysteries of life.

Willie Dixon died of heart failure Wednesday in Burbank, California.

At age 76 he followed brethren like Hutto and Waters into a boneyard that has now claimed all but the very last few of this country's great and genuine bluesmen.

As the composer of hundreds of songs, the longtime house producer for Chess Records, and a bassist and singer who cut many of his own records, Willie Dixon is being remembered around the globe as a primary influence on a Sixties generation of long-haired white boys who hit it big with rock-and-roll covers of Dixon classics like "Spoonful," "Little Red Rooster" and "You Need Love."

But I will remember Willie Dixon as the great articulator of the blues.

"Listen to the message in the blues, the message in the blues is the most important part. This is what my people need to know," he told me. "The blues have been neglected all the way around. Nobody has actually pushed the blues, they always went on their own. The world has always underestimated the blues, like people didn't know what they was talking about when they talked the blues. If outsiders didn't have the experience, then naturally they wouldn't know."

Willie Dixon never tired of schooling those outside the blues experience — rooted in slavery, poverty and misery — to its message of endurance and hope. He especially enjoyed passing it to young black children far removed from the music's beginnings in Deep South towns like his Vicksburg, Miss., birthplace.

To that end he formed the Blues Heaven Foundation a decade ago and was a chief participant in Chicago's "Blues in the Schools" program, which donates instruments to students and conducts classroom blues workshops.

And he was also a kind host to many a writer and musician who made the pilgrimage to his southside Chicago home; people like my colleague David Zurawik, who played blues harp long before he wrote for a daily newspaper.

In 1969 a friend needed a ride from Milwaukee to Chicago to fence some stolen saxophones and flutes. David says he refused the favor until he learned that the trip involved a visit to Willie Dixon's house.

Remembering the visit, Zurawik said: "Willie hadn't said two words when he came down the basement where his sons were practicing, took the bass, and said: 'OK, let's do it.' He started a bass line to Hoochie Koochie Man or Little Red Rooster and my mouth was hanging open — Willie Dixon was playing bass and I was blowing harp to one of his tunes that I'd heard 9,000 white guys play on the record player in my basement. Then he said — 'OK boys, let's eat' and everyone went upstairs for a big pork chop dinner. Willie asked me if I liked stewed yellow turnips and I lied and said, 'Oh yeah. I love 'em' and he piled them up. They were so bitter, but I ate them and even asked for more. But the main thing about the visit was that this was a purely gracious act by a man whose music was being ripped off left and right. If anybody had the right to tell two white guys who showed up at his door to go to hell, it was Willie Dixon."

I last saw Willie Dixon in 1983 at Muddy Waters' funeral, when he said of Muddy's death: "The blues has no where to go but up. It's been down too long."

A photograph of the composer hangs on the pink walls of my Highlandtown row house with an inscription that says. "To Rafael, a great writer... Willie Dixon."

It is priceless to me, a wonderful treasure, but until just now it hadn't occurred to me that Willie Dixon never read anything I had written.

But he knew that I wrote about the blues, and through the blues I wrote about the history of his people, and that was enough to qualify.

January 31, 1992

Chapter 15

Changing Times

New Canton rises atop painful memories

THE ROAD WAS COMING, AND THE PEOPLE OF CANTON HAD TO ABANDON homes their families had lived in for generations.

It was 1965, and an urban superhighway — a double-decked monster called the East-West Expressway — was going to lop a long slice of life out of Southeast Baltimore and cast a shadow over what was left. To make way, about 300 families were forced to surrender their homes to the city for an average of less than $5,000 — the prevailing market value, according to appraisers at the time, but less than similar houses were going for outside the neighborhood.

Anna Kuhn cried for three days after the city paid her $6,000 to take the home at 1214 S. Decker Ave. that she and her husband had bought for $6,000 12 years earlier. They moved to Dundalk and had to assume a mortgage on their $10,900 single home.

"Ain't that a damn shame?" she asks, still hurt some two decades later.

"While it was still standing I'd go in and look and it was empty, I'd go down there when my Brian was just a baby and I'd cry and sit him on top the stove and say: 'Brian, this is where Mommy and Daddy used to live.'"

Planning for the expressway took 40 years and cost taxpayers about $15 million.

In the end, in 1969, a team of socially and aesthetically minded architects persuaded the state that a double-stacked, 16-lane highway cutting through the heart of the city and across the mouth of the Inner Harbor to Fort McHenry was not in Baltimore's best interests. The solution was the Fort McHenry tunnel — the last link in Interstate 95.

That decision is credited with saving the Inner Harbor and Federal Hill — two other neighborhoods in the path of the planned expressway — and thereby preserving the opportunity for Baltimore's downtown renaissance of the 1980s. But the bureaucrats scrapped the road just a little too late for the people of Canton. The houses had already been boarded up and the bulldozers had rumbled.

For the next 20 years, the vacant lots that spread two blocks north from the Boston Street waterfront were nothing more than scruffy hosts to pick-up soccer games, moonlit beer parties, ethnic festivals, field mice, and a garden or two.

They stayed that way until the early 1980s, when developer Louis J. Grasmick suggested to his friend Mayor William Donald Schaefer during a walk down Boston Street that the Canton waterfront could be Baltimore's "Gold Coast."

The result was high-rise condominiums on the water and a real estate boom that turned the area into one of the most lucrative housing markets in Maryland.

Part of that boom was the building of a new community — which has almost nothing in common with the old except a ZIP code — over the memory of a neighborhood that ultimately had been razed for nothing.

In 1986, according to city records, Baltimore sold 6.7 of the 11 vacant acres to developer Theo Rogers and a group of associates for $420,018.

Now standing on the properties — some of which were taken for less than $3,500 — are stylish urban town houses selling for $136,000 to $235,000, according to the developer. The older houses nearby have increased in value as a result: Real estate agents say traditional Canton row houses currently sell for as high as $79,000.

The Canton Square development of 133 town houses is filled nearly to capacity. Only about 20 units are unsold, according to the developer.

With resale prices still climbing, many of the neighborhood's old-timers and their relatives feel a lingering pain over the Canton boom.

While the rest of the 11 acres was set aside for the private Canton Harbor Nursing Home and an indoor soccer arena still in the planning stage, the town houses don't quite make sense to the people who can't forget the way things used to be.

"If the expressway had been built, you'd say, 'Well, who'd want to live there anyway?'" said Mercedes Stevens, who lived with her parents in a house at 1242 S. Decker Ave. and whose aunt, sister and several cousins also lost homes.

"But even if I have forgotten it, the [Canton] renaissance is putting salt into the wound. You go back there now and say, 'This was mine, and now other people are living here.'"

Helen Wisniewski, whose father, Demitro Iwancio, received $3,600 for his house at 1116 S. Kenwood Ave., was more to the point.

"When you go to see what they're putting up where you used to live," she said, "it's like sticking a knife in your heart."

Destroyed along with Anna Kuhn's home and scores like it — stolen, Mrs. Kuhn says, by "the crooks in the city" — were corner grocery stores such as Kitko's, neighborhood saloons such as Whitey Stefan's gin joint, the old National Lumber yard and filling stations such as Tolan's Garage.

Torn down were the private and usually paid-for homes of hundreds of families, mostly older Polish clans such as the Wisniewskis, and German folks such as the Woolshlegers.

A way of life tumbled down with those homes and haunts — habits such as housewives hosing down the gutters in the summer, fathers coming home from the vegetable "packing house" with green tomatoes to be dipped in flour and egg and fried up, and a liberal definition of extended family that is rarely seen today.

"People would walk off the sidewalk to squirt down the *street*," said John Woolshleger, whose father received $5,000 for a house in the 1100 block of South Lakewood Avenue. "We didn't know what dirt was."

"Leaving Canton was the furthest thing from our minds," said Anna

Buddemeyer, who was 10 years old in 1966 when her family had to leave its home at 1218 S. Ellwood Ave. — a house that has since been razed.

"The street pole is still there in front of the house. We used to play jacks under the streetlight, and the women would glitch-glotch and all the men would meet down the bar."

"Everybody talked to each other back then — I know, I've lived in Canton 55 years — not like it is today," said Evelyn Schoor, 79, whose home in the 1100 block of S. Curley Street sits beside the planned route of the highway. "They all mourned when they had to go, and what they got for their houses wouldn't buy them another."

That lingering sense of betrayal, set against hundreds of millions of dollars in development along the Boston Street waterfront, has made for a splintered Canton, a neighborhood split between fixed incomes and big incomes, the lifestyles of the old working class and the new professional class — between people who won't ever forget what happened to their friends and relatives in the 1960s, and new residents who don't even know there was a neighborhood before they came.

Larry DiLegge, 39, has a foot on each side of the divided neighborhood.

Not only did he go to school there, play ball there and drink many an underage beer in Rose's Bar — another business knocked down for the phantom expressway — but Mr. DiLegge grew up to own a corner bar next to the Canton Square town houses and now lives in the development with his own family.

And as much as Mr. DiLegge would like to see Canton Square fold into the older community that has thrived by the water for more than a century, he doesn't see it happening any time soon.

"I remember these blocks when they were other people's homes. It's unsettling. There's a distance between the two communities," says Mr. DiLegge, who hopes his work with the fledgling Canton Square Neighborhood Association will help bridge the gaps.

"The [old residents] see us as strangers, people they have no connection with."

But, said Mr. DiLegge, "There may be a bridging as long as we have a common enemy."

That enemy, which has brought together communities from Fells Point to Highlandtown in a broad watchdog group called the Waterfront Coalition, is runaway development along the waterfront on the other side of Boston Street from Canton Square.

One side effect of this development — this move to change an old working waterfront into a community of luxury condominiums and boat slips — is a plan to widen Boston Street to six lanes and turn it into Boston Boulevard, an East Baltimore equivalent of Martin Luther King Jr. Boulevard west of downtown.

Today, Boston Street is an uneven, barely paved remnant of a Canton that was an industrial giant — a heavily traveled, truck-and-train-bearing stretch of pothole-riddled asphalt that begins at the edge of Fells Point and runs east to the city line of Dundalk.

"I've got a deck out back here," said Mr. DiLegge, pointing at sliding glass doors that look out at Boston Street. "And when I stand out there I feel like I'm living in Ocean City without a beach — it's like looking at Coastal Highway."

Highway officials envision a smooth new road, but one that residents fear will cut them off completely from the harbor.

And so, along with seemingly endless battles with city planners over height limitations for the condominiums, public access to the waterfront and the number of units allowed in each project — "We try to get a handle on one thing and it all keeps coming," said one resident — the coalition of community groups has accepted the new folks from Canton Square for the fight.

Beyond that, said Rev. Lee Hudson, the pastor of Messiah Lutheran Church on O'Donnell Street, it's going to take more than a common enemy to create harmony in Canton.

"The big danger is that there will be one Canton south [of O'Donnell Street] and another to the north, and the new residents will come in with the expertise and set the tone for everyone," Mr. Hudson said. "We have to find a gentle way to convince [the new folks] not to close themselves off. The window of compatibility will only be open for a short period of time. If it closes, it will be very difficult to reopen."

But the sense of being deceived, still felt by the old residents, works against cooperation and compatibility.

According to one city planner who asked not to be named, that feeling threatens to overshadow nearly every project proposed for Canton by the city or developers.

"They bring it up no matter what we try to do down there," the planner said. "They are gun-shy."

City officials are sensitive to the outcry about the way the planning for the East-West Expressway was handled.

"It would appear that having cut this swath through East Baltimore, we forgot about [residents]," said Harry McCulloh, head of the city's interstate transportation division since 1972. "But there was 40 years of study before we agreed what to do. We went into acquisition and demolition well in advance of these changes.

"The residents say they didn't get fair market value," Mr. McCulloh said. "But no amount of money would be worth what was taken from them."

One of the enduring legends of East Baltimore, in fact, is that for many of the elderly people who lost their homes in Canton, the move was fatal.

"They were dying of broken hearts and dropping like flies," said former state Delegate Raymond A. Dypski, who retired from the General Assembly last year after building a political career on the fight to save his Canton neighbors.

Mary Potocki Lasek and her parents lost their home at 1216 S. Ellwood Ave. to the expressway, and soon after, Mrs. Lasek's mother died.

"To this day I say it's what killed her," she said. "So many of them died off in those first years of leaving."

"On my block alone, I would say about 20 people died within two years of having to move," said Ms. Stevens. "There was one lady who had a heart attack and died the day they came and stenciled 'Property of the City of Baltimore' on her front door. It seemed like within a few months there were all these people just dying."

Few of the new Canton Square residents are aware of it.

Some express a belief that the cultural gulf between the working and the professional, the old and the new, can be bridged with simple courtesy and old-fashioned neighborliness. But no one is completely convinced it will happen, particularly since many of the town houses have been bought for investment.

"My idea of Canton will always be the old ladies and the neat-as-a-pin houses," said Karen O'Connor Williams, who moved into 1102 S. Kenwood Ave. with her husband and teen-age son last August.

"I feel I'm part of Canton, and I want the [other residents] to know it. The friendliness they show me will be responded to. You find the down-to-earth people around here, and that's what I love."

It might surprise some of the older residents that people like Mrs. Williams and Mr. DiLegge — East Baltimoreans not all that different from themselves — are living in new town houses.

Mr. DiLegge himself even finds it a little hard to believe.

"Sometimes I relate more to the old ethnic side of Canton than the new homeowners I'm living next to now," he said. "For the most part, I would say the people moving in here are Yuppies."

That kind of talk makes Phyllis Walton and Bill Hopkinson mad, even though they admit that with a two-career relationship, a health club membership, no children, a nearby slip for their boat and a trendy in-town address, it's easy to label them.

Yuppie or not, the couple love Canton, were quick to join the Canton-Highlandtown Improvement Association, and say they will work to bring the old and new together.

"You have to understand that we're all in this together," said Ms. Walton.

"It's not our fault that these houses were built, but we do want to preserve the continuity of Canton. The [older residents] don't want the neighborhood taken from them. They want to keep the same look of Canton if nothing else. They don't want a Miami."

"Unlike the high-rises," said Mr. Hopkinson, "this is a neighborhood, and because of that I think we'll be able to merge with the old Canton."

Until then, said Mr. DiLegge — whose New Year's Eve party brought together friends from the old and the new for a comfortable good time — there will be two Cantons.

And in memory of those who were displaced, it may always be this way.

"I think we got a raw deal, a very bad raw deal," said Clinton Buddemeyer. "We were displaced, every one of us.

"You run into somebody from back then, and that's all you ever talk about — our life back in Canton."

June 19, 1988

When the old seamen's bar is turned
into a surf shop

IT IS ABOUT 10 O'CLOCK ON A HUMID WEDNESDAY NIGHT IN FELLS POINT, and I am sitting in the neighborhood square, filled with anger and sadness, staring at 805 South Broadway.

Cars circle the block endlessly looking for places to park; gangs of young people with bad haircuts and teeth too big for their mouths circle the block endlessly, looking to connect with people who look like themselves; and I keep staring into the windows of 805 South Broadway, my mind circling around memories from 1963, 1964, 1965, 1966... endlessly.

I can think of no building, except the Macon Street row house in which my father was born and raised in Highlandtown, as important to my identity as 805 South Broadway.

For most of this century the three-story brick building was known to foreign seamen, tugboat men and neighborhood regulars as Karcz's Cafe, a cool, dark bar where the front door was locked and you were let in only after someone peeked out the round window in the door and looked you over.

But to my family it was always "Miss Agnes and Mr. Simone's," and we went down Broadway to visit there just about every Sunday night after dinner.

My eyes glazed Wednesday night as I forced spirits from the past to appear behind the plate glass.

There was Miss Agnes (Karcz), eating steamed crabs with my mother, drinking Cutty Sark and water with my old man, decorating the bar for Christmas with life-size manger scenes and buying me my first record player.

Behind the bar was her husband, Simone Garayoa, a veteran of the Spanish Civil War and a tugboat man like my dad. He loved talking in his native tongue with my father and giving me and my little brother bags of Wise potato chips and Coca-Colas in small, green-tinted bottles.

He always called us "Champ" and cooked squid stuffed with their tentacles and sauteed in their own ink for his special friends. Mr. Simone was the nicest man in the world.

I played football in the street with their sons, Mark and David, when the Fells Point square was a parking lot, and I went up to the Recreation Pier with their daughter, Kathy, to play and listen to Smokey Robinson records.

Of all the regulars in Karcz's Cafe, including a wonderful Spanish gentleman named Mr. Steve who quietly smoked cigars, the one I remember best is Mr. Oley, an aged Norwegian seaman with wire-rimmed glasses and a cane who threw back shots of whiskey until the day he died and spoke in a voice like a yodel.

"Oooh, oooh, oooh," Mr. Oley would sing to us from his bar stool, pointing down at our little giggling faces with a crooked finger. "I like-a you, you like-a me? Oooh, oooh, oooh."

We liked Mr. Oley.

And then the Expressway the City Never Built was supposed to cut through Fells Point, and the Garayoas sold their bar in the early 1970s for money that wouldn't buy a good station wagon today.

Then Karcz's Cafe became a florist shop. Not long after that, Miss Agnes died. Then Mr. Simone died, and sometime in the last year 805 South Broadway stopped being a flower store.

I sit on the square in Fells Point and stare at the building, filled with anger and sadness, shaking my head as the spirits of my childhood vanish into the fluorescent glare of 1990.

Miss Agnes and Mr. Simone's is a surf shop.

I park my car in a lot just beyond the corner of Bond and Thames streets where a good buddy and I used to sit on the ledge of an abandoned warehouse, drink beer and watch the sun go down over the city before developers made a straight hemline out of every loose thread that was Fells Point.

I'm on my way to the square, to sit and brood over what was, what is and what will never be, but before I get there I see old friends sitting on the corner, sipping beer on a humid Wednesday night in Fells Point outside a bar that has been in the woman's family for decades.

I almost never go at night anymore to Fells Point; the place where I was served my first beer in a bar at age 16 (with Kathy Garayoa); where I had my first date with a girl I would grow up to marry; where I taught my daughter, Amelia, to ride a two-wheel bike without training wheels so she would have some sense of the place.

Once in a while I visit in the daytime — to buy chicken at the market or stare at the water where the tugboats my father worked on once docked — but I can't take it anymore at night. At night I see gangs of people alien to what I remember of Fells Point roaming the streets for good times, and they bring out emotions I'm ashamed of.

But I made a special visit Wednesday night. I forced myself.

On my way to the square, I stop to talk to the couple outside the bar they own at Bond and Thames, friends I hadn't seen for a while, people I was happy to see.

"I'm writing a story about the death of Fells Point," I say.

"Fells Point's not dead," says the woman, ready to argue. "We're here, aren't we? This is my father's bar, and I stay here for him, to keep his memory alive. Fells Point isn't dead."

I lay out the evidence: Karcz's Cafe is a surf shop; the old Baker-Whiteley tugboats, sold to a sinister company that fired its union workers in 1984, are long gone from Thames Street; and Mrs. Veronica Lukowski, perhaps the oldest lifelong resident of the neighborhood, died June 9.

It doesn't register. They seem not to know who Mrs. Lukowski was.

At Mrs. Lukowski's funeral, her sons, Gilbert and Jerome, remembered their father slaughtering pigs and chickens in the back yard of 1718 Thames Street, the Seaman's Cafe where boarders were taken in and pickled green tomatoes floated in barrels of vinegar in the basement, where Mrs. Lukowski still did laundry on a washboard until she died.

Her sons said there wasn't a reason anymore to go down Broadway, to visit the neighborhood that gave them life. Fells Point, they said, is gone.

But the couple sipping beer outside their family bar, after admitting that sentimental reasons keep them in Fells Point, offer me proof of a pulse.

"Guess whose screen door I saw open just the other day?" says the man. "Old Miss Fronie, her place is still a bar just like it was when they closed it after her husband died. The bar's still there, got a picture of John Kennedy on the wall."

"I seen her up the market a few weeks ago," says the woman, turning to me. "Now there's real Fells Point. Miss Fronie is Fells Point... Almost 90 years old, still goes to Mass and the market every week."

I had never heard of Miss Fronie anywhere around Broadway.

"Where's her house?" I say. "Will she talk to me?"

"Sure Miss Fronie'll talk to you, hon," says the woman. "She's got a bar right between the Waterfront Hotel and the Cat's Eye, right on Thames Street. Looks just like it did years ago."

But the more we sit and compare notes — is Miss Fronie the mother-in-law of a widow named Eleanor Lukowski on Ann Street, didn't her sons used to work on the tugboats? — it slowly becomes clear that Miss Fronie and Mrs. Lukowski are one and the same.

"That's what I'm telling you," I say. "She died. Her screen door was probably open so real estate people could come and look at it."

The man falls silent, and the woman starts to cry, quietly, from the corner of her eyes.

She doesn't try to argue with me anymore about whether Fells Point is dead or not. She just sits and cries, and I kiss her on the cheek and excuse myself to go sit on the square and brood, filled with anger and sadness.

June 24, 1990

Wrecking ball can't remove memories of East Lombard Street

As Baltimore's Jewish community celebrated its legacy in a climate-controlled museum, the very past being remembered tumbled in dust around the corner.

Bulldozers demolished five derelict rowhouses that had stood witness to life both robust and rogue on East Lombard Street for more than 100 years.

The buildings were razed starting May 30, the same weekend the Jewish Historical Society opened its exhibit, "Fertile Ground: 200 Years of Jewish Life in Maryland."

For some, bygone years came to life outside the museum as the end came for 1010 through 1018 East Lombard Street.

"A lot of people showed up with their memories," said George Dausch, who owns the property and had the buildings torn down. "A lot of Jewish people came down and stood around to watch."

Because the buildings had so deteriorated, Mr. Dausch said, many of the observers said the demolition "should have been done years ago."

He said city inspectors refused to enter to verify that the sewer and gas lines had been capped, fearing disease from used hypodermic needles.

Said Sid Traub, who intends to buy the land from Mr. Dausch to expand his nearby warehouse of novelties: "There is no historical significance to those buildings."

Perhaps not the way they were at the end: vacant, collapsing and carpeted with trash, empty booze bottles and dope needles.

But if history is measured in racks of meat butchered to order, bushels of fish beheaded and cleaned, and coops of chickens sold live and slaughtered, then something more than bricks came down when the rowhouses were razed.

"To understand Lombard Street," said Irving Spivack, whose family owned a poultry store there, "you have to understand that mostly it was all Jewish."

The five buildings housed Brotman's for kosher meats, Lesinsky's for fresh fish, and Cohen's and Yankelov's for chicken.

The block had stores one after the other — with an Italian deli or fruit stand here and there, and a bazaar where fat women sat on wooden crates plucking chickens by hand.

Just after the start of World War II, Harry Tulkoff began buying up most of the block to make his "Flaming Hot" horseradish.

The Tulkoffs sold out in 1979 to the Traub family, known for its line of Baltimore postcards, and the Traubs sold to Mr. Dausch's Durable Steel Products Co.

Durable Steel expects to sell the lots back to Sid Traub when the rubble is cleared.

Although the pungent and lusty bustle began fading in the 1950s, old-timers regarded the demolition with sadness.

"There must have been a half-dozen places to get chickens," recalled Sam Rubin, 81, who grew up a few blocks away on East Baltimore Street. "My mother would ask me to help her take chickens back home on holidays."

One Polish woman who traveled from Canton with her mother, one of thousands of gentiles who also went to market on Lombard Street, remembered the warmth of the just-slaughtered chicken against her body as she carried it home.

Even some of the laborers who helped topple the structures felt bad.

"I knew when we started that we were tearing down the chicken place," said Thonnie Smith, 45. "I used to come over from the West Side to get a live chicken and have him killed, maybe 10 or 15 years ago, for a couple bucks. When you got a chicken killed on Lombard Street you knew you were getting a fresh chicken."

Michael Meyer Yankelov, 87, said his cousin David Yankelov was the last man to sell live chickens on Lombard Street, continuing on through the 1970s after the others were long gone.

A few businesses, such as Attman's Delicatessen, thrive as part of a group widely known as Corned Beef Row.

But most of the neighborhood has given way to blight and vacant lots.

"It's sad," said Moe Gordon, who grew up on Lombard Street in the 1920s.

"But let's be pragmatic, no one cares. Even if you saved the buildings, you can't bring it back, you can't put the pickles back in the barrels and the olives on the sidewalk and the storekeeper who would come out and stick his hand down in a barrel of herring, pull out a fat one, wrap it in old newspaper and give it to the customer for a quarter.

"You can't bring those people back. Lifestyles have changed. When I tell my own children about the old days they say: 'So what?'"

So what?

So some of the best years of Paul Wartzman's life were spent there, running the streets and hanging in his family's bakery in "good old days that sometimes weren't the good old days.

"There's never been anything like Lombard Street. I used to fight one of my best friends on the chicken coops. We'd roll around on the coops, and flail our arms; the chickens would be screaming. It was fun," said Mr. Wartzman, 65.

"They had the ritual schochet who killed the chickens. My memories would be to carry the chickens over and watch him kill the chickens.

"It was frightening, the razor would always be on his lips and he'd take it out and cut the throat of the chicken and let them hang there. The blood had to come out ritually.

"It would hang for awhile, and I'd take it back to the customer in the chicken store. I did it for tips, maybe a penny or two in the early '30s."

Mr. Wartzman recently noticed a piece of sky stretching north to Baltimore Street where bricks used to be.

"I happened to be down there getting a corned beef at Attman's," he said. "It's sad, a sad thing when you see a whole culture and era going by your eyes."

Barry Kessler, 34, curator for the Jewish Historical Society, said he witnessed the demolition.

"I walked over to watch and thought, 'These buildings have been in the heart of the Jewish community for a good hundred years, they might still have some stuff left in them.'

"I felt like I was taking my life in my hands; but I went in with a garbage can and collected whatever I could grab."

Now, said Mr. Kessler: "We have the greatest collection of horseradish labels on Earth."

The labels, customized for different markets around the country, were left behind in 1979 when the sons of Harry Tulkoff moved to an old brewery complex in Canton.

"My family started buying up that side of the block in the early 1940s," said Martin Tulkoff, 56.

He said that after his father came from New York, he ground horseradish but also sold fruits and vegetables.

"He had a nice display set up with a pyramid of oranges and one day a woman pulled an orange from the bottom and the whole pile fell. Dad said, 'That's it, I'm going into horseradish only.'"

Bernard Fishman is the director of the Jewish Historical Society, which occupies a modern building on land where rowhouses once stood between two synagogues on Lloyd Street.

He said it would have been nice to have saved 1010 through 1018 East Lombard Street, but raising the money to renovate the synagogues was burden enough.

"In general, those older buildings were very poorly documented, but they were the bread and butter of the late 19th century. But they didn't stand out as extraordinary," said Mr. Fishman.

After the 1968 riots dispatched the last of the old neighborhood's lingering stalwarts, the city began looking for ways to revitalize the former Jewish marketplace.

But Amy Glorioso, a city planner, said hopes for bringing back the strip for retail have been abandoned.

"We wanted Lombard Street to come back, but no one large user like Tulkoff wanted to be there anymore," said Ms. Glorioso. "We're trying to work on the design of the [planned] Traub warehouse to make it as friendly as possible, maybe brick with some windows. But it's going to be a challenge to develop that block."

Irvin Spivack, 50, recalls the neighborhood in its heyday, when all of his grandparents owned businesses. Hyman and Sarah Brotman were the butchers on his mother's side, and a chicken place was run by Solomon and Ida Spivack.

He said the fierce competition was balanced by mutual respect.

"Everybody was trying to grab the guy walking down the street. When it came to business, everybody was out to get you, they wanted your customer, enough was never enough," he said.

"But outside of work they were all friends. Now, as far as I'm concerned, it's the end. If you didn't have the synagogues, Lombard Street would just be another street."

June 16, 1992

Tales of old Fells Point

GILBERT LUKOWSKI WANTS TO READ HIS OBITUARY BEFORE HE DIES.

As the tough old stevedore nears 70 — having stood by as friends and family took tales of Baltimore to their graves — he has become anxious for his own stories.

"When I was growing up, the foot of Broadway was the greatest place in the world," he says, riding through cobbled streets transformed in a lifetime from one of the city's roughest neighborhoods to some of its most expensive real estate.

Mr. Lukowski stares through a gray rain at his old neighborhood, and everything he sees is dead. He sighs: "They say nobody remembers, but I think about it every day."

The Daily Grind coffee house and the Orpheum Cinema above it used to be Mooney's rope shop. BOP Pizza at Broadway and Lancaster Street was a pool room and boarding house. The recently installed fortune-telling parlor at 1716 Thames St. was a barbershop fronting a bookmaking operation.

Across Durham Street from old School No. 6 (now the Lemko House for seniors), a farrier shod horses. At the corner of Aliceanna and Ann streets, a woman in the habit of dressing like a nun made a living turning worn shirt collars inside out and sewing them up for another year or two of wear.

The building that houses the Cat's Eye Pub once served as headquarters for a private "pleasure club" for drinking and gambling, where carnal recreation could be obtained for half-a-buck, a dollar for something special.

And at the end of Fell Street, where warehouses have been converted into condominiums, stood a "car float" — railroad tracks on pilings that were used to move rail cars onto barges. At night, drunken drivers tended to mistake it for a bridge. Savvier street urchins used the float to launch their naked bodies into the Patapsco for summertime dips.

Gilbert Joseph Lukowski was born into all of this on Feb. 17, 1925, at his maternal grandmother's house at 807 South Ann St., spitting distance from the harbor waters that have washed over his entire life.

Roman Catholicism dominated the neighborhood of immigrants and, when the priests a few doors away at Saint Stanislaus would not recognize the unsaintly name of Gilbert, he was baptized Gabriel.

"My mother liked the name Gilbert," he says of his legal name. "But they called me a lot worse than Gilbert on the docks."

The middle of three sons born to first-generation Americans Edward and Veronica Lukowski, Gilbert spoke only Polish until he was "about 4 years old and started to run the streets."

In the 1930s, those streets jumped with working people, animals pulling wagons or waiting to be slaughtered, businesses catering to seafarers, and characters who landed on Thames Street from ports around the world.

"This was the most diverse neighborhood in the city — Greeks, Poles, Irish, Jews, Spaniards, blacks, Turks," says Mr. Lukowski, remembering a community of rag shops, stag bars, chandleries, vinegar works and row-houses with white wooden steps that residents turned upside down when they didn't want anyone to sit on them.

Known as "Harrigan," his father was a coppersmith's helper and a long-shoreman until he fell into the hold of a ship. He then became a bootlegger, selling illegal booze until Prohibition was repealed and he opened the Seamen's Cafe in a former soda fountain at 1718 Thames St. The family lived above the bar. Harrigan Lukowski died in 1967.

Mr. Lukowski's mother, known to locals as "Miss Fronie," worked for pennies in neighborhood tomato and strawberry factories. At home, she pickled green tomatoes, cucumbers, onions, and pig feet in the basement. Live pigs were butchered in the backyard; coal was conserved in summer by warming tubs of bathwater in the sun.

Horse manure, coveted as fertilizer for vegetable gardens, was plucked from the street.

"We were all poor, only we didn't know we were poor because your house was spotless and you always had something to eat," he says, remembering the thrill of stealing empty 5-gallon cans from the local tin can warehouse and selling them to bootleggers.

Such thievery and mischief often caught the attention of the neighborhood constable.

"The police never bothered to chase you back in them days," laughs Mr. Lukowski. "They'd yell after you: 'I'm going to your house to tell your mother and father.' You stopped running because no matter what that cop did to you, it was better than getting it from your mother and your father."

At 16, Gilbert Lukowski began working on vessels of questionable sea-worthiness — "bum boats," which picked up work that fell through the cracks and carried last-minute items to departing ships. These were the days when a nickel-a-ride ferry between Fells Point and Locust Point made sister villages of the cross-harbor neighborhoods.

"My father would give me a nickel to go over to Locust Point to cash brass [coin pay vouchers] for the stevedores who drank in our bar," he says. "I'd walk all the way around the harbor just to save that nickel. A nickel was something. You could run up the street and get a good coddie [fish cake] for a nickel."

Before long, he was making a dollar's worth of nickels every hour for unloading sacks of coffee, crates of canned goods, bags of sugar and anything else ships carried.

"If you stood on the corner in the summer when the stevedores were busy and you were big enough, you went to work," he says. "Nobody asked you how old you were in them days. It only mattered if you were big enough."

In 1950, Mr. Lukowski was elected president of the International Longshoreman's Association ship carpenters Local No. 1355, known as "the wood butchers." Ever since, he has split his career between elected union jobs with No. 1355 and dockside labor with the cargo handlers of ILA Local No. 829. For the past 20 years, he has administered the local ILA pension plan.

"To make a different life for myself," Mr. Lukowski left his mother's home in 1950 after marrying an Italian woman from Milton Avenue named Katherine Mazzie. The couple bought a house between Edison Highway and Herring Run Park and raised three children there.

He explains: "When I was coming up, if you wanted to play on grass you had to go to Patterson Park. I wanted to give my kids something better than growing up on cobblestones."

Yet for years, he and all of Veronica Lukowski's scattered children and grandchildren returned to the old neighborhood every weekend to visit.

Mrs. Lukowski died in 1990 and her family recently sold her home — the one with the wooden bar and the nice portrait of John F. Kennedy on the wall — for about $160,000.

These days, the only time Gilbert rolls through the neighborhood is in the morning to pick up a newspaper at Jimmy's Restaurant on Broadway. He says hello to the few people he still knows, the ones who are still alive, and moves on.

After touring his old neighborhood for an hour the other day, Mr. Lukowski parks his car in front of 1718 Thames St. and sees ghosts in the plate glass window.

"It's not just the times or the places, it's the people I miss," he says. "Once my mother was gone, that was the end. My mother was the center of the family, not this house. The family doesn't see each other like we used to anymore."

Silent for a moment as he gets ready to leave, Gilbert Lukowski says: "It's over for me now. When I want to be with my family, I go down to the graveyard and talk to my mother."

March 5, 1994

Lexington Market: Luster fading from hometown jewel

IT REMAINS THE MOST EXOTIC BAZAAR IN ALL OF BALTIMORE.

Some 212 years after it began as an open air market frequented by gamblers and ruffians, Lexington Market is a 266,000-square-foot adventure for palates seeking foods from goat meat to raccoon to hog jowls.

But today, the characters on the fringes of the nation's oldest, continuously operated public market are not the romantic rogues from the seedling years of Baltimore Town. Too often, say some merchants and customers, they are belligerent beggars, thieves, drug addicts and falling-down drunks.

As the neighborhood around Lexington Market continues its decline in the wake of the abandonment of Howard Street by the Hecht's, Hutzler's and Stewart's department stores, the luster is fading from a hometown jewel.

"I think it's still as exciting to come down here as it ever was," said Theodore Edlow, 67, who sells frozen yogurt and remembers the days when women in white gloves shopped at the market after taking their tea at Hutzler's. "But in 20 years, I've seen the class of people who come here change.

"We get a good crowd for an hour-and-a-half at lunch. The rest of the day is on the low end."

Said Yogurt Tree employee Michael Jackson, 35, who grew up working in the market: "There's too many people here with no money and nothing to do."

Market officials — planning an ice cream festival for July 21 — argue that downtown is no different from anywhere else; that in this day and age, anything can happen anywhere.

In less than two weeks, this has happened on the streets around Lexington Market:

• Just before 4 a.m. on June 27, one man was killed and another injured when a gunman opened fire on the occupants of a parked car. Police called the dead man an "intended target."

• On July 4, about 2:15 a.m., more than a dozen men sprayed gunfire into a crowd of about 200 people a block from the market, wounding at least five people. Of the gunmen, police said: "They just wanted to see people run."

• And about 8 a.m. Wednesday, just outside a market entrance, a homeless man whacked an acquaintance with a hatchet, sending his victim to the Maryland Shock Trauma Center with a deep gash in his neck.

None of the incidents is directly related to Lexington Market. But the market suffers by association, as the streets around it become a nocturnal magnet for hordes of young people looking for kicks between the bars' closing time and sunrise. Crowds sometimes grow to 700 people or more, police say.

"What you may have are some carrying guns," said Maj. Leonard Hamm, commander of the Central District. "It has nothing to do with Lexington Market. It's kids coming to one area to socialize."

To combat the problem, cars simply cruising the area will be routed out during hours before dawn, the commander said.

And Crazy John's, an all-night pizza joint on East Baltimore Street where many kids hang out, has agreed to close on Sunday and Monday from 1 a.m. to 3 a.m.

Joanne Dolgow, director of promotions for Lexington Market, resents that middle-of-the-night incidents and a hatchet attack between drunken street people have hurt the market's image.

"We don't want outside things to destroy the good thing we have here," said Ms. Dolgow, noting that arrests by 18 full-time security officers are largely confined to shoplifters and pickpockets. "Lexington Market is still a clean, safe, secure place to shop."

Yesterday, one police officer in the market warned a lunchtime shopper that the man who had just asked her for money was a known pickpocket.

And that, says Carmen Caltabiano, is exactly the kind of nuisance that has cost him 25 percent of pizza sales in the last five years.

"Everyday, as soon as you park your car, people are asking you for a dollar," said Mr. Caltabiano, owner of Italian Stallion pizza and a market tenant for 12 years.

"The drug dealing has calmed down a bit, but physically, the neighborhood has deteriorated, with trash and boarded-up buildings.

"The hospital people don't make the two-block walk like they used to. There's not as many tourists as there used to be."

Mr. Caltabiano, who pays $50 a square foot to lease his stall, says rent goes up about 5 percent every year. "Rent goes up and our sales go down," he said, adding that he is among at least five of the market's 140 merchants trying to sell their businesses.

"I'm leaving, I'm disgusted," barked Tony Serio, who has spent 60 of his 70 years selling produce at his family's stall.

"You don't have the people who really buy like they used to and you hear too many words you don't want to hear."

Said his son Sam: "It's just not a fun place anymore."

Yet, there is nothing quite like it.

When the Ringling Brothers and Barnum & Bailey Circus came to town in March, trapeze artist Vivien Larible and her family made the trip to

Lexington Market for fresh fish, squid and sea scallops that they took home to cook on the circus train.

Roasted turkeys sit fat and golden for sandwiches carved as fresh as the ones your grandmother makes for a Thanksgiving snack.

If you don't care for a whole sandwich, you can buy a turkey neck for 50 cents.

A bag of roasted peanuts sells for 45 cents and smells divine.

For some, such images are indelible.

Westminster's Richard Krebs missed the "coconut man" so much that he wrote a letter to *The Sun* in March, asking if anyone knew what had become of him.

Wrote Mr. Krebs: "He started with a whole coconut, holding it with the finger tips of his left hand. In his right hand was a small ax. With deft strokes he cut off the outer shell… he would cut a hole in the end of the partially peeled coconut and pour the clear, sweet liquid into your container, to be taken home."

Michael Houvardas has watched his chocolate cookie profits steadily decrease at the Berger's Bakery stall, but vows to stay.

"I see the bad, I see it going down, but your publicity makes us go down even more," said Mr. Houvardas.

"But people come from many states just to see this market, like the aquarium or a museum. We have to protect the Lexington Market the way we protect those things."

July 8, 1994

Stove shop now a warm memory

JOE THALER WASN'T SURE HOW HE'D FEEL WHEN HIS FAMILY'S CENTURY-OLD stove shop was torn down.

A year ago, he said: "Maybe I'll look back for the last time and shed a tear, but then maybe again I won't."

He didn't.

The bulldozers were at the Thaler building in Old Town Baltimore this week, slowly bringing down a seven-sided, 19th-century building where five generations of Baltimoreans had bought stoves and stove parts. Mr. Thaler, great-grandson of founder Lorenz Thaler, went out of business in early 1993, selling the building to the city for $72,500.

A couple of days ago, he went back to the corner where Central Avenue crosses Gay and Madison streets to see what the city had done with his legacy. He found them razing it for new housing.

"I'd agree that the building wasn't worth keeping. I figured it would've cost me a quarter-of-a-million dollars to renovate it," said Mr. Thaler, 68, pointing his cane through the chain-link fence surrounding the site. "But they could have saved a lot of this stuff. That tin ceiling alone is worth a fortune and those light fixtures . . . you just can't buy 'em anymore."

In the heyday of cast-iron coal burning stoves, up to 30 employees worked at the George J. Thaler company, talking to each other through tubes that snaked through the three-story building.

And in its last years — long after oil, gas and electric power had made wood and coal stoves into curiosities — the company was a place to go for things no one else sold, like the odd gas cock for a 1925 Oriole range. If the part didn't exist, the Thalers could fabricate it in a sheet metal shop on the second floor.

The company did business for 133 years, including making tin and slate roofs for a time.

Joe Thaler was behind the counter for the last 49 of them. Around him stood 50 tons of stove parts — 5,000 bins of parts from floor to the 16-foot ceiling.

"I needed a special kind of hinge once when I was renovating my house," said City Councilman Anthony J. Ambridge, whose district includes the old store. "They had piles of stuff, but Mr. Thaler went right to the part without blinking an eye. He was probably the only human alive who knew where that part was."

But the odd hinge, castings — and every now and then a stove — were not enough to keep the Thalers in business, not even when wood-burning stoves become trendy again in the 1970s.

Mr. Thaler suffered a stroke and a heart attack; longtime customers became leery of going into a changing neighborhood; and there wasn't enough business for the fifth generation — Joseph Thaler, Jr.

The company's building wasn't particularly elegant; no one ever pushed all that hard to have it declared a historic building. The Baltimore Museum of Industry on Key Highway inherited much of the Thaler office — about 100 linear feet of old stove and plumbing catalogs — and odd fixtures that are displayed from time to time.

Now, sitting in his car in front of the store, Mr. Thaler seemed untroubled by the rubble of what used to be: big shards of storefront glass shattered on the wooden floor, toppled shelving, bricks in a heap.

"The slum landlords always tried to chisel us for discounts, and every time they reminded me I'd mentally add 20 percent to the price," laughed Mr. Thaler. "But the only memory that really comes back to me is that this place was loaded with stoves and parts."

Just before driving away for the last time, he said: "I think my father and my grandfather would feel the same way I do. We're done using it; tear it down and do something else."

September 30, 1994

For 1910 pharmacy, a bitter prescription

WHEN THE BELL RANG IN THE MIDDLE OF THE NIGHT, F. ROWLAND MCGINITY, Sr. would stick his head out the second-floor bedroom window to see who needed help on Eastern Avenue.

His father, John, had founded McGinity's Pharmacy in 1910, and neighborly service was a hallmark of the family and the times back in the days when Highlandtown was a genuine urban village.

By the early 1960s, police were telling McGinity not to dispense drugs after hours unless they were on hand to protect him. Today, people brazenly sell drugs and sex across the street in Patterson Park.

But the crime and noise and street trash that were eating into the good life in Highlandtown were not enough to put McGinity's of East Baltimore out of business.

It was the health care insurance industry that doomed the independent corner druggist, according to F. Rowland McGinity, Jr., the third-generation pharmacist at Eastern and Ellwood avenues known to all as "Doc Frank."

McGinity's last day of business is July 10, when it joins the Patterson movie theater and Illona Restaurant on the scrap heap of recently defunct Highlandtown landmarks.

"The writing is on the wall, and the safety net is fraying," says Frank, who still mixes ointments by hand and spends hours chatting with elderly patients who often are more lonely than sick. "You've got to be blind not to see it."

Under certain health maintenance and managed care plans, Frank is paid $3 or less to dispense drugs and compounds that often take him a half-hour to mix the old-fashioned way at the back of the store.

According to the National Association of Retail Druggists, such cost containment contributed to the demise last year of about 40 independent pharmacies a week. Mail-order prescription companies have also taken their toll.

The association says it has been independents such as the McGinity family — druggists working to solve problems for patients who also are neighbors and friends — who have brought about innovations in the industry.

Now 47, Frank started in the business as a kid, crushing ice and mixing lemon phosphates. He holds out his hands to show noticeably enlarged muscles between the forefinger and thumb. He says: "See that? It's called pharmacist's hand. You get it from mixing compounds. You don't see it anymore."

McGinity's business was bought by Rite Aid, and Frank will join the staff of one of the chain's half-dozen or so outlets within a few miles of his store, which filled its 2 millionth prescription in 1984. Frank's mother and father, Evelyn, 81, and F. Rowland McGinity, Sr., 82, will continue to live above the store. Still standing in the basement are wooden cages in which medicinal alcohol was locked during Prohibition.

Helen Przybylski, a year younger than the pharmacy, grew up down the street from the store. She says she rarely cries, not even at funerals. Yet she felt a tear come to her eye at news of the closing.

"I was devastated. I knew his grandfather, Dr. John, and when I was little they had an ice cream parlor with iron chairs," she says. "They said they'd transfer my records to the Rite Aid. Frank was very capable; sometimes he'd advise you better than your doctor."

Frederick "Fritz" James, a 74-year-old resident of the South Decker Avenue rowhouse where he was born, remembers going to McGinity's before he was old enough for school. His 98-year-old mother, the drug store's oldest customer, has her prescriptions delivered to the Canton nursing home where she lives.

"I used to go down with a dime or a nickel," says James, who remembers the model fire engines that the store's founder, city fire commissioner John J. McGinity, had on display. "One of the druggists would say: 'Come here, I'll make you something special,' a chocolate soda or a sundae. It was a good old drug store where you sat down at the counter, and they knew you by your first name."

The soda fountain was taken out in 1967, when Frank's father, known as Rowland, remodeled to concentrate on prescription medicine alone.

"I wanted to run a pharmacy and not have to watch the school kids who were coming in and beginning to steal," explains the elder McGinity, who closed the store only on Christmas and Easter.

Nowadays, says his son Frank, you have to sell lottery tickets and disposable diapers and shampoo to turn a profit and he'd rather work for somebody else than turn his family legacy into a convenience store.

"It's an emotional thing, something Frank's been thinking about for a long time," says Helen Getzel, who has worked at McGinity's for almost 20 years. "They've always been there. On that corner, there's never been anything else."

July 3, 1996

Images of another time

THE PICTURES JIM LEWIS MADE WERE SIMPLE IMAGES OF FAMILY, AND neighborhood, of a time before the first World War when negatives were made of glass and the sight of a working man running around Fells Point with a camera was charming and odd.

Before his death at 79 in 1960, James Houston Lewis took thousands of pictures: his wife lying across their sun-swept bed on Orleans Street; a 1907 view of East Baltimore rooftops echoing Dickens' London; Catholic girls posing for First Communion shots in a backyard portrait studio: and local hooligans in bowlers looking as if they're ready to rob a mail train.

A fraction of his work — 45 prints taken between the late 1890s and 1921 — is on display through June 22 at Baltimore's Peale Museum on Holliday Street.

It is not just something sentimental found in the rafters after an old man's death (although it is that, too), but an artful document of the way working people lived in the days before America became obsessed with taking pictures of itself.

The Peale has a wealth of historical photographs about Baltimore — more than 125,000 pictures of everything from the Great Fire of 1904 to the building of the Jones Falls Expressway — but not much of what Jim Lewis found important.

"What is fascinating is seeing people we can relate to doing things we still do today: enjoying family and taking care of their homes," said Richard W. Flint, who first saw the pictures when he was curator of photographs at the Peale. "It was the people he knew, people in a particular time and a particular place."

Lewis' wife, Theresa, is shown in a 1911 photo standing near a kitchen window filled with light, quietly reading the label on a can of food. Behind her, in the shadows, stands a floor-to-ceiling china cabinet of glass and wood.

It is for images such as this that the exhibit is called "Poetry on Glass," poetry written across glass with shadows and light.

"He'd come up the stairs with a print in his hand that was still wet and say: 'Didn't I get the light on this one!'" said Jack Hennessy, 54, who remembers that his grandfather habitually disappeared into his basement darkroom after big Sunday dinners.

"He was a hell of a character," Hennessy said. "He quit Poly but had books on everything from primitive sexual practices to the complete works of

Dickens. He taught himself plane and spherical trigonometry when he was in his 40s, working out the problems just to see if he could do them."

His passion seemed to help others get through their problems. Lewis spent his childhood on Bank Street, then moved with his new bride to East Pratt, near the original Obrycki's, followed by Orleans Street and finally, from 1913 until his death, on Southern Avenue off Belair Road.

In those neighborhoods, he was the man who came to your door with a picture he'd found in his files after one of your relatives had died. It was usually taken at an oyster roast or crab feast or during hours whiled away on the porch, and often provided a family with their only image of a loved one who had passed on.

Said photographer Robert Creamer, who made the prints for the exhibit: "We owe a great debt to the fact that instead of having some artistic ax to grind, Lewis captured the people of his time. To look at these pictures and have them look right back at you, that's the most fun."

None of Jim Lewis' cameras survived him, although several on display are similar to those he would have used. When 500 of his glass negatives were found in wooden boxes in the basement rafters on Southern Avenue, many were still sheathed in paper from the J. Sussman Photo Stock Co. at 223 Park Ave.

It was slow, arduous work to take pictures in the days before plastic film, but Lewis — who worked without three fingers on his left hand after an accident as a printer's helper — never tired of it.

"It wasn't like shooting a roll of film. With glass, you took pictures one negative at a time," said Dean Krimmel, curator for the exhibit. "You coated the glass, put it in the camera, made the shot, took out the glass, put it in a case and stored it in the dark before reloading the camera. You either caught the moment or you didn't."

Lewis caught his moments on panes of glass hand-treated with a silver gel, some measuring 4 inches square and others 6 inches by 8 inches.

At 79, Estelle Farrell is the only one of Jim and Theresa's three children still alive. She is shown in a 1921 picture of what was then bucolic Gardenville, crossing a meadow with her brother Jim and a neighbor. It is one of the last images her father made with glass.

"Any extra money Dad made he spent on photography. He always had his camera — it became part of our life," Farrell said of the man with a quizzical smile who worked in the freight office of the Baltimore and Ohio Railroad from 1920 to 1955. "He had his moods, and sometimes he'd sit off by himself and daydream, but he loved good times and his family.

"When his pictures were especially good, we'd be happy for him."

January 15, 1997

The excesses of success

NOURISHED BY BIG-MONEY WATERFRONT DEVELOPMENT, CANTON'S WORKING-class roots have blossomed beyond a Realtor's wildest dreams, transforming the old Polish colony into one of the sexiest neighborhoods in Baltimore.

Boston Street is becoming the Charles Street of the 21st century. Ordinary rowhouses that sold for less than $20,000 a generation ago regularly go for $100,000 and up. Simple saloons that offered pickled onions and cheap draft have been remade into twenty-something hot spots with good menus, pastel paint jobs and improbable names such as Looney's and Dooby's.

In less than 10 years, Canton has emerged as a miracle in a city where more housing is razed than built.

And the Sanders family — which traces its Canton heritage before World War I, when a great-grandmother landed from Poland as a child — is sick of it.

The Sanders are so frustrated with side effects of the revival — noise, parking nightmares, all-night lines at the automated teller machine down the block, belligerent outsiders and unruly drinkers who mistake flower pots for urinals — that three households in the extended family have decided to move to Glen Burnie.

"My mother worked her whole life at American Can inspecting the ends of the cans. It would be amazing to her to see how they're renovating that place. She loved new things," said Dale Sanders, who grew up in Canton and raised four children there with his wife, the former Joanne Cwik.

"But it's like the Boardwalk down here on weekends, and when the bars close it's another story. People run across your car hoods, urinate wherever they feel like it. Cars get broken into."

"Unless I'm at church or meeting some friends for breakfast, I see no familiar faces, no old-time friends," said Joanne Sanders, who continues the Polish tradition of having her house blessed each New Year in honor of the Three Wise Men's visit to the baby Jesus. "It would be a neat place to live if you didn't have to pick up all the empty pizza boxes and whole cases of empty beer bottles."

Dale and Joanne Sanders have lived in a converted shoe-repair shop in the 2900 block of O'Donnell St. since 1970.

They grew up in the neighborhood and have fond memories of an asphalt playground on O'Donnell Street where 1950s grown-ups played cards under a pavilion while kids splashed in a concrete wading pool. It's now a swath of green space used by homesteaders to gossip, exercise their dogs and leave the droppings for others to deal with.

A few doors away, daughter Debbie lives with her husband, Charles Riser, and their two children. Around the corner and up the street, son Dean (entrusted to take the family's homemade kielbasa recipe into the next century) lives on Fait Avenue near Potomac Street.

Instigated by the Risers — who want something more wholesome and serene for their children than a seven-day-a-week street party — all of them have staked out several acres of family-owned land near Marley Creek.

The Risers hope to be gone by summer, with the Sanders to follow within a year.

Family members say they'll miss the old neighborhood and will continue to attend Mass at St. Casimir's and commute to O'Donnell Street so the children can stay in their Catholic school.

And they'll be cashing in for the kind of money that would have bought entire blocks of rowhouses in the old Canton.

The Risers bought their two-story brick house for $28,500 in 1983. Few blink when they say they're asking $180,000 and calls have been frequent. Five houses away, next door to Provident Bank, the Sanders say they have been offered $300,000 for the three-story home they bought for $8,000 from the cobblers who owned it before. Houses command less the farther you get from the action on Boston and O'Donnell Streets, and Dean Sanders' home on Fait Avenue is probably worth about $60,000.

"I hate the way the neighborhood is now, but I love it in my heart," said Debbie Riser, whose children say they won't move to Anne Arundel County unless their grandparents come along. "It's not the neighborhood I grew up in, and it blows my mind that someone would pay $180,000 for a little rowhouse in Canton."

Canton's problems might be aggravating to residents, but compared with the violent crime across the city, they are largely nuisance complaints.

Maj. Timothy Longo, commander of the Southeastern District, said his officers have taken to giving out criminal citations for offenses such as public urination and noise instead of making arrests. Dog droppings come under animal control, he said.

Of 306 citations handed out in Canton from October 1996 to the end of last year, Longo said, the most numerous offenses were drinking in public, theft under $300 and going to the bathroom in public.

"Quality of life isn't always a police issue, but I can tell you, Canton is one of the nicest areas in this district, partly because of revitalization and partly because of neighborhood spirit," said Longo, who has selected Canton as one of three neighborhoods, along with Patterson Park and O'Donnell Heights, for a permanent team of officers on foot, bicycles, cars and horses who will be in the community every day.

"At the point you throw up your hands and say, 'That's it, I'm out of here,' you do a disservice to what you've worked so hard for. The strongest thing a community has is its willingness not to give up."

Longo's exhortations are a little too late for the Sanders family.

"If you're right here on the square like we are, it's worse than Fells Point," Charles Riser said.

January 24, 1998

Chapter 16

Mack and the good life

I MET A STORYBOOK'S WORTH OF CHARACTERS DURING TWO SUMMERS AS THIS paper's Ocean City correspondent, from adolescent runaways looking for rock and roll and shelter to a legendary, dying mayor with an eye for last hurrahs wherever they might be found.

But none of them, not the drifters with the carney, the students from overseas, the Boardwalk preachers, not even the endless waves of beautiful young women, captivated me like Watterson "Mack" Miller.

Mack died in his sleep early July 9 at the age of 83. Born into money and status, the grandson of one of America's great newspaper editors and an heir to the wealth of the *Louisville Courier-Journal*, Mack spent his last years as a poor laborer, a self-described "garbage man" living alone in a shack among the vessels of West Ocean City's commercial fishing docks.

Although he built no hotels, sold no treats or trinkets, never traded real estate or held public office, I believe Mack passed on something more substantial than any of Ocean City's power figures whose names will pepper future histories of the resort. They made fortunes by the sea. Mack stumbled into town after drinking one away.

"My experience," he said once, "has been that people like me just as well as a garbage man, and probably better than they did when I was a chicken s... playboy. I didn't have half as many friends or get a fourth of the smiles from pretty girls when I was young as I do today.

"I must have been one mean SOB in my past life to have had it as hard as I have," he said, affirming his belief in reincarnation. "I wouldn't want to do any of it over."

The story of Mack Miller so intrigued me that I would drive over the Route 50 bridge to his book-stuffed plywood shack as often as I could — a rare visitor to his home, enjoying evening talks about the spiritual world, history and literature, his travels and the seductiveness of alcohol.

Always, I would end our conversations with a polite plea for permission to write a book about his life. Politely, he always refused.

Mack was born the grandson of Henry "Marse Henry" Watterson, a former Congressman and Pulitzer Prize winning editorial writer who combined two Louisville papers to establish the *Courier-Journal* in 1868. He was later hailed by H. L. Mencken as "the most distinguished editorial writer on the American press."

Brought up in proper Kentucky society, Mack responded enthusiastically as a teen-ager to the jolt of hard liquor. When his famous grandpappy reserved a spot for him at the family paper, thinking the boy would take the reins one day, Mack opted for drunken afternoons at a backwoods swimming hole instead.

Labeled incorrigible at age 16, he was sent to prep school in Massachusetts and managed to graduate before escalating his drinking career at Dartmouth. Taking the easiest courses the school offered, he dropped out after his sophomore year and began drinking and romancing his way through Europe and Northern Africa in the 1920s and 1930s. Before his grandfather died in 1922, he arranged for Mack to have a try-out as a reporter for the *New York Times*. The bottle interested him more.

"I saw quite a lot of Europe from the bottom of alcohol glasses," he said. "My money was going very fast and finally the men in white coats were whooping off in the near distance."

In 1937, miserable and broke after drinking away his inheritance, and finding himself nearly deserted by friends once it was gone, he took the advice of a woman who told him: "Mack, you're the most unhappy SOB I've ever seen. I don't see how you could be more unhappy if you were sober."

He began walking to the Eastern Shore looking for work. The hard labor of oystering and building fishing shacks didn't bother Mack as much as a depression that shadowed him for more than a year after his last drink.

One night, alone at the table of the old lunch wagon he had turned into a home, he placed a pistol to his head. He said that before pulling the trigger, he heard a voice urging him to try prayer. Shaking off the idea, he again put the gun against his temple and again heard the voice.

"I dropped to my knees and cried: 'God help me,' and it was like a bright light going on in my head."

The depression lifted, never returned for more than a day now and again, and while Mack subscribed to no particular religion, he decided to "behave," living a humble, unassuming life that would be pleasing to God.

In between his work as a janitor at the Castle in the Sand hotel, his reading, regular meals of raw eggs and nearly raw ground beef, and his heroic swims a mile into the ocean and back, Mack tried to help any alcoholic that crossed his path. He said most of the old rummies he knew from the fishing docks eventually committed suicide, but a few stayed sober for a year or more with his advice.

His primary motivation for granting interviews — he became an annual feature for the small resort papers — was to preach the gospel of sobriety, using his own life as an example of alcohol's rewards.

Although he never attended an Alcoholics Anonymous meeting, getting their message out was more important to him than the shame his story brought.

"You must admit," he said, "that it's a little humiliating to be a garbage man when you had all the opportunities in the past."

After my last summer covering the beach in 1984, I began writing letters to my friend. Like our conversations, the letters including requests to write a book on his life. I received the following reply in late October that year.

"Have you considered writing the life of the founder of A.A.? His is a far more inspiring life. He built a religion for alcoholics and his disciples are legion. Think how an inspiring biography of such a man would influence the budding alcoholics... There are millions of A.A.'s who would be delighted to read it... With a story of me, you would influence maybe a thousand; with the founder of A. A. you might influence a million."

That December I drove to the shore for what proved to be our final talk. Still holding out hope that he might change his mind about my project, I taped the conversation. He remained opposed to "a biography of a non-entity" and I filed the tape away, not listening to it until a reporter called from Ocean City to tell me that Mack had passed.

Playing it back last week, I heard a sweet, humble and alert voice rise from the tape as we spoke about this life and the next:

"When I'm a little depressed," he said, "I hope this is the last life and there won't be any more. But when I'm not depressed I think, well maybe the next one will be a little bit better and maybe, if I'm exceedingly good for a life or two, maybe I'll get to a planet of the blessed and start a new life."

July 21, 1986

Abe Sherman, news dealer, is dead

ABE SHERMAN AND HIS CELEBRATED CRANKINESS HAVE PASSED ON TO JOIN the ranks of such Baltimore luminaries as Mr. Diz, Polock Johnny, Rudolph "Sun Lies" Handel and the Great Dantini.

"Baltimore's characters are a dying breed," said Philip Sherman, son of the 89-year-old news dealer who died of cancer Wednesday night. "There was only one Abe Sherman."

For nearly 80 years — many of them from a green wooden kiosk in the middle of Calvert Street between the old post office and the city courthouse — Mr. Sherman supplied Baltimore with newspapers and magazines from around the world.

And if his impatient, salty tongue could tolerate your presence long enough — a prospect that was greatly improved if you bought something — Mr. Sherman would also supply you with fierce opinions on just about anything.

Mr. Sherman had little patience for "just browsing" customers.

"He was a great philosopher," said U. S. District Judge Edward S. Northrop. "When our offices were on Calvert Street, I'd talk to him nearly every single day, and in the morning he'd outline what was in the paper and give me my marching orders."

A decorated veteran of both World Wars and the 29th infantry division, and a man who volunteered as a private during World War II while in his 40s, Mr. Sherman was severely patriotic.

"He couldn't stomach the hippie generation," said Judge Northrop. "When I tried the Berrigan brothers for pouring chicken blood on draft cards, he was quite upset.

"And he had plenty to say about the [1968] riots — all of it purple prose. He had his likes and his dislikes, with no hesitancy about speaking about them. He felt people had a duty to support the United States. He didn't like people who had other views."

While personal war stories were among his favorite conversation — Phil Sherman said yesterday that as his father lay suffering from cancer of the esophagus, he read aloud to him chapters from "The History of the 175th" and "29th, Let's Go" — Abe was far better known for his caustic personality.

He gave up his spot beside the Battle Monument in Calvert Street in 1970 because he said the smog was killing him.

Calvert was a public spot where he couldn't quite tell people who got on his nerves to hit the road. But after moving into a store at Park Avenue and Mulberry Street, a joint simply called "Sherman's," he refined his practice of tossing browsers and other idlers out the door.

"He was a cranky, gruff old fellow," said Russ Smith, editor of the weekly *City Paper*. "People expected him to be that way. You go in there and he hassles you right away, so my trick was to pick something up and then you could browse."

Mr. Smith, who said he visited Sherman's twice a week, said he often saw the old man giving some unfortunate the heave-ho.

"He'd say, 'Get out of here!' and the person would say, 'What do you mean?' and he'd say, 'Get the hell out of here right now.'"

The dusty store — reminiscent of the hippie generation he so disliked, with posters of the Beatles, Bob Dylan and marijuana plants on the walls and ceiling — was open yesterday.

A hand-made sign said: "No Browsing Girlie Magazines." A similar sign tacked onto a shelf of kung-fu literature read: "Limited Browsing on Bruce Lee Books."

The newspapers ranged from the *Times-Picayune* of New Orleans to *Pravda*, and the magazines from *Dog Fancy* to *Vogue*.

The only thing not on sale was yesterday's *Evening Sun*, which carried front-page news of Mr. Sherman's death. All copies had been put aside for family members.

Dozens of regular customers stopped by yesterday, many learning of Mr. Sherman's death from a note on the door saying the store would be closed today, Friday, for the owner's funeral, which will be at 1 p.m. at the Sol Levinson funeral establishment, 6010 Reisterstown Road.

"The thing that sticks in my mind is that beneath his [grouchy] attitude was a decent man who loved his country," said Ken W. Scott, a member of the serial department of the Enoch Pratt Free Library who came by daily to stock the central Pratt's shelves. "His gruff manner was just his way. Everybody said, 'Oh, that's just Abe,' and left it at that."

Phil Sherman said he hasn't decided whether to continue the business. For one thing, he said, it just wouldn't be the same without Abe. For another, the seven-day-a-week business is a lot of work.

Born in 1898, Abe Sherman was the son of a Lithuanian immigrant named Moses. Raised on Pennsylvania Avenue near the Lafayette Market, the son remembered touring the ruins of the Baltimore Fire of 1904 at his father's side. He began hawking papers by the age of 8 or 9.

His son Phil said yesterday that Abe was his father's formal, given name. "A-B-E, that's it," he said.

Mr. Sherman opened his kiosk at the Battle Monument with a $1,500 World

War I bonus. Along with the government clerks and laborers who stopped by for a paper were such uncommon folks as Babe Ruth and H. L. Mencken.

His caricature, so often used in the political cartoons of his friend, *Sun* artist Richard Q. Yardley, was marked by an ever-present cigar clenched between his teeth, eyeglasses, and the kind of thin cap favored by cabdrivers and certain horse players.

Mr. Sherman's last home was in the Westminster House apartments in the 500 block of North Charles Street, four blocks from his store.

"People make great cities, and Abe Sherman was one of the people who made Baltimore what it is today… He was an institution who added to its liveliness, color, personality and character," said Gov. William Donald Schaefer, a man Mr. Sherman admired.

"He'll be missed," the governor added. "And I'll miss him when I stop by his shop."

Mr. Sherman's wife of 40 years, Ann, died in 1963. His son Philip is a lawyer and brigadier general in the Maryland National Guard and his second son, Lee, teaches at the University of North Carolina. Survivors also include four grandchildren and seven great-grandchildren

Such characters as Abe Sherman — genuine, unaffected spirits who gradually gain legendary status without the aid of a public relations office — seem to be on the wane these days, said Phil Sherman.

It was Mr. Diz who gave Baltimore balloons, bubble gum and bad racetrack tips, and Polock Johnny who gave it sausage. The Great Dantini provided magic, and Rudy Handel reminded everyone who passed *The Baltimore Sun* building that you can't believe everything you read.

And it was Abe Sherman who gave Baltimore a piece of his mind and the news hot off the presses for more years than most of us have been alive.

April 17, 1987

Hurdy gurdy man's grandson keeps memories alive

LOCKED AWAY IN A SMALL GARAGE BEHIND A LITTLE ITALY ROW HOUSE ARE the childhood dreams of Anthony "Corky" Schiavo, memories that lie deep in a musical contraption known as a hurdy-gurdy.

The hurdy-gurdy belonged to Mr. Schiavo's grandfather, and Corky, like many little boys long on heart and imagination, had a special relationship with the old man. His grandfather was Charles "Chess" Cirelli, who died in March 1961 at the age of 83.

Chess Cirelli was a hurdy-gurdy man, a guy who made music all over Baltimore by cranking a handle on a cart-drawn player piano, a paisan from Italy who believed he was every bit a musician as Guy Lombardo or anyone else.

"He always said he didn't work for a living, that he was a musician. He took it serious and he worked hard. That thing weighs 648 pounds, and it was hard work pulling it around," said Mr. Schiavo, 58. "He was born in Genoa and always said his father sent him to Rome to become a musician."

Mr. Schiavo, a carpenter, and his younger brother Gino are the keepers of their family's legacy, a treasure nearly a century old and the last of 16 hurdy-gurdies their grandfather owned throughout a long career that faded in the 1950s.

Still painted bright red and green, as it was the last time Chess Cirelli cranked out "Sidewalks of New York" or "O Sole Mio," the turn-of-the-century invention is sheltered in a small backyard garage on High Street in Little Italy, about a block from the Eastern Avenue row house where Mr. Cirelli lived for many years with little Corky.

"I was raised with my grandfather; my mother wanted somebody to stay with him after his brother died," said Mr. Schiavo. "Nobody [in the family] has the interest in the hurdy-gurdy that I got, because I was the only one who went around with him. He was my buddy. I was his mascot.

"He wouldn't take me with him during the week, but on Saturday he'd pull it uptown and take me. We'd begin at 6 a.m. on a route — up Lexington Street, up to Guilford, stop on the corner. People would throw money out the windows. We went from corner to corner.

"People would give him loaves of bread, canned goods," Mr. Schiavo remembered. "Other times we'd start up through Baltimore Street, up near the [old] fish market, and he ate and drank the whole time he was out.

"He had a copper kettle on the wagon that [tavern owners] would fill with draft beer and he drank it as he went around. He sang along with the hurdy-gurdy once in a while when he was half-potted, and he'd come home in the evening, sometimes not until 9 o'clock, and you could see two red lanterns burning on the back as he walked home."

"Hard work," Mr. Cirelli was known to tell anyone who took the time to ask. "Like a horse."

From the turn of the century through the Roaring Twenties and well into the 1940s, hurdy-gurdies were common in East Coast cities with strong Italian communities — Philadelphia, New York, Boston and Baltimore.

At one time Chess Cirelli had acquired so many that he rented them out to other men for $1 a day, back when President Street near the harbor was known to locals as "monkey row" because that's where the grinders kept their furry helpers.

In a 1959 "I Remember" column for the *Sun Magazine*, Mr. Cirelli said, "I never took a monkey with me. No sir. I don't like monkeys. Bears either."

Chess Cirelli's dislike of animals lasted until the day he died, but technology put a bad spin on the days that made the hurdy-gurdy a street favorite.

"Radio was getting bigger and bigger, and then people had stereos," said Mr. Schiavo. "After the war he tried to get back to the streets, but it was nothing there and it was too hard for him to pull it. I was with him when he died. He died in bed of old age. He was wore out."

The surviving hurdy-gurdy, the old man's favorite out of all the ones he owned, has fared better.

It hasn't been tuned for several years, but with nothing more than the right tempo on the crank it yields a rich, turn-of-the century saloon sound, the feel of a street carnival.

Chess Cirelli often tested the magic after he retired, Mr. Schiavo said, "taking the hurdy-gurdy outside on the pavement and playing just so people would stop and talk to him about it — his toy, his hobby, his living, his everything."

Corky Schiavo frequently does the same. Not long ago, on a bright Saturday afternoon, he removed the tarps that cover the instrument, wheeled it out of the garage and set up music-making at South High and Trinity streets.

A crowd gathered in moments — old-timers from the neighborhood who were kids when Chess Cirelli walked the streets in his heyday before the war, tourists from Harborplace, motorists blocking traffic catch a tune and families walking to neighborhood restaurants for supper, urging shy children to go stand next to the hurdy-gurdy for pictures.

Corky Schiavo smiles as he cranks the box, which he would like to see preserved in one of the city's museums, and waves to passers-by.

"Hey," he calls out. "You remember the hurdy-gurdy?"

"Oh it sounds lovely," says an elderly woman.

"The good old days," agrees an old man with a baseball cap.

July 2, 1987

'Hot Rod Mary' and her love for life

SOME OF MARY DOBKIN'S CLOSEST FRIENDS STOOD YESTERDAY ON THE baseball diamond named in honor of Baltimore's "Aunt Mary" — disgusted that the field had decayed into a weed-choked dump, but cheered by memories of the little old lady who helped needy kids grow up through America's pastime.

They were just a few of the many people around Baltimore and the country who mourned the passing of Aunt Mary, who died Saturday night at the age of 84 after dedicating more than 50 of her years to helping young people.

"Ain't this ridiculous? This used to be our field. How did this happen?" asked Walter "Bud" Reichert, one of the many men who volunteered to coach a team for Miss Dobkin.

"If she saw this field... I know Aunt Mary..." put in Marge L. McCardell, the mother of a former player.

"Yeah," said coach George Miller as he looked over the tall grass and trash on the ball field behind the Armistead Gardens neighborhood in East Baltimore. "She'd have been calling [Governor] Schaefer."

The cronies of Mary Dobkin — whose life of joy despite ill health and poverty was celebrated in a 1979 television movie of her life starring Jean Stapleton — weren't sure why or how Dobkin Field in Herring Run Park became such a mess.

But they had no trouble describing the charged-up life of a woman who fled czarist Russia as a baby, who was too poor to own shoes in this country, wound up having the better part of both legs amputated because of disease, and didn't mind asking anybody for anything if it might help the thousands of kids who played ball for her.

"She'd call me up and say, 'Mr. Maranto, I want you to take the [station] wagon over to Stone's [Famous] Bakery on Lombard Street and pick up a loaf of bread,'" remembered Charles J. Maranto, who coached Dobkin teams for 35 years. "I'd come back with 200 or 300 loaves that they gave her, dump it all in her living room, and the next day it would be gone. She'd given it all away. Everybody took advantage of Aunt Mary."

Marge McCardell remembered how she met her friend of more than 20 years.

"One day, my youngest son, Mark, came home and said, 'Mom, I'm going to play ball for Mary Dobkin,' and I said. 'Who's Mary Dobkin?' and he said, 'It's some lady who lives on the hill who walks with crutches, and she's going to get us uniforms.'"

Ms. McCardell said she once asked Aunt Mary why she took an interest in so-called "bad kids" — teams, according to one man who watched them play many times, that "looked like a bunch of dirty-faced kids who needed haircuts."

"She always took these bad kids — she could take a bad child and make a beautiful child out of them, and once I told her, 'I know why you do it. You were a bad child yourself, weren't you?' And she said, 'Yes, I was.'"

Together, they remembered a woman who was crazy for corned beef sandwiches and loved to take long drives in the country to get homemade ice cream, usually chocolate.

They talked of a sports-happy lady who fielded good teams and was ready to drive to Hershey, Pa., on a minute's notice to watch a Baltimore Clippers hockey game; who liked to drive fast and take sharp corners, earning her the nickname "Hot Rod Mary" from her ballplayers; who fell in love once when she was young but didn't marry the boy because he was Catholic and she was Jewish.

She was a fan of quiz shows, the Orioles, almost any kind of music, her annual Christmas party giveaways and, of course, her kids.

"I want to get as many of her old players together as I can and have them autograph a ball to put in her casket," said Mr. Maranto, hoping to get it done before the 9 a.m. funeral today at the Sol Levinson funeral establishment, 6010 Reisterstown Road.

Baltimore Mayor Clarence "Du" Burns said yesterday that he knew Mary Dobkin from the beginning of her career as a volunteer in the 1940s. He called her a pioneer in integrating Little League baseball in Baltimore.

"She went a long ways in bringing black and white together," Mr. Burns said. "She was a great lady — poor, didn't have anything herself; she was just interested in kids."

Asked how a city-owned field dedicated in honor of a person he described as a close fiend was allowed to go to seed, Mr. Burns said he didn't know.

"I'd like to see us memorialize her in a way that will last, because even if we fix that field up, it will be a mess again in two or three years," the mayor said. "I want to see something different, something that will stay around."

Mr. Burns said he didn't know what might be appropriate but promised that he would put his mind to it.

One thing that Aunt Mary mentioned often before she died, according to her friends, was a desire to have a display of her life's accomplishments set up at the Babe Ruth Birthplace museum at 216 Emory St.

"We've got all of her artifacts in our archives... many of her items of memorabilia chronicling her involvement with children — photographs, gloves, trophies, stuff from the movie they made — but we've never been able to get funding for a permanent display," said Michael L. Gibbons, a spokesman for the museum. "It would take about $5,000, and we could do it. But we need the money."

John Steadman, a sports columnist for the *Evening Sun* who was in charge of the Mary Dobkin Children's Fund charity for many years, said that Aunt Mary — who didn't work and lived on Social Security — developed a sharp sense of amateur fund raising through the years.

"People would almost run when they saw her coming, because she always wanted something," said Mr. Steadman, noting that when he first met Ms. Dobkin she came to his old office at the *News American* saying she didn't have enough money to buy a baseball for her team.

"She always had a tale of woe, and in her own way she got things accomplished — she was incredible at being able to elicit the damnedest support," he said. "She knew when someone would help her or slam the door in her face. Some of her kids were so poor they would keep their uniform after the season and wear it to school."

Former Orioles manager Earl Weaver, reached at his home in Miami yesterday, said Aunt Mary once told him he should "take a lesson" on their shared passion — saying the Orioles would win more games if he had taught them bunting more.

"I told her Little League baseball and big-league baseball were two different things," Mr. Weaver said. "But I held high respect for her, for the things she accomplished, and always enjoyed just being with her.

"Just to see the look on the kids' faces when they had Mary Dobkin night at the stadium and they'd present her with a trophy was special," the retired manager said. "She touched a lot of lives."

And as for her baseball savvy, Mr. Weaver added, "Evidently when she formed her first team she had to know what she was talking about, or she wouldn't have held the youngsters' attentions."

August 24, 1987

Divine remembered

THE MAN THEY BURIED IN THE SUNSHINE AT TOWSON'S PROSPECT HILL Cemetery yesterday afternoon grew up as a chubby, kind-hearted and mis-understood kid from Lutherville named Harris Glenn Milstead.

But he triumphed as a star of the somewhat sordid screen: a comical sweet-natured actor-as-transvestite that a world of hipsters embraced as sim-ply Divine.

"Divine, like all great actors, was a man of many faces," said John Waters, in whose films and fraternity Divine was the perennial star.

"To his family and his friends he was Glenn... what to even a most liberal parent must have been a puzzling career in the beginning turned into a liveli-hood that I think they grew to understand.

"But to his friends, and there were many of them from all over the world, he was Divine — Divvy to many.

"To his other friends in Baltimore, he was the fantasy relative everybody deserves, funny, giving, sort of like a male Auntie Mame. And at Christmas — well, Santa himself was never so upstaged.

"To me," Mr. Waters continued, speaking to about 300 people gathered for the funeral, "I lost a lifelong friend, a business partner, a confidante, a co-conspirator, and an actor who could say the words I wrote better than any-body...He left the mark of Divinity, as we used to joke, everywhere."

Mr. Waters, who was enjoying the glow of the success of his most recent film "Hairspray" until Monday, when Divine was found dead in Los Angeles of heart failure, was followed at the lectern in the Ruck Towson funeral establishment by the Rev. Leland Higginbotham.

Mr. Higginbotham has been the Milsteads' minister since Glenn was a young boy.

As the Baptist minister spoke, the deceased lay behind him, blacksuited in a nickel-grey casket, the curve of his belly and the shine of his pate sug-gesting the image of Alfred Hitchcock.

Although Mr. Higginbotham referred to his old friend by no name other than Glenn — "a boy who was always sensitive to the feelings of others" — it was apparent that he understood the hard fight the youngster endured to become Divine.

313

"He and his parents spent many hours with me trying to figure out what was going on; it was an agonizing period," Mr. Higginbotham said. "I as a pastor felt totally inadequate to help in any way.

"But although Glenn took the painful road to find himself, at last there was reconciliation.

"The tragedy is that he was cut off right at the point of becoming who he really is, and the world will never see how that flower could have unfolded."

March 15, 1988

Old soldier gets final call at the Dead Eye

CAPTAIN RALPH EVRAN FORD, SR. OWNED MORE SUNKEN BOATS AND BARGES than anyone in Baltimore, a string of deep-sixed derelicts on the harbor bottom from Curtis Bay to Canton.

Boats that might sink he brought ashore, and the ones that refused to sink he docked in the shadow of the Hanover Street Bridge where they bobbed yesterday on green water his mourners stared at to remember a man who loved boats, any boat, all boats.

Among his prizes were a tugboat named for himself, leaky wooden buckets that sat on blocks for years, and an auctioned city yacht named for William Donald Schaefer.

"No matter where he went he was always coming back to this waterfront," said Rose Mary Ford, after they buried her father. "From Curtis Creek to Pratt Street to Boston Street and then down to this marina, he was never leaving sight of the water. He saw water every day he lived."

A peculiar legacy for the son of an Ohio farmer.

Belligerent, intelligent, crude, crafty and proud, Ralph Ford came to Baltimore during the Great Depression to join the Coast Guard and found himself in the Army when the United States entered World War II.

He told tales of knife fights with Japanese who captured him on Guadalcanal; of killing enemies and watching buddies die; and of being on the deck of the USS Missouri — a GI decked out in a naval officer's uniform for the sake of a photo — when Japan surrendered. Those experiences earned him a Purple Heart and a military burial yesterday morning at the Crownsville Veterans Cemetery.

And his warm, crusty heart entitled him to a wake crowded with friends. Whether they met him last week or 30 years ago, they repeated stories Captain Ford told from his stool under the head of a caribou in the Dead Eye Saloon in South Baltimore.

Yesterday the stool was draped in black crepe with a huge basket of red carnations on the seat.

Captain Ford died on the waterfront early last Monday morning after cursing that "last call" had come early at the Dead Eye and retiring to the shipping container he called home. He had lived in the 20-by-8-foot steel box at the Baltimore Yacht Basin marina for the last 10 years.

He was 70, told everyone he was 80, played and sang Hank Williams' songs whether you wanted to hear one or not, and chased women to the end.

"I was his last girlfriend," said a gray-haired woman named Betty Lynn, "but I think I was on his lower list."

When David Ridge met Captain Ford he found a second father.

"I met him down on Boston Street about 20 years ago; we were trying to raise one of his tugs that sank," said Mr. Ridge, who, in the loose ranks of harbor titles, prided himself as Captain Ford's first mate. "We got that tug up, but it's sunk down at Curtis Creek right now."

Even the old captain's namesake found its way to the mud.

"When you're driving east on 695 going over Curtis Bay look to your right and you'll see a large tugboat with its bow sticking out of the water," said Dan Davis, the marina owner. "That's the R. E. Ford, Sr."

Captain Ford owned boat yards on several Pratt Street piers back in the 1950s. When Baltimore began to groom itself for tourists in the early 1970s, Captain Ford was chased over to Boston Street, where he lived in a trailer until fire destroyed that boatyard. He moved to the Middle Branch of the Patapsco near Hanover Street in the early 1980s.

"Finished with engines" after years of driving pilings, pushing barges and ferrying supplies to ships on anchor, Captain Ford spend the last years of his life collecting boats, playing guitar, handling boat lines for free beer, and enjoying the status of being Ralph Ford.

"He was completely different from anyone, one hell of a man," said Ralph E. Ford, Jr. yesterday, raising a Budweiser to his father's memory and looking out at one of the last boats the old man bought. "He was Ralph Ford — just Ralph Ford, that's the way he lived, and he lived his whole life like that. When you met him, you met *him*, you didn't meet anyone else."

March 10, 1992

Fells Point bids farewell to man of character

RUTH GOETZ STOOD IN NOONDAY SUN ALONG THE 500 BLOCK OF S. WOLFE St. yesterday to watch an eight-piece brass band, a couple hundred mourners and a lone bagpiper march south to the harbor.

"I've seen it in New Orleans," she said, "but in my 70 years I never seen it on Wolfe Street."

Never in Baltimore, as best anyone can remember, until the funeral of H. Jefferson Knapp, III, local character nonpareil.

"Jeff wanted a Viking funeral where they put your body on a boat and light the funeral pyre at sea, but all he had was a rubber dinghy," said Larry Benicewicz, a friend who flew the brass band into town from the Crescent City. "We gave him a New Orleans send-off instead."

Jeff Knapp was a generous barkeep, an incorrigible prankster, and a slavish scene-maker known as the Abe Lincoln of Fells Point for reasons carved into his face.

He died Saturday at age 63, setting off rounds of waterfront fetes in his honor that lasted until the bars closed this morning.

Yesterday they eulogized him, cried and danced for him, and cremated him.

"Jeff was always the spirit behind an impossible lifestyle," said Megan Hamilton, who carried a basket of flowers to give to mourners and spectators lining the street. "He couldn't [party] without style, and if he couldn't do it his way he'd just stop. He must have been ready to go."

Some thought it beyond coincidence that Mr. Knapp passed away a week before the Fells Point Fun Festival, where for the first time public drinking would not be allowed.

In front of the funeral parade as it left the Lilly and Zeiler funeral home on Eastern Avenue was a man carrying a floral arrangement of carnations shaped like the letters V.T.N.F., which stood for Mr. Knapp's beverage battle cry: "Vodka Tonic No Fruit!"

Behind it marched his brother, Phil Knapp, carrying a large color photograph of the deceased taped to a stick. On either side were Jeff Knapp's four children and his grandchildren. Next came the tuba, drums, trumpet and trombone of the Treme Brass Band playing Old Rugged Cross, followed by a gang of mourners whose ranks swelled as Thames Street neared.

Bringing up the rear was Wayne Francis, piper for hire, who played "Amazing Grace" before Mr. Knapp's open coffin and blew a spirit of Eire that snaked through the narrow streets and alleys of Southeast Baltimore.

The procession turned onto Thames Street from Wolfe, paused before the Cat's Eye Pub where Mr. Knapp is best remembered by tugboat men and Ph.Ds as the blasphemous wit who gave away drinks like water. It then rolled along to "When The Saints Go Marching In" toward the new promenade where his name and motto are chiseled in a brick his son Gary painted gold the night of his father's death.

There, a man who was once a minister stood on a platform, held a Bible and gave the final blessing.

"Jeff's stories will be told and retold for years to come," said P.J. Trautwein. "The way he used to take wedding pictures and have them developed in time to give to the bride at the reception; the first time he dressed up as Lincoln to dedicate the Tomb of the Unknown Wino in the Fells Point square to the dismay of then Mayor Schaefer; when he staged the Sputnik crash on Thames Street."

And now, Mr. Trautwein said, Herbert Jefferson Knapp, III has been reunited with his late Cat's Eye commandos Kenny Orye and Ralph Miller, who succumbed to the party a few years before him.

The preacher said: "All I can say to you in the Great Beyond is this: 'Watch out! They are together again and they are on the loose.'"

October 1, 1992

Pete Covacevich, Fells Point barkeep

PETE'S AT 906 S. WOLFE ST. WAS THE KIND OF WATERFRONT JOINT WHERE stevedores brought in stolen hams off the docks and the local priest dropped by to bless the meat before it was divvied up.

"The priest said as long as a few of the hams went to poor people, it was all right," said Anthony Covacevich, who today will bury his father, Peter A. Covacevich — last owner and barkeep of a family saloon that began at the turn of the century.

Pete Covacevich died of pneumonia Monday at Church Hospital after fighting cancer for more than a year. He was 72 and lived his entire life in Fells Point.

Today, a new generation of drinkers knows the tavern off the corner of Wolfe and Thames streets as the Red Star. It's unlikely that any of Pete's regulars guys known as John the Dutchman, La-Dee-Dah, Grumpy, Banjo Eyes and the One-Armed Watchman would recognize the place.

The Covacevich family sold the business in 1984.

The bar that Pete Covacevich ran served National Boh, Gunther and Arrow 77; it sold homemade codfish cakes two for a nickel during the Depression and when World War II broke out the price for a coddie jumped to a dime; and it stayed in business for most of the century catering to cannery workers, tugboat men, truckers and longshoremen.

"My father had a good head on his shoulders, he could converse with anyone and he was good-hearted," said Anthony Covacevich, a Fells Point resident who passed up the family business for a law degree. "But he could tell you where to get off in a minute, if you know what I mean."

Pete Covacevich was born above the family bar, established by his namesake grandfather after he immigrated from the Baltics in the late 1800s. He graduated from St. Stanislaus grammar school on Ann Street and attended Loyola High School for two years before going to work in the bar.

Over the years, as the saloon passed from father to son over three generations, it was known as Pete's Place, Tony's Cafe and then Pete's once more. When the late Mr. Covacevich was a little boy and his mother, Mary, ran the kitchen, it was famed for shrimp soup and oyster sandwiches.

When alcohol was illegal in the United States, the bar was closed, but, according to Genevieve Covacevich Zientak of Canton: "The day Roosevelt lifted Prohibition, the front door opened and we were back in business."

In 1953, Pete Covacevich married the former Josephine Roslan and the couple had one child, Anthony. Mrs. Covacevich died in January.

In his later years, Mr. Covacevich volunteered most of his spare time to St. Stanislaus Roman Catholic Church and was the regular bartender for parties and dances at the church hall for the last 15 years.

"Pete missed the last dance, the one in April, because he was so sick," said Mrs. Zientak, his sister.

A Mass of Christian burial for Mr. Covacevich was to be offered at 9 a.m. today at St. Stanislaus.

In addition to his son and his sister, Mr. Covacevich is survived by a brother, Edward Covacevich of Canton.

May 13, 1993

Lavonda "Bonnie" Hunt, whose bar paid lavish tribute to Elvis

LAVONDA "BONNIE" HUNT, THE GOOD-HEARTED REDHEAD WHO PRESIDED over cold beer and the eternal memory of the King at Miss Bonnie's Elvis Shrine, died of a heart attack Tuesday at her home above the East Baltimore tavern where she made her living. She was 62.

The landmark barroom at the corner of Fleet and Port streets featured a 15-by-12-foot mural of Elvis on the side of the building. a jukebox packed with Elvis hits, and hundreds of Presley artifacts, including a jar of red clay from the singer's native Tupelo, Miss., and an iron pole from the gates at Graceland.

Such curios, enhanced by the quiet hospitality of Bonnie Hunt, attracted visitors from around the world.

"I like running this bar," she said. "It's my life."

In recent years, it was often a lonely life.

On many nights, a man with a thirst could walk inside the narrow row-house saloon and find Miss Bonnie sitting at the bar with her thoughts and a small glass of wine, alone in the twinkle of Christmas lights and enveloped in the voice of the King.

Although pilgrims yearning to soak up Elvis stopped by now and again for a drink — and the place was known to jump with poetry readings and holiday parties — Miss Bonnie's Elvis Shrine suffered from a lack of regulars.

She blamed poor business on drunk driving laws, the wane of the traditional neighborhood bar, "harassment" from the liquor board, intolerant neighbors and simple misfortune.

A bitter, years-long feud with her neighbor resulted in nearly a dozen appearances before the liquor board for noise violations and a zoning dispute over the mural.

That may explain why she always harbored a suspicion that unknown forces wanted to take away her bar for their own profit. Such headaches, she said, led to a heart attack and three strokes.

Yet, until the end, she never stopped smoking.

Never stopped drinking.

And never stopped loving Elvis, whom Miss Bonnie claimed to have met once in the check-out line of a Florida supermarket.

Of the scores of Presley images hung throughout the bar, she said: "Every way I turn, he's smiling at me."

Lavonda Hunt was the seventh of 10 children born on a farm outside of Savannah, Ga., to Dolphus and Zerie Hunt.

Married at 14 — the first of five marriages to four men — she moved to Baltimore with her first husband in the early 1950s.

During her years in Baltimore, she worked as a barmaid at various waterfront gin mills. For a time, she moved back to Savannah and was living in Ohio when Elvis died in 1977. She bought the bar that bears her name in 1981, about the time her last marriage ended. The celebration of Elvis began slowly, but once customers found out she nurtured a special passion for the King, they began giving her presents: busts of the singer, thermometers embedded in tin images of Presley under the words "It's Cool;" and Tennessee license plates emblazoned: ELVIS. One pennant said, "Elvis: 1935-to- Forever."

At the end, there was nary an inch of paneling not covered with something related to Elvis Presley. The bar will be closed until the family figures out what to do with it.

Services will be held at 11 a.m. tomorrow at Duda-Ruck funeral home, 7922 Wise Ave., in Dundalk.

She is survived by two sons, Wayne Mosley and Dene Mosley, both of Dundalk; two sisters, Laverne Kicklighter of Dundalk and Vella Tippins of Canton; a brother, Houston Hunt of Baltimore; and five grandchildren.

September 2, 1993

Author's acknowledgements

I would like to thank Sharon Snyder for putting in a good word for me with *The Sun* circulation department back in 1977 and the late Cordella Metzger for hiring me to dispatch trucks despite her doubts.

I would like to thank Russell Smith, co-founder of the Baltimore *City Paper*, for taking on a young poet who had never written a newspaper article. I would like to thank his partner, Alan Hirsch, for paying me once in awhile.

I would like to thank Deborah Rudacille for making it as easy as possible for me to pursue my craft in the early years.

I would like to thank all of my city editors — Dale DuPont, Rebecca Corbett, Tony Barbieri, Mike Adams and Jim Asher — for leaving me alone as much as possible to do what I wanted.

I would like to thank the immortal Jay Spry and the irascible David Michael Ettlin for teaching me to be a newspaperman.

I would like to thank my editor on this book, the kind and conscientious Scott Shane.

I would like to thank photographer Jim Burger — the coolest mensch in the world — whose work has graced all of my books.

I would like to thank my colleagues who volunteered to proof read the manuscript: Jonathan Bor, Heather Dewar, Peter Hermann, and Dion Thompson.

I would like to thank Amelia, Jake, and Sofia for amusing themselves for countless hours in the newsroom everytime Daddy had to go into work for "just a few minutes."

I would like to thank Manuel and Gloria Alvarez, my parents, for being proud every time my name appears in print and trusting that you could actually make a living in this business. Mom also checked the book for typos.

I would like to thank Elisabeth.

Above all, I would like to thank my readers

About the author

Rafael Alvarez was born in Baltimore in 1958 and educated in Catholic schools. He is a 1976 graduate of Mount St. Joseph High School and earned an English degree from Loyola College in Baltimore in 1980.

His first book, a collection of short fiction titled "The Fountain of Highlandtown," was published by Woodholme House in 1997. That same year, he wrote an episode of the "Homicide" television series. A second book of short stories — "Orlo and Leini" — will be brought out by Woodholme in late 1999.

Alvarez lives in the Greektown neighborhood of East Baltimore and is the father of three teenage children: Amelia, Jake and Sofia.

He enjoys the music of Johnny Winter, the prose of Stuart Dybek, and the photography of Jed Kirschbaum.